PRAISE FOR
SWIMMING TO THE HORIZON

"As a social worker, Zak Mucha did a job for seven years that most people wouldn't do for seven minutes. His clients were the people most of us cross the street to avoid. But there's no clinical snobbery or academic posturing here. Mucha's gift, as a writer and on the street, is his ability to cut through assumptions and pretensions—and in the cases of his clients, psychosis—and make a connection. *Swimming to the Horizon* is a brave, compassionate, often hilarious book about the true cost of helping others, and all that we get in return."

—Trey Bundy, Journalist at *The Center for Investigative Reporting*

"Zak Mucha begins this extraordinary book wondering if he genuinely wants to help his psychotic, criminal, and often drug-addled clients or if he's an adrenaline junky trying to resolve the conflict of being both a writerly sensitive type and a tough guy. In fact, not so very unlike those he seeks to help. We should remember that the road to hell is paved with good intentions. Only the person with such a questioning, personal investment can do street-corner social work with people society has thrown asunder. Erik Erickson noted that for those labeled delinquent, their greatest need and only source of salvation can come from someone who refuses to confirm them in their criminality. Few have the courage; even fewer have the verve to really write about it. I love this book."

—Jamieson Webster, Psychoanalyst and Author

"Imagine if *The Wire* or *Justified* had been about social workers, and you'll have an idea of how gripping, heartbreaking, and funny this book is . . . but it's not fiction. Zak Mucha's combination of honesty, furious compassion, and irresistible storytelling makes him one of the most important contemporary public intellectuals."

—Dogo Barry Graham, Zen Monk and Author of *Kill Your Self: Life After Ego*

"There is quite the open secret in social work and mental health treatment—much of the work done with those who are most in need and most vulnerable involves situations no books describe and no theory prepares you for. Those of us who choose this work find ourselves flying by the seat of our pants, trying desperately to find a way in with our clients while trying to keep them and ourselves safe in impossibly risky circumstances.

"In clinical circles, if we tell the stories as they truly happen, other professionals are often aghast, uncomfortable with our unconventional interventions. Zak's stories are a beacon, a bright window into what it is like to endeavor to walk alongside, rather than look down on, those who this world has punished again and again. The stories are incredibly touching, funny, and well written. This book is a must-read for anyone doing this work seldom written about. It is a must-read for those in clinical circles who cannot imagine this work. Actually, everyone should just read this book."

—Pfeffer Eisin, MA, LCPC, Director of the Erikson Institute DCFS Early Childhood Project, Psychotherapist, and Fellow Swimmer

"This is a compelling and readable book of stories about real people and hard times. I know lots of people who are proud of their inherited wealth who wouldn't last a day on the mean streets of Chicago. Zak Mucha celebrates the dignity and humanity of people whose lives are filled with trauma and adversity and yet somehow manage to survive. This book is a memoir, though it's mostly about other people. At the same time, it is (or should be) a textbook for real social workers—you know, the ones who actually work with people and communities that desperately need help."

—Joel Dvoskin, PhD, Former President of the American Psychology–Law Society, Former Acting Commissioner of NY State Office of Mental Health

"People say the word 'empathy' a lot these days. This book gives you a look at what it means and what it takes to actually do it. Walk the streets of Uptown with Zak, and you may hear the ghost of Nelson Algren, another great chronicler of Chicago life, laughing at these often unexpectedly funny stories of everyday battles with addiction, mental illness, and possibly the greatest enemy of all: bureaucracy. With humor and grace, this book shows us the missed appointments, the paperwork, the trips to the hospital; the run-ins with landlords, psychiatrists, and cops; the long, hard, and fearless work it takes to forgive ourselves for being human."

—Annia Ciezadlo, Journalist and Author of *Days of Honey*

"Intense and real. I found this book difficult to put down. From one mental health professional to another—kudos to Zak Mucha for his willingness to work with our community's most difficult clients, and the ability to write about it."

—Nicole S. Kluemper, PhD, Author of
See Jane Fly: A Memoir

SWIMMING TO THE HORIZON

Swimming to the Horizon: Crack, Psychosis, and Street-Corner Social Work

by Zak Mucha

© Copyright 2024 Zak Mucha

ISBN 979-8-88824-225-4

All rights reserved. No part of this publication may be reproduced, stored in a retrieval system, or transmitted in any form or by any means—electronic, mechanical, photocopy, recording, or any other—except for brief quotations in printed reviews, without the prior written permission of the author.

Front cover collage: *Enigma* by Bridgette Bramlage

Published by

3705 Shore Drive
Virginia Beach, VA 23455
800-435-4811
www.koehlerbooks.com

SWIMMING TO THE HORIZON

CRACK, PSYCHOSIS, AND STREET-CORNER SOCIAL WORK

ZAK MUCHA

VIRGINIA BEACH
CAPE CHARLES

For Alice Vachss, who reminded me when I was in the middle of this

In her essay, "Playing, Wild Thoughts, and a Novel's Underground," Siri Hustvedt wrote: "We remember and the meanings of what we remember are reconfigured over time. Memory and imagination cannot be separated. Remembering is always a form of imagining. And yet some memories remain outside sequence, story, and felt human time . . ."

Even so, it should be noted that while this is a personal story, all identifying features of characters in this book have been altered or disguised to protect their privacy. Any resemblance to persons alive or dead is coincidental.

PART ONE

1

The iced slop of Chicago sidewalks in February are treacherous enough. On this sidewalk, a psychotic young man named Jamil was screaming and throwing wild, roundhouse punches at me, long white bandages unraveling from his hands. We had just been up in his pay-by-the-month hotel room, where I was trying to coat his blackened, frostbitten fingers with silver nitrate paste before applying new bandages. Jamil wasn't having the clinical approach, so now it was zombie shadowboxing on Lawrence Avenue.

This was Uptown, where the city corralled its poor, psychotic, homeless, and addicted. I ran a street-level mental health team, and Jamil was the crisis of the moment.

In the dead of winter, he had spent two homeless weeks nearly freezing to death and running from us in hopes of avoiding the lousy housing options we had to offer. His previous landlord had evicted Jamil after catching him in his room with a full can of gasoline and plans to do something ugly with it. The police had to help me hospitalize him.

One day, after weeks on the run, Jamil showed up at our office and gave our program assistant, Stella, a look at his fingers—swollen, white, and blistered into balloons. We got him to an ER, where a doctor said Jamil might lose his fingertips. To prevent that, we had to locate and catch him twice a day to apply the silver nitrate.

As Jamil swung at me on Lawrence Avenue, I wondered what went through the minds of the people passing us by on their way to work. A cop car coasted past, and I tried to flag it down, but the officers inside stared straight ahead. Jamil ran back inside the hotel, and I followed him to his room, where he had left the door open.

Jamil had grown up in foster care, group homes, and mental institutions. Now he was an adult in our program, where people ended up when no other programs were effective. The worst part of the job was never really knowing the right thing to do—the mythical tried-and-true solution—in situations like this. I stood in Jamil's room and considered calling the cops to assist with a psychiatric hospitalization, which would have been easy to justify, thanks to his acute psychosis, violent behavior, and refusal of medical treatment. He wouldn't let me touch his hands, but I still didn't hospitalize him, and I would never know if that was the right call.

Over the next few weeks, as the doctor predicted, Jamil lost several fingers to gangrene. Over the next few years he continued to get drunk, high, tasered, hospitalized, arrested and evicted from his hotel rooms until there was nowhere left to put him but a psychiatric nursing home.

Maybe that day in his room he had appreciated not being hospitalized and punished for behaviors he couldn't control. Or maybe he didn't register anything at all. Hard to tell.

• • •

Historically, Uptown was a cluster of problematic city blocks that kept social workers of all sorts employed for decades. Prior to World War II, the hotels in the neighborhood catered to the upper and middle classes. Chicago mayor "Big" Bill Thompson lived in the Edgewater Hotel while he was in office and Jimmy Hoffa stayed there when he was in town. To escape prohibition raids, Al Capone used the coal tunnels that ran under the taverns and nightclubs on Broadway. In time, the moneyed began moving to better neighborhoods, their vacancies filled by displaced people from elsewhere.

The hotels became rooming houses, the interiors chopped into smaller units to provide housing for the returning servicemen without families. Appalachians from Kentucky, West Virginia, and Tennessee came north as the Southern mills and mines closed. Later, Cambodians and Vietnamese began to arrive on the edges of what had once been called Hillbilly Harlem, noted by *True* magazine in 1970 as one of the most violent neighborhoods in America.

Uptown also became one of the few racially integrated—though not peaceful—neighborhoods in a deeply segregated city. During that time, the Black Panthers, the Young Lords, and the Young Patriots created a temporary alliance between radical African Americans, Hispanics, and working-class Whites, prompted by the extreme poverty and police brutality in the neighborhood. But the displaced kept coming, as Uptown had the cheapest transient housing on the north side.

Social services became entrenched in the neighborhood during the Johnson administration's War on Poverty and the deinstitutionalization of the state mental hospitals. The area became a shunt valve for the homeless and mentally ill. Community mental health agencies popped up and attracted discharges from the hospitals.

One man I knew, who had been repeatedly hospitalized for vociferously interrupting Catholic masses, told me, "Uptown is the mentally ill ghetto. They ship us all here."

Even that has changed. I still live and work in the neighborhood, but the gentrification that had been promised—or threatened—since the 1970s has come to pass, displacing most of the folks who keep property values down.

• • •

This book is about those last years before gentrification knocked down the homeless shelters and chicken-wire flophouses. Former transient hotels and psychiatric nursing homes have been converted into luxury microsuites. Chain mattress stores have replaced mom-and-pop junk shops. Taverns that once had Lexan sally ports now sport repurposed wood and serve craft beer. Occasionally I run into a former client from the old neighborhood, but it doesn't happen much.

Before real estate money transformed the neighborhood, I ran an Assertive Community Treatment (ACT) team, a mental health program for clients suffering from severe and chronic psychotic disorders, drug addictions, homelessness, incarceration, poverty, and medical issues stemming from lives at the very bottom of the socioeconomic scale. I became the program's supervisor simply because no one else at the agency wanted the job. I was fresh out of school and learning as I went along. I had no clue what I was doing. Like a lot of people who end up in the social work or psychology fields, part of the reason I ended up doing this work in the first place was born out of a childhood urge to understand the adults around me. As a response to childhood trauma or the childhood responsibility of being a caretaker for others, emotionally or otherwise, some of us gravitate toward the helping professions in order to prove our worth. For me, that instinct was mixed up with two somewhat conflicting aspirations: to be a writer and to be a tough guy. I had models to mirror in both directions. Before I went to college, I bounced around jobs through my twenties—hanging sheetrock, moving furniture, working as an artist's assistant, a journalist, a novelist, a staffer at a juvie shelter, a teacher in women's prison, a labor organizer, and a bouncer. Once, in desperation, I tried to convince a Mongolian I knew from the truck yard to become a boxer, and I would be his trainer. We were both sick of carrying furniture, but he wouldn't do any roadwork.

I had tried working a couple of entry-level social-service jobs but always felt like an outsider. As a union organizer on the Ohio-West Virginia border, I was a stranger telling people how the union had the answers they were looking for in their lives.

Before that, I worked in a locked juvenile facility for adolescents who had been removed from their homes by child protective services. The unit was violent and often erupted into full-on brawls. The boys—some who had committed homicides, sexual assaults, or arsons—were living under the old "Boys Town" model of receiving gold stars for making their beds or brushing their teeth. They were all instructed to consider the unit and staff as family, a directive which, given the families these boys came from, was either a lie or a compounded insult. They were locked up precisely because of their families.

Both of those jobs seemed to hold a sort of missionary aspect. I was an outsider who could never be a part of the community, telling others from a distance how they ought to be. I often thought of the awful stereotype of the social worker, the well-meaning do-gooder who could leave the clients at the end of the day and go back to their safe homes in quiet neighborhoods without ever really understanding who their clients were or what they were going through.

I disliked school, but I disliked everything else even more, so I enrolled. I was older than most of my classmates. Despite my reservations, social work sounded like a portable degree with open-ended possibilities, and I figured I would find a path once I graduated.

I enrolled in a seminar with a professor employed by a domestic violence program that provided therapy for "men who batter"—clinical lingo to avoid stigmatizing those who one day might become "men who don't batter." The professor's clients were court-mandated to counseling. None volunteered, but each had a choice: counseling or jail. A big problem, the professor explained, was that most of the men possessed two sets of values. They told their counselors one thing but behaved differently outside the office. The professor backed this up by charting the cognitive distortions of men who batter, explaining how the flow between emotions, thoughts, and behaviors completed a full circle.

"They know what they do is wrong," the professor said, "but they go home and do it anyway. If I ask whether they would approve of someone slapping their mother, they get really angry, but they'll hit their own partners." To believe that a person can actually have two sets of values, one has to rationalize that a distortion exists somewhere, he said. I suspected the distortion belonged to the professor in believing a person could have two sets of values. His court-mandated clients, I assumed, were simply willing to play along with the therapist to stay out of jail. It sounded a lot like school. If school was time served, the internship was my education. I volunteered to work in the psychiatric unit of Cook County Jail. My duties were to provide therapeutic services of some kind for the men on my tier, an open room with thirty bunks, one guard, and an open row of toilets and showers. Some of the men I would see again and again over the years.

Manny was a tiny, soft-featured client, quiet and acquiescing with a self-diagnosed anger problem. I felt a physical repulsion for the man. He was in for domestic abuse and violation of probation. I assumed he behaved like a total coward with every person on the planet but his wife. I was wrong. During my second shift, Manny went off on an inmate twice his size. He jumped his opponent, not in the day room or on the deck where the guards would have intervened, but in the back storage room with no guards watching and nowhere to run. Three guards eventually had to pull the other guy off Manny and then hold him down until he stopped fighting. After they handcuffed him to a bench, he sat vibrating and grinding his teeth. With half his face swollen and one eye filled with blood, Manny approached my supervisor and requested therapy. Our first sessions were dead silent. We just sat in a tiny therapy room where the security chairs—too big and bottom-heavy for one person to lift—took up most of the floor space. He kept his body protected, arms folded, head down. He claimed to be hard of hearing, so I dragged my chair closer. I tried to slow my breathing and allow him to make eye contact. I gained some begrudging respect for Manny's maniacal devotion to his fragile self-esteem. He wanted to kill anybody he thought had insulted him. He didn't bother measuring potential opponents first. He wasn't a bully. He responded to a true sense of life-threatening terror provoked not only by physical threats but—and more frequently—threats to his sense of self. When he felt disrespected or diminished by someone, he was propelled to attack, to kill the perceived source of the threat. I thought of the domestic violence professor and the quote often paraphrased and attributed to Margaret Atwood: "Men are afraid women will laugh at them. Women are afraid men will kill them."

"What's it feel like when you go off?" I asked.

"Nothing," Manny said. "I don't know."

I walked him through the physiological changes that any human body goes through when a threat is perceived.

He found physical responses that sounded familiar. "It's like a tunnel," he said. "I can't see anyone but the person I'm pissed at. Like a fog and my arms and legs are shaky and don't weigh anything. Vibrating and not there. I have to do something to bring them back, you know?"

"Do you know how your face changes?" I asked, seeing his aggravation rise toward me and my questions.

"It doesn't."

"The hell it doesn't."

His baby face was so soft and seamless when calm, like he didn't have a concern in the world. But the transformation was truly extreme. He didn't believe me until I described it: furrowed brow, clenched jaw, flushed coloring. Listening to my description, he felt along his jawline and forehead like a blind man.

I had been working with Manny for seven months when one of the jail psychiatrists needed a client to keep another intern busy. He approached Manny. "If your therapy with Zak isn't working out, let me know," she said, offering to hook him up with a new psychologist with a better pedigree than I had. In my next session with him, Manny told me about the offer. I reminded him that if he felt like the sessions weren't helping he should let me know and we could quit. My feelings wouldn't be hurt.

He was confused by some advice the doctor had given him. "She told me I had to let go of my past."

"Did she say how to do that?"

"No! What the fuck!"

Manny stayed with me. And I hoped his wife would use his incarceration as an opportunity to get out of town.

In the psychiatric unit of Cook County Jail, many men saw their time inside as a natural occurrence, just a part of life in the world. To them, incarceration was something to be tolerated, but not a consequence of anything they had done wrong, nor an opportunity to redirect their life's path. Most of the guys had learned to say what they had to say in order to get through it.

One man confessed to me during a group session, "My problem is I'm addicted to stealing. I just can't keep my hands off other people's shit."

"What do you do with the stuff you steal?" I asked.

"What?"

"I mean, do you hoard the stuff, keep it under your bed and really treasure it?"

"No, I sell it for money."

"Okay. What do you do with the money you get from that?"

"I buy dope."

"Okay, so if you had the money, would you steal?"

"No. I'd buy dope."

"If you had the dope, would you steal?"

He thought for a half-second. "I wouldn't care about money."

"Then the problem isn't stealing," I said. "The problem is that you're not a successful thief. You have choices here. You can find a different way of getting money, stop using dope, or learn to steal better—unless the plan is to keep coming here."

In group sessions, we charted the risks and gains for various crimes, whether stealing a car, fighting at a taqueria, or smoking crack. We looked at the difference between committing a push-in burglary on Wilson Avenue versus a burglary in some posh suburb where the gain could be more than a DVD player, but the risk of arrest was much higher. In diagramming the consequences of economic crimes, we illustrated how simple the decision was when a person had nothing to lose. The downside consisted merely of having to avoid arrest—a plan usually made while running down the street once the act had been committed.

The main problem with working in the corrections system is that every client, no matter what brought him into jail, had the same treatment goal: getting out of jail. Anything else was secondary. At one point during my jail internship, my supervisor tipped me that one of my professors had said I needed to "soften up a bit" based on a heated discussion between myself and the advisors regarding my final thesis on qualitative interviews with skinheads. They thought I should keep editing with only their vaguest suggestions, which were not written down anywhere. I thought I was being hazed. I asked my supervisor what she thought. "I think you're fine," she said. "But I'm in the jail. What do I know?"

After graduation, I went back to Uptown and took a job with a community mental health agency. Some of my old pals were less than enthusiastic about my new social-work career. One guy, after I told him a couple of work stories, said, "You're just an adrenaline junkie trying to look like a nice guy."

2

SPRING 2006

Another friend, a police officer with thirty years of martial arts training and life experience over me, also voiced concerns over my new job.

"It sounds dangerous," he said. "Do you carry anything?" When I said I didn't, he offered me a yawara stick—a little baton that fit neatly in the palm of my hand—for self-defense. He pulled out his own, attached to a keyring, and demonstrated how to pop a rowdy in the sternum or crack someone's skull if I were really in trouble. He finished the lesson by wrapping his own hands around my wrist and leveraging the baton against the bone, dropping me to my knees. I didn't know what to expect from the job, but I was certain I couldn't carry weapons. I knew I was to be a therapist for clients who were suffering from acute and chronic psychotic symptoms. And I knew my job wouldn't be to hang around the office much. I would be in the neighborhood, visiting clients at home, providing therapy and assisting with housing, Social Security and disability benefits, medications, and legal issues. The office filled a two-story building on a quiet residential block of wood frame houses and courtyard apartment buildings. The agency made a wise move not to advertise for business. The upscale neighbors gentrifying the block regularly complained about clients throwing cigarette butts in their yards, sitting on the stoops, and drinking and pissing in the alley. The front door of the office opened to a waiting room and an elevated reception area. Beyond the first secure door at the side of the reception desk, two hallways led to treatment rooms and staff offices. My supervisor gave me the tour and directed me to a desk in a narrow group office shared by six case managers and therapists. The desks were generic pressboard jobs from an office supply catalog, all matching. Case managers ran in and out of the office while I sat at my desk, browsing through case files and giving a cursory read of the employee manual on subjects like infection control and fire extinguisher safety. I read service notes and intake assessments at my desk for the first three days, bored silly. The next few weeks I rode along with case managers, meeting clients and seeing the various buildings in the neighborhood that were part of the routine—single room occupancy (SROs) hotels that served as low-income housing, the pharmacy, the public aid office, the medical clinics, and the discount grocery, which during the first week of each month when Social Security checks were disbursed was like one of those apocalyptic movie scenes with people stocking up before the impending crisis kicks off. I rode with one case manager, Brandon, who was so reserved that I couldn't tell whether his demeanor was low-grade depression, mild autism, or an honest response to a new guy tagging along. We were picking up Karl who, Brandon warned me, was painfully shy and beyond overweight. Generally, Karl did not speak. He could rasp or grunt, and he didn't like new people. We found Karl in front of his building, trying to distribute his girth equally between his cane, the wrought iron fence behind him, and his own distressed knees. He was the most immense human I'd ever seen. His legs bowed inward at the knees and each step looked bone-grindingly painful. Karl's case management was limited to driving his five hundred pounds to the grocery store once a week. He refused any other medical, therapeutic, or psychiatric services. Brandon introduced me and Karl refused to acknowledge my presence. "Where do you want to go?" Brandon asked Karl.

"Nggh."

"Dominick's?"

I hung back at the grocery store and watched Brandon fill Karl's shopping cart as Karl pointed in the general direction of items he wanted. Brandon later claimed that Karl could hold in-depth conversations about politics, natural law, and animal husbandry but would only do it with Brandon. I felt like I was being pranked by both of them. If this was the entirety of the job, I decided I would quit.

• • •

LeFlore had been passed down by a series of case managers whose primary duties consisted of stopping by his room every night to provide a cocktail of serious antipsychotic medications—and when out in the neighborhood, keep him from screaming obscenities at his ten-foot-tall invisible friend. Wrapped inside layers of clothing flecked with chewing tobacco, LeFlore was the prototype of the ambulatory psychotic: matted dreadlocks, random teeth, and rotten clothes. The pockets of his jacket contained Slim Jims and cans of sardines, to which he would help himself during group therapy sessions. Every so often, he would simply scream, "Don't you fuck with me!" I hadn't seen LeFlore since my internship at Cook County Jail, where I'd had to sit next to him in group sessions and prompt him throughout the hour to quit pointing across the room and snapping off curses at his hallucinations. Sometimes he would smile and calm down with my reminder—sometimes he would glare back at me.

We picked up Le Flore at his hotel. As he came out to the van, he saw me in the passenger seat and pointed.

"I know you," he said. "You finish school?"

"Yeah."

"You work here now?"

"Starting this week."

"You a social worker now?"

"Yeah."

"Where did you go to school?"

I told him.

"I think I heard of it," he said, which is what folks say when they're being polite. "How much money you make a year? Eighty thousand?"

"Nooo."

"Forty?"

"No."

LeFlore whistled a note of disbelief and shrugged. If I wasn't even making forty grand a year, I couldn't be that smart.

• • •

After a few days of shadowing my coworkers, my supervisor called me in.

"I think we have a client for you," he said. "Two people from emergency services went to outreach to this client yesterday because he didn't come to an intake. He has a psych appointment he's supposed to go to, but he might need to be hospitalized."

I didn't know what this meant. The client, Bobby, had been in the hospital for the last three months and had been recently discharged to a hotel room and outpatient care. The emergency services team of two people visited Bobby in his room, but he had been "sexually inappropriate." Apparently, he had come to the door wrapped in a bed sheet and refused to get dressed. So, the women had sat down and tried to ask questions.

The intake process is a matter of introducing a person to the services they could receive through any of the agency's programs and also assessing which programs would best benefit the potential client. One of those standard questions is: *What kind of services do you think you need?* In response, Bobby had leaned forward, placing a hand on one knee of each woman and responded: "Sexual release. And fucking."

The intake team had ended the interview, gone back to the office, and put in a call to my supervisor, who had then handed the case to the new guy. I was to bring Bobby to the office for his scheduled psychiatric evaluation. I went to Bobby's hotel, which had been a grand place seventy years earlier, but was now one of the larger, and safer, SRO hotels in the neighborhood. The lobby smelled like urine and cheap cigarettes, but the top floor had an abandoned ballroom and indoor swimming pool that hinted at how the place had once been reserved for the moneyed class.

I eventually found the manager and asked him about Bobby.

"I can't have him acting up and making people uncomfortable," he said. "He shouldn't even be here. This is for senior citizens mostly."

I would soon learn the hotel was mostly not for senior citizens but was one of the few places that would take tenants who were on disability. They charged a disproportionate amount for rent but offered month-by-month rental agreements and cut some slack for tenants like Bobby, who sometimes caused problems in the building. I explained that we were trying to keep Bobby on his medications, so he wouldn't be acting up. I said we appreciated that he was looking out for our guy.

"I'm not," he said. "I'm looking out for my job. His neighbors told me he's banging his head against the wall all night. He does it again; he's out of here."

"I'm going to get him to the doctor."

"Yeah, go ahead. Good luck."

Outside the door of room 510, I prepared myself to find some scrawny letch of a guy sitting in the dark, bottles of booze and overflowing ashtrays covering every flat surface in the room. I braced myself for a confrontation, figuring this guy wouldn't want to go and might even be offended by the intrusion. I knocked and waited. A chubby man wearing only a pair of boxers opened the door. He had a bowl haircut and the wide cheekbones of an Aztec under layers of fat. "Can I help you?" he asked in a child's passive voice.

"Are you Bobby?"

"Yes."

"I'm Zak. You met a couple of my coworkers yesterday. You have an appointment over at the office to meet with a psychiatrist."

"I didn't make an appointment."

"No, they did."

"Um. I don't think I need it."

He tried to shut the door. I gently held it open. "Maybe not. But you ought to go prove you don't need it."

I was already making up rationales for things I hardly understood. I had no clue here, and suspected Bobby knew this.

"Mmmm. I don't know about that. I don't have anything to prove, really."

"The only reason you might want to is so you don't have to go back to the hospital." I stopped talking when I noticed Bobby staring so intently at me that he could probably see the wall through my head. "Bobby?" I said.

He was listening to something else.

"Bobby, are you taking your meds?"

He came back for a moment. "I don't like them. I don't need any more. I have a lot."

Bobby stepped back to let me in. The narrow walkway connecting the door to the room provided space for the sink, refrigerator, and toilet. He had full bottles of antipsychotic meds—Haldol and Risperdal—lined up on his little kitchen table. The prescription dates were from four months earlier. The room itself was spotless, an open square with one window, one bed, one dresser, one television, and one clock radio. The bed was made with the sheets pulled taut. Cans of soup and boxes of Ramen were set in ordered rows on the bedroom dresser.

Bobby didn't want to see the doctor. I suggested if he didn't go, he would be breaking the agreement he made in order to get out of the hospital. I explained that the building manager was complaining about something—I didn't say what—and the doctors sent me because they were concerned. I continued pulling rationales from the air like a magician pulling silk handkerchiefs until Bobby relented. He stepped out of his underwear and put on shorts and a T-shirt. I took him outside to the car. Bobby and I sat and waited to meet the psychiatrist at one of our agency's buildings. I didn't know anyone on staff, and no one knew me. Having just met Bobby, I asked him some generic questions but his only response was to begin listing various female television meteorologists. He said they worked out of town a lot and had odd schedules, so he didn't get to see them much.

"My wives come and go," he said. "They're busy. They see me sometimes and we have sex, but they leave without saying much. I should not talk about this much because my parents met in Washington and the government knows how they met and they are reading my thoughts."

"Your parents?"

"The government. They are reading my thoughts. They talk about me in their meetings, trying to figure out how to keep me from doing things."

"Like what?"

"I'm not telling. But sometimes I leave instructions for the economy, like they could take those instead of my life. But they never do what I say. They don't want my advice. They just watch me."

I asked myself the question that would become a mantra for a while: *What the hell do I say to that?*

Bobby wasn't staring blankly at the wall or boring a hole through my head with his eyes but was focused on one single spot floating in the air between us. At times, he seemed to go totally blank, almost inert, like a screen saver, in response to whatever was happening internally. I tried to separate facts from his delusions and as I asked more questions, Bobby just stared and giggled to himself. I felt my face beginning to flush. I wanted to ask someone what the hell I should do now, but everyone looked busy.

And then Bobby couldn't shut up. He said George Bush regularly intercepted his thoughts and that he wanted to write a letter telling the president to knock it off. When Bobby's social worker showed up, she had to force a smile to look less distraught at seeing him. She asked if he remembered her from yesterday. He said he did.

"Are you hearing voices now?" she asked.

"Yeah, some."

"Are they telling you to do things?"

"Sorta."

"What are they telling you?"

"Umm, that I should go now."

Bobby stood up and politely excused himself. I followed him down the hall and coaxed him back, explaining that we still had to check in with the doctor. He followed me back to the office and when the social worker couldn't get any more answers, we were excused. While we waited in the doctor's office, I told Bobby to jump on the scale, aiming to distract him for a minute. He weighed 267. Eventually the doctor, a slender woman with an open smile, came in and sat down.

"And how long have you been working with Bobby?" she asked me.

I looked at my watch. "About half an hour."

The doctor went through the standard evaluation questions. Whether Bobby was hearing or seeing things that might not be there. Whether he felt like others could read his thoughts or wanted to hurt him. She checked whether he knew the year, the day, and the name of the president of the United States. And she asked if he was taking his medications.

"I have eleven wives I want to fuck," he said.

"Oh, my."

"I have to go now," Bobby said and got up again to leave. I corralled him back into the office, offering to give him a ride home. I checked my watch. I had my first intake interview at one o'clock. My schedule was starting to feel hectic.

"Can you get on the scale?" the doctor asked Bobby.

"I know how much I weigh," Bobby said. "All you people want to do is weigh me."

The doctor lowered her eyes and silently mouthed the word "hospital" to me. I knew she meant he had to go to the hospital, but did that mean I was to take him? Which hospital? Did I call an ambulance? The cops? As we walked back to the waiting room, I looked in on Bobby's social worker and she waved the involuntary commitment form at me. Bobby and I waited in the lobby. Every few minutes he grew restless and would lumber toward the door. I followed him out each time and directed him back to the row of plastic chairs. An hour passed and no Medivan or ambulance came. I went back to the social worker and explained that I had to get back to my office for an intake.

"You can't stay with him?" she said.

"Not much longer."

"I don't think anyone here can."

I didn't understand why not. There were people all over the place, walking around, sitting alone in their offices. I didn't know if protocol demanded that whoever brought the client to the appointment was responsible for the hospitalization. I couldn't tell if I was the new guy getting jerked around. None of this was in the employee manual. I would understand later that crisis work—hospitalizations, suicidality, potential violence—always takes priority over scheduled therapy sessions, intake interviews, and staff meetings. And I would learn that my days on this job were simply going to be chaotic.

"Can you just wait until people get back from lunch?" the social worker asked.

I waited until a young woman, who radiated a soothing calm, was able to stay with Bobby. Her office was softly lit, a Tibetan scarf over the lampshade, her diploma on the wall. I thought she was going to have to fend for herself if Bobby decided she should audition for his delusional harem. When I left, he was staring through her skull. I got back to the office in time to sit down for an intake with Standish, a Vietnam vet with a greaser's ducktail. Standish had been mugged at gunpoint for his Social Security Disability Insurance (SSDI) money.

"I'm not racist," he said. "But these niggers are gonna kill someone."

He was out of money and out of meds and shook throughout the interview. He left huge gaps in his story but it was a relief to speak to someone who seemed to occupy the same plane of reality as me. We agreed to meet the next day to get emergency meds from the psychiatric clinic. Back at my desk at the end of the day, I saw an email from the calm, soothing social worker.

"Bobby never made it to the hospital."

The email suggested, for future reference, that I not leave clients alone in an empty room when they should be hospitalized.

Without thinking, I wrote back that I hadn't left him alone; I'd left him "in your office."

She never responded. I was angry. The next morning, I went to the hotel and knocked on Bobby's door. Bobby answered in his underwear again and offered a warning.

"If you're coming to tell me one of my wives is cheating, I'll kill her."

"That's not it," I said, adding that if one more complaint about him went to the building manager the hotel would kick him out.

His threats against his imaginary wives also had me worried he might threaten an actual person, or worse. I tried to explain that he might benefit from a hospital psych exam, but I couldn't tell if he heard me—he just stared at my face with no expression on his. I repeated myself and waited. He stood up, put on his pants, and grabbed a notebook and a baseball cap.

"Let's go," he said.

This surprised me.

We left his keys at the front desk for safekeeping, and I took him to the hospital.

A hospital worker showed me how to fill out the involuntary commitment papers. "He'll probably be out in five days," he said.

3

I found Standish in the office waiting room the next day, hunched over in a plastic chair. His knees were angled over his lap and his fingertips would have reached the floor if he extended his arms. While other clients there wore layers of mismatched clothes, inappropriate for the June weather, Standish's shoes were shined like mirrors under the cuffs of gray dress pants topped by a maroon polo shirt. He had not been dressed like this yesterday. According to his old intake records, Standish had a history of slipping away from treatment once his immediate problems were solved. I stored this information away, not certain what it meant. Maybe Standish only came in when he ran out of options and was truly in crisis. Maybe he came through to hustle case managers when he needed some extra cash. He said he had been diagnosed with schizophrenia and post-traumatic stress disorder years ago. I didn't see any psychotic symptoms, at least not as acutely as I had seen in Bobby or LeFlore. But I hadn't seen Standish react to anything other than an intake interview, and I had no other intakes with which to compare his. He didn't have enough money for food or the rent coming due in two weeks. Beyond that, I was only certain that Standish was big and angry and refused to discuss why he was no longer receiving psychiatric services from the Veterans Administration.

"Fuck them, no way," was all he would say.

He spat out snippets of his history, flashes of frustration crossing his face before he passed into calm again.

"There's things I'm not going to tell you," he said, momentarily centered. "I don't know you yet and I might not ever."

"Yeah, you have no reason to trust me. If you decide you do later, okay."

I could feel my words hitting the brick wall Standish projected.

He suspected me for even agreeing with him that he shouldn't trust me. I felt awkward and wanted him to relax. But here was this guy who stood a head taller than me, had twenty years on me, had done two tours of duty in Vietnam, and now was stuck depending on me to keep him from being homeless. I had no right to say, "Trust me," and expect anyone to do so—especially in a relationship where a power imbalance hung over every conversation. During my internship at Cook County Jail, if I expressed any beliefs about the fragility of a client, their dependence on my skills, or my inability to help them, my supervisor would set me straight.

"These people are much tougher than you think," he said. "They have survived everything without starving to death before they met you. If you were to die tomorrow, they would be just fine."

• • •

Standish said he needed his meds. I could do that. If he had been seeing psychiatrists at the Veterans Administration, he should already have meds, but he said he got mugged and lost them. I had a bunch of questions because his story didn't make sense. I could have demanded a timeline of his last appointments and permission to contact his doctor before scheduling a psychiatric appointment, but he would have bolted. I had the vague feeling I was being played, because the implication behind his limited disclosure was, "If you push me, I'll quit this."

I knew that feeling. Ultimatums were always challenges for me, whether they came from a girlfriend or an employer. I'd had some unfortunately short relationships with both and I didn't want to push anyone into that corner. I didn't want my clients to feel like they had to give up power in order to talk to me. The job wasn't supposed to be a power struggle. I had to shove my ego down a bit. Standish needed meds. So I called our emergency clinic, unaware of the proper procedure to get them. In order to finagle an immediate appointment

I said the case was dire. Standish and I went to see a doctor in another office. Dr. Radler didn't seem very impressed with Standish, or me for that matter.

"Now, what is the problem?" he asked. Standish told pieces of his story—the nursing home, the flophouse, the mugging. He didn't have any paperwork and he hadn't been to see his old psychiatrist in months. Last month he had filled some scripts at Cook County Hospital, waiting eight hours for a ten-minute appointment and a refill. The process hadn't encouraged him to return. The doctor fired off a string of questions as if Standish wasn't in the room.

Why didn't I have any discharge papers for the client?

Why didn't the client have any prescriptions or money?

Why wasn't the client still seeing his previous doctor?

Why couldn't the client remember his exact dosages?

"I think I know what I was taking," Standish said, "if you'll let me talk."

"I cannot write a prescription based on what you think you know," the doctor said. "You know or you don't."

"I know I was diagnosed with PTSD. I was at the VA for years."

"Why are you not getting your medication from them now?"

"A lot of reasons. I've had it with them."

Standish adjusted his coat sleeve, and I saw the tattooed chains around his wrist.

"Were you in Vietnam?" the doctor asked.

"I did two tours of duty," he said proudly.

"I do not understand." The doctor settled back into his leather chair. "What is the purpose of war? To shoot people for what reason?"

Standish didn't answer.

"Did you kill people?"

"Yes."

"Did you kill a lot of people? With a gun?"

The doctor mimed sighting down an invisible rifle and jerking back with the recoil. Trying to dry his sweaty face with his shirtsleeve,

Standish measured the distance between himself and the doctor. I was too far from the desk to physically intervene.

"What's a lot? Standish asked carefully.

Dr. Radler continued explaining the futility of the Vietnam War and US imperialism in general, oblivious to the possibility Standish needed psych meds precisely because he had been to war. But even if Standish had never seen combat, even if his story was complete bullshit, he was obviously coping poorly with many things in his life and fighting to retain his composure in front of two strangers.

The doctor made that sanctimonious clucking noise with his tongue. "Protector of our country and now you are homeless," he said.

I interrupted. "What we need right now are the meds Standish lost. He's been without for nearly two weeks."

"I see no discharge papers here."

"He wasn't discharged. He was mugged."

"You look very big to be mugged," the doctor said to Standish.

I tried to push him back onto the point.

"Okay," the doctor said. "I will help."

He picked up a copy of the Physician's Desk Reference and flipped through to find pharmaceutical mugshots for Standish to point out his meds and dosages. We got samples from the nurse's station to hold Standish over. When we got out to the sidewalk Standish began taking full, deep breaths again.

"I was just about to fuck him up," he said. "Motherfucker is telling me what I did was wrong? Where was he? In college, protesting? You see how close I was?"

"I saw that. Glad you didn't."

"You think you could have stopped me?"

"You think I'd bother?"

He laughed and I handed him the paper bag of Seroquel and Depakote. We smoked cigarettes and watched the traffic for a while. In the office he had looked like a frightened old man. Outside, he looked twenty years younger. In the office, all the power belonged to the doctor.

In the car, Standish slumped again as if he were waiting for a slap to the back of the head.

"I still don't have food money," he said.

I was embarrassed for the guy. He'd had to sit through a grilling about his military service to get psychotropic medications, and then he had to ask for food money from a guy young enough to be his son. I didn't like being embarrassed, not for myself or anyone else. I took my bit of the agency's petty cash fund, and we went to Aldi's. I waited in the van until Standish returned with enough Ramen noodles, bread, and lunch meat to get through the week. He looked nervous again. I stayed quiet as we rolled back into traffic.

"Can I get two bucks to get a DVD to watch?" he asked." I need something to do." The request deflated my embarrassment for his suffering pride. I was offended he took me to be such a soft touch. Maybe my assessment had been completely off, and he was just a siphon with a good story.

"No," I said. "Go to the library. Stuff's free." Even as the answer left my mouth, I saw ripples of anxiety rolling off of him, and the hard features of his face went slack. He nodded firmly as if he had made a decision.

We drove back to Wilson and Broadway, a notorious corner that exemplified what the neighborhood had to offer. A preacher from the Jesus Hotel testifying through a megaphone. Guys dressed as Statues of Liberty passing out flyers in front of Popeye's Chicken. Neighborhood players selling crack, begging for change, or hustling whatever at the El station. Two methadone clinics and a Salvation Army were within walking distance. Gang violence was never particularly organized in the neighborhood, but Wilson and Broadway was always the scene of some dispute that prompted random shootings.

Standish was staying at the Wilson Men's Club on the other side of the El tracks. The Wilson was one of the last chicken-wire sleeping room SROs in the city. The rooms were cubicles with a cot, a bare light bulb hanging from the ceiling, and barely enough room to stretch out.

Each floor held dozens of cubicles, all topped off with chicken-wire ceilings. The bathrooms were shared, the noise could be unbearable, and the fire escape doors over the alley had signs posted: *Do Not Throw Urine Out The Windows!*

I dropped Standish at his door. I learned two weeks later that Standish had walked in and borrowed money from the juice man in the hotel. The interest was twenty-five percent a week and when his next Social Security check came, Standish didn't have rent. I didn't see him again until he was three days away from being homeless.

• • •

Leonard got tacked onto my load after his case manager, Leslie, hit a wall and went to my supervisor.

"I think he needs therapy," she said. "He doesn't want to stop being homeless. It's crazy."

I took Leonard on. I didn't have any reason to reject anyone. When I walked into the treatment room to meet Leonard, he was screaming at Leslie, arguing that she owed him money, not wholly a delusion. The agency provided payee service for those who could not, for whatever reason, handle their own money effectively. Often, the Social Security Administration would decide a person could receive disability benefits as long as another person or organization accepted the role of the client's payee. The payee had to pay the client's bills and dole out the remaining funds. By the time clients reached our agency, they had typically burned so many bridges that family and friends were done battling with them over money. I had run into Leonard outside the office before. He stank from the sickly-sweet layers of booze his body processed twenty-four hours a day. He would park his shopping cart on the sidewalk outside the office door, usually asking another client to keep an eye on it in exchange for a cigarette. Beneath Leonard's baseball cap I saw wide, flat cheekbones framing a nose that had been pounded crooked years ago.

He stopped screaming at Leslie and spoke in a halting voice, every syllable a huff. "This is unfair," he told her. "You have my money and I want it now."

As he pounded the desk with the flat of his hand, I saw each long fingernail packed with black dirt. "I am holding onto your money to get you an apartment like you said you wanted," she said.

"Well, where's my apartment?"

"It takes time. It will be ready by Wednesday, and you can move in."

"Forget it. I'm better off without."

Leonard received the average $674 a month in Social Security benefits, which left him very little to live on after the rent was paid. Several SRO landlords had refused Leonard tenancy due to his criminal record, and he had survived just fine on the street without it. On the street with 674 bucks seemed preferable to being under a roof with a hundred dollars to last the month. He didn't want to stay in any of the homeless shelters. They had too many rules, and you could not protect your belongings—or even your own body. Leonard stayed at the edges of the crews who slept in tents beneath the viaducts on Lake Shore Drive.

"This is your therapist," Leslie said, using my arrival as an opportunity to slip out. "You two should talk."

"What are we supposed to talk about?" Leonard asked.

"I'm a therapist here. My job is to talk to people about whatever they have going on and help with whatever problems they have to figure out."

"What do you want to talk about?"

"Up to you. Anything bothering you?"

"Big things. Revolutionary things."

"Okay, like what?"

"I'm spiritual. I talk to God. My real name is spiritual, a mix of wolf-turtle."

"Okay. What's that mean?"

"I'm Oglala Indian, but that's not all of it. I believe in a higher power. I can't live in His ways, and I want to. I'm too much of a carnal mind. I can't get away from this."

He gestured like a frantic magician, swirling the air in front of his chest as if he could coax something invisible out of his body. I jumped in without much plan.

"I think I get it. You have a working relationship with your spirits, right?"

"Yeah."

"You talk to them, right? That's what you're supposed to do if it feels right. Other people don't have that kind of relationship and it freaks them out a little to see someone who does. They see you talking and no one's there."

"God is everywhere, man. I see the signs. See this?"

Leonard opened his coat to reveal two pigeon feathers tied with string and pinned to his shirt. "That's a sign."

"Of what?"

"God's glory. It was left for me on the sidewalk to tell me what I have to do."

"What is it you have to do?"

"Praise Him."

It was better than the answer I feared: kill them.

Leonard got signs from God all the time. Nearly every moment of the day provided a divine message to be plucked from the mundane air. People kept telling him he was delusional and that the voices were not God but a symptom of a mental illness. Leonard didn't believe this. For him, as for many, the idea that God was passing notes was much easier to swallow than the idea that he didn't have control of his own brain. If Leonard saw a motorcycle cruise past, for example, it was encouragement from God that he should continue on his path.

"See?" he said. "*Motorcycle* means to change through life. *Motor* means motivate and *cycle* means to cycle." He smiled, showing me a row of broken uppers. "I'm on my path," he said. "I don't know if I want to be inside an apartment. All those material goods, they corrupt. I'm not concerned about my physical body. I want to work on my inner self."

"That's admirable," I said, pointing to the big, sloppy numbers written across the back of his hand from a recent arrest. "But how many times have you been picked up in the past couple months?"

"Oh, yeah. I was prospecting."

"Where?"

"At the McDonald's by the drive-thru. They don't like that. But it wasn't bad. The captain let me sleep in the cell. He woke me up with everybody else then let me go back to sleep. It was nice. I asked if I could stay another night."

"You don't want an apartment, but sleeping in the lock-up is okay?"

"It's better than being outside."

"Okay. Is an apartment better than jail?"

"Sure."

"If jail's better than outside, wouldn't an apartment be better than outside, too?"

"I guess."

With my hands I placed A, B, and C at different levels in the air between us. "Sure. If A is better than B, and B is better than C, isn't A better than C, too?"

"Yeah. Sure."

"Having a roof over your head is going to give you more time to focus on the spiritual end of things, right? You get your material body indoors and you can focus on the spiritual much easier. You won't have to spend so much energy protecting the material and physical so much."

"I don't want to be too materialistic."

"You're not getting a penthouse on Lake Shore Drive. Where in the Bible does it say you have to sleep under a viaduct? Look at the religious leaders, the good ones. Martin Luther King had a house. Moses had a house. Gandhi had a house." I didn't know if Gandhi lived in a giant shoe, but I figured Leonard didn't either.

"I'll think about it."

"That's all you have to do," I said. "If you move in and decide you don't like it, then you can move back out. Your choice."

I walked Leonard to the door, and we found his shopping cart unattended in the rain. I went back to the garage and found an industrial-size garbage bag for him to cover his belongings.

"You are my spiritual brother," he said, unfurling his own garbage-bag poncho and slipping it over his shoulders.

While this statement made me feel good, I suspected he would be disappointed later because I had done nothing to become his brother. If that status was so easily ascribed, it would be easily taken away.

4

Schoolwork doesn't prepare anyone to navigate this job. A couple of coworkers guided me through documentation processes and organizational procedures while managing their own overflowing caseloads. I got a brief primer on the bureaucracy of the Social Security Administration, the Department of Mental Health, the Department of Human Services, Medicaid billing, and subsidized housing programs. People tipped me off to the best times to visit Public Aid (before 9 a.m.) and the best time to call (never). Also, the best route to apply for subsidized housing, where to schedule a dental appointment for an undocumented resident with no Medicaid, and how to negotiate payment plans for security deposits on client apartments. The textbooks could describe the proper manners to present when meeting a client: make eye contact, lean forward to show you are listening, and utter polite, nonjudgmental noises at appropriate moments to prompt more talk. But I had to come up with an answer to why any client would want to take meds and stop drinking. No client was going to listen to me because I had a master's degree. Not long ago, to me and my pals, a college degree had been a sign of softness. If a guy came onto the truck yard and clearly looked like he was carrying a degree, we would place bets as to how soon he would quit. For a long time, I assumed all jobs were like that: let's see how much grief the new guy can take.

• • •

During my first weeks I didn't have enough clients to fill an eight-hour day, but two months into the job eight-hour days became a luxury. I was proud to be working longer hours than other people. I knew that feeling was a holdover from manual labor jobs where we would compete to see who could work the hardest, carry the most loads of drywall. Anyone who didn't volunteer to work harder than the next guy was, in our estimation, less of a human and not to be relied upon. To some extent this is simple macho pride. We knew, logically, that the harder we worked, the more money the boss made while our wages stayed the same. But it was a safe and righteous way to measure ourselves. As long as those measures were in place, we were better than the boss who sat in the air conditioning all day. But this wasn't a truck yard, and we weren't working an assembly line. I couldn't look at this job like I would a semitrailer to be loaded and emptied by 4 p.m. I had to change the way I measured my value each day.

I had an urge to hurry clients toward some stability. This wasn't shift work. It was a continuous, unbroken series of problems and responsibilities, one day building on the next with intermittent breaks to repair whatever had gone wrong during my off-hours. It was bailing water out of a boat that had too many holes.

I got a lot of clients who were described as "nice" by the referral sources, and I learned this adjective should be taken as a warning. One man I interviewed, Davone, was "sorta homeless" because he couldn't stay with his sister for long. And his probation was about to be violated because he'd gotten picked up for trespassing, a charge that could mean anything from standing on a known drug corner to letting himself into an apartment that wasn't his. He wanted a letter from a social worker, hoping that would keep him out of jail.

"I feel depressed a lot," he said. I gave my default response to clients who described depression resulting from the lousy situations in which they lived.

"That makes sense."

Who wouldn't be depressed if they couldn't stay out of jail for more than a month at a time? Davone bowed out of the intake interview when I informed him I couldn't write a letter of recommendation to his probation officer until after he began participating in services.

"Oh," he said. "I need it on Monday."

He thanked me for my time and ended the interview. Davone's sister called two days after his interview, asking if I could bail her brother out of Cook County Jail. No, I couldn't. Just because a person couldn't stay out of jail didn't mean they were mentally ill. The compressed schedule of seeing clients back to back all day helped me compare their needs, symptoms, and levels of participation in our program. I gauged who was drifting away because they didn't need services, who was falling away because of psychosis or severe depression, and who was malingering and hoping to score the mythical "free rent" other clients spoke about. I took whichever clients were thrown at me with new-guy enthusiasm and no complaints. Because of this, a lot of my referrals came with prison records that disqualified them from other caseloads. During one intake, a man tried to explain away his murder conviction and fourteen-year incarceration.

"I didn't do it, pretty much. But I took the blame. See, I had a girlfriend and a friend. He was a guy and, see, I would have sex with my girlfriend, but my friend, he would sometimes have sex with my girlfriend, too. But when he did, he would give her money. And this one time he didn't give her money and she killed him. I confessed to it because I wasn't in my right mind at the time, but I didn't really do it." The best interpretation I could make of this was that he was a sometime pimp who had killed a john. With no provisional diagnosis other than substance use and, possibly, depression, he walked away from the agency after learning he wouldn't get a free apartment and spending money in exchange for declaring some sort of mental illness. He would have gladly accepted any diagnosis in lieu of having to support himself. Another interviewee with a record tried to tell me he had never done time. Instead, he said, he had simply done nothing for twenty years.

"I just stayed on my mom's couch. I was depressed."

He knew enough to stick to his story. Maybe Mom had given him all those tattoos while they were watching *The Price is Right*. To distinguish between genuine therapy clients and murderers who wanted free apartments, I assessed clients by their behavior. If someone wanted services, they had to participate. When the former pimp or the twenty-year couch surfer would come in reeking of booze, demanding assistance because they were living in a shelter and starving, I had a default response: "You were able to get money for booze. How do you get money for food?"

One kid was referred to our agency after he aged out of an adolescent group home. Scabs and scars, bloody red and pale white, tattooed the inside of each forearm. He quoted Nietzsche and bragged of an extremely high pain tolerance: "I pulled off a perfectly good toenail just to see if I could."

Another man came in announcing he knew the machinations of the racist conspiracy between our agency, the court system, and his ex-wife. Nearly vibrating with anger, he demanded help filing a lawsuit against the agency but repeatedly refused any psychiatric evaluations or case management services. During our few sessions, the man would work himself into such a frothing rage that I shifted my weight so I sat balanced on the edge of my chair, one leg coiled with my foot against the wall behind me. If he was coming over the desk, I could at least meet him halfway.

5

"I need money now," Standish snapped. "I don't even know where I'm going to get my next meal. I don't have rent for this month. They're going to put me on the street."

His rent was due on the fifteenth and his SSDI check wasn't coming until the beginning of the next month. He had already borrowed money from the juice man at the Wilson Men's Club and the interest kept rolling at five-for-four every week. Standish was probably the only resident at the Wilson Men's Club with an ironing board. He kept his wardrobe hanging neatly from the chicken-wire ceiling of his cubicle and each morning he splashed the communal bathroom with a gallon of bleach.

The curdled smell of discarded food, blunts, and human waste permeated the air of the Wilson. Televisions and radios blasted constantly, and residents yelled throughout the night. Standish didn't take his Seroquel because he didn't want to sleep too deeply against the chances of a desperate crackhead pushing through his flimsy door at three in the morning. The budget we had established would have barely gotten Standish through the month, but he'd torpedoed that by borrowing against his next SSDI check. Now that chunk of money would go to the flophouse loan shark, who Standish didn't have the luxury of avoiding.

We sat in my car and made plans. He was about to be on the street, so I dropped the big, ugly situation in front of him as honestly as possible.

"You're going to have to get out of there," I said.

"And do what?" he asked.

I kept my voice level and said he would have to be homeless for a while. Standish didn't absorb my answer. He didn't like it, so he wouldn't accept it.

"I don't have to split if you can pay the rent," he said.

"I can't. You'll have money again on the third of the month when your check comes. But if you don't cut that loan off, you're going to end up owing the juice man two month's rent by the end of next month."

We figured out how the interest would compile and I ticked off days on the desk calendar. Standish would be on the street for almost three weeks. We sat quietly for a minute as the information sunk in. "When we finish this stretch, you'll have the money again to get back into a place and get back on track," I said.

He fumed, staring out the window. "I do not want them throwing my stuff out onto the street. I seen 'em do it—just kick a guy's shit out and then have cops drag him out of the place."

"Why should you have your stuff thrown out? We're going to walk in the front door and carry everything out like moving day." I expected him to erupt. "I can store your stuff in the garage," I said. "You won't lose a thing. Sound fair?"

"I guess, but this is bullshit."

"It is and you should be pissed."

"I don't want to be evicted. From this place? That's the lowest of the low."

"Who's getting evicted? You don't have to tell anyone at the hotel your business. It will just look like you're moving out. We're going to walk out the front door in broad daylight like men. Fuck the Wilson. Anyone asks, give them a fake address. Who cares what they think? You've been saying the building is all crackheads anyway."

I slowed down and repeated immediate objectives: We don't look at the big picture. We take the pieces of this and handle them one at a time. And we pay off the debt so it doesn't keep growing.

"I promise you, this will feel worse before it feels better," I said. "But if we navigate it correctly, we'll get this done."

"I ain't moving back in there, either," Standish demanded. "I'd rather be in jail. If I have to stay in shelters for too long, I will end up in jail. Some shit I ain't putting up with."

I agreed that we would find him a place by the beginning of the next month. As I said this, I felt a flush of anxiety. I didn't know how to guarantee an apartment in three weeks. Standish wasn't pleased. He had no friends who could put him up. He hadn't talked to his family in years. "A viaduct is better than a nursing home," he said, pissed off at the world and at me for not being able to change it. All I could do was set a moving date.

• • •

Leonard moved into one of the hotels in the neighborhood. Reluctantly, he allowed me to help him fill out the application, and he coughed up the thirty-five bucks that went to a credit and criminal background check. For $425 a month, he got a room with a bed and a bathroom. The walls had been painted over so many times that the layers rounded every corner of the room. His window looked at a wall across the gangway. No kitchen, no fridge, no stove, but he was allowed to keep his shopping cart in his room. He had $175 to live on for the rest of the month.

Leonard didn't adjust well to his responsibilities. If he happened to appear at the correct hour for an appointment, he was either a day late or a day early. Or he would come in when I was out and scream at the secretaries for wasting his time. One day I was in a therapy session with a woman who said she had been privy to a Satanic ritual in her childhood and wanted to examine her dreams when there was a knock on the door.

"Sorry," my supervisor said. "But could you come to the lobby? It's sorta an emergency. It's Leonard and he's getting upset."

While the dependable chaos of Hurricane Leonard was irritating, I couldn't reasonably expect a person receiving directives from God to adhere to an appointment schedule. I hoped if I did my job, Leonard would find a reason to stay sober, out of jail, and off the street. But if I proposed any goals without Leonard's explicit understanding and motivation, they would be of no value to him.

When I stepped into the lobby, the secretaries were trying to ignore Leonard's barking. When he saw me, his voice soared. "They said . . . They told me . . . I need my money!"

"What are you doing?" I asked in a bored monotone that sometimes seemed to settle people who were looking for a good screaming match.

"I need money," he said. "Now I got me an apartment, but I don't have any money."

"I'm talking to someone right now," I told him. "Give me five minutes. You got something to read?"

"Uh, yeah."

"Why don't you read for a couple minutes? I'll be right back."

He pulled a little leather-bound Bible out of his bag, each page marked in a neon rainbow of highlighter marker, every margin crammed with his own ballpoint-pen notations. All anyone saw from the perch behind the reception desk was me mumbling to a screaming man who, in response, sat down quietly and took out a Bible. It looked like a good trick. After the therapy session, I found Leonard still nose-down in the annotated book. We took a walk to the gas station for coffee.

"How do you like your apartment?" I asked.

"It's a little small."

Christ. "You had all the room in the world before."

"I guess. Listen, I want to live right. I want to clear my record." Leonard showed me a court order to answer a citation for panhandling. He'd missed the court date. The fine had gone to collections and now he was being ordered to pay five hundred dollars.

"Where was this mailed to?" I asked.

"My mother's." Leonard pulled the envelope out of another pocket, showing me his mother's address.

"Did you used to live with her?"

"Yeah. She was my payee, but she was messing with my money."

"How long ago did you live there?"

"Maybe a year ago. I don't go over there much because she was why I went to jail. Now she has an order of protection against me."

"For what?"

"Because she was messing with my money."

I let the subject drop.

"What do we do about this?" he asked, tapping the letter with his finger.

"We go to court and fight it."

He didn't like his apartment and he didn't like his medications, but he wanted to go to court to clear his name. I would follow his lead.

• • •

Bobby didn't want to take his meds. He preferred his delusions. He thought naked starlets were hanging on him every day. Meds and case managers were interrupting the honeymoon. He didn't want to wait for my help after his Medicaid benefits had lapsed. He filled out his public aid application all on his own, listing his seven fantasy wives as dependents, before growing tired and stuffing the incomplete forms into a mailbox. He and I later visited the public aid office and explained the circumstances of that particular application, offering a corrected version without Tyra Banks listed as Dependent Number Three. The hospital called. Bobby was ready for discharge from another five-day stay, and I talked to the hotel manager, who was not going to evict him. I picked Bobby up, not liking the idea that he was being set loose before a Labor Day weekend, when he would go unchecked for four days.

"This is probably as good as he'll get," a nurse told me. "You two can go as soon as I find his paperwork."

"You can keep him for the weekend if you want."

"Oh, no. The doctor said he's stabilized."

Another staff member led me to Bobby's room. "I can't get him to come out," he said. "You try."

Bobby sat at a little desk in his room.

"Hey, Bobby. Remember me?"

"Hey, Zak."

"Ready to go?"

"Almost."

He hunched down again, scribbling on a notepad protected by the crook of his arm. I peeked at the list: *Women I Would Like to Marry and Then Fuck*. Beneath the list of celebrity candidates, Bobby signed his own name, along with President Bush's, and included detailed instructions for how the announcement should be presented to the people of Cambodia.

I drove Bobby back to the hotel and took him to his room. All he wanted was to stay out of hospitals and nursing homes, so we agreed on a plan. Bobby would work with me and a doctor to find a medication he approved of, and he would meet me every day so I could make sure he took his meds. Then Bobby took his meds in front of me, we had a couple cigarettes, and I left. The next morning the hotel manager called.

"You have to come here and get your friend. He's at it again." Apparently during the night, Bobby had gone door-to-door, wearing nothing but his boxer shorts and asking his neighbors if they had any porn magazines. When I got to the hotel, Bobby wasn't in his room, so I went down the street to a used bookstore that kept some porn on the back shelves, hoping to find him browsing, and checked with the owner.

"You happen to see a Native American, maybe Mexican-looking guy, baseball cap, big grin, in here buying porn?"

"Yeah! Him? He was in here yesterday. He bought three of the same issue. I tried to tell him he was wasting his money, but he just kept staring at me. You want me to not sell anything to him anymore?"

"No, his money is good."

"Is he dangerous?"

"He's okay. He just likes to look. What was he buying?"

"Oh, really straight vanilla stuff. *Playboy*."

In the afternoon, I found Bobby in his room and braced him on his neighbors' complaints.

"Oh, that wasn't me," he said, giggling.

"Whether it was or not, the manager thinks it was and he wants to call the cops on you."

"Oh."

"Yeah. If you want to keep this place, I think you're going to have to go back to the hospital for a little bit."

"I don't want to go back. If you make me go back, I'll kill my neighbors."

"You're going to kill people? You have to go back."

"I don't want to."

"I know, but that's not a choice now. I talked to the manager, and he said he could hold the apartment if you went to the hospital, but he can't have another complaint. If he gets one more, he says, he's going to force you to move. Going to the hospital now, whether you need it or not, is going to show the manager that you're willing to take his advice. It may be good advice. Were you bugging your neighbors? A little bit?"

"A little."

"Were you hearing voices last night?"

"A little bit. I didn't do everything they were telling me to, but I did a little bit."

"Okay. Then maybe we should go to the hospital."

"I don't want to."

"I know. I wouldn't want to, either. But your choices are the police or me. Now, you know me a little bit, right?"

"Yeah."

"The police, who knows what they can be like? If one is having a bad day, his wife was giving him a bad time, whatever, they take it out on us. You want to go with them, or do you want me to take you?"

"I guess you."

"Okay. Put some pants on."

The front-desk girl at Lakeshore Hospital did a polite double-take when Bobby and I came through the door. "It's us again," I said. Bobby did his Queen Elizabeth wave for the orderlies. He promised not to kill his neighbors when he got out.

• • •

I went back to the hotel, where the manager did not want Bobby back. But the manager was on vacation, so I pressed his second-in-command.

"I know for certain," the manager's assistant said. "We did not want him back before this."

"But Bobby's paid up through this month and the next. If you can't take him back, he's going to need his money and his security deposit today so I can find him a new place."

The assistant manager considered this.

"If Bobby has a room paid up, I expect he can move back into it," I said. "If he continues to be a problem, then we'll find a new place for him, okay?"

"I guess that's okay. The manager won't like it."

A week later, the hospital discharged Bobby and I visited him at home. He answered the door in his underwear.

"Hi, Zak. C'mon in." Orderly rows of Campbell's soup cans, family-size bags of Reese's Peanut Butter Cups, and boxes of ramen noodles lined his dresser.

"I went to the store," Bobby said.

He had also moved the refrigerator within an arm's length of the bed. "It felt a little crowded in the kitchen."

The hospital psychiatrist had dumped Bobby's previous prescription and put him on Clozaril, considered the "last chance" antipsychotic.

"I realize I was having delusions," he told me. "I don't have seven wives. And voices were telling me to do some silly things. But they get so persuasive sometimes. Like, I don't have an ID."

"You mean it expired?"

"No. When before, when I was hearing voices, they told me to get rid of them all. Birth certificates and everything. So I drew all over them and tore them up. My birth certificate, I don't know how to get another one. But they sounded so convincing at the time. It made sense. I tore up my Social Security card, too."

"Okay, where were you born?" I could request a new birth certificate from Cook County Records easily enough.

"Saigon."

Damn. I broke the news to Bobby that he would have to get his blood tested every other week because Clozaril presented a risk of heart problems, seizures, and a rash of other life-threatening side effects. Anti-psychotic medications all came with a range of ugly side effects that people had to weigh against the possible reduction of symptoms. But Clozaril was the most severe and used only when a person didn't respond positively to any other medication regimen.

"Never mind, then. I don't like needles. I like Haldol better."

"But you weren't taking it."

"It was a lot of trouble doing that twice a day."

"This?" I mimed opening a bottle and popping a pill in my mouth. "That's too much hassle? C'mon. It's either that or going to the hospital a few times a year."

"I don't like needles, so I won't do that."

"Okay, then no Clozaril."

"And no Haldol."

Goddamn.

• • •

Time and resources were the primary barriers to progress with all clients. If I had fewer clients or more hours in the day, I felt I would have been able to do more, help people stay housed, stay healthy, reduce symptoms, or take fewer drugs. As I spent more and more time at the office or running around the neighborhood, I didn't really notice the pressure I placed on myself to fix all of those problems. My car—a crappy but dependable '95 Chevy Cavalier—became my second office, where I would write up intakes between visits, make phone calls, and eat lunch. There was always more to do. There was always a crisis unfolding somewhere on my caseload.

To adjust to the pressure, I had to triage the work. I had to learn to distinguish between severe symptoms, addictions, adaptive responses to living at the very bottom of the socioeconomic ladder, and sometimes just lousy human behavior.

Malingering—where a person faked symptoms for some sort of benefit—was a problem, too. People put on not-guilty-by-reason-of-insanity defenses to achieve the secondary benefit of not going to jail. They faked a range of symptoms to gain access to Social Security and Medicaid benefits. Clients hospitalized themselves to get a break from the shelters and viaducts, a couple of spa days with air conditioning, television, a bed, and three square meals. Choosing a psych unit over a homeless shelter could simply be a survival tactic. Sometimes the hospital is the best possible choice.

6

Sometimes the job felt like I was actually making some impact in the world, and I was desperately proud of this. I'd pretty much bounced around during my twenties, tethered only to vague plans. I had quit drinking several years earlier when I was twenty-eight. No great melodrama prompted the decision, but I knew alcoholism ran in the family and, until recently, I had surrounded myself with heavy drinkers. To that point, I'd never considered not drinking, and I couldn't figure out why my life was not playing out the way I wanted.

I'd gone to New York to get serious about writing—having realized that sticking with manual labor would eventually strangle my real ambitions—however minuscule the odds of earning a living that way.

I scraped by in Dumbo, a then industrial, working-class Brooklyn neighborhood developers would soon begin gentrifying within an inch of its life. I scored an apartment roughly the size of a parking space, which wasn't bad for a freelance writer with no steady income. But after a year the writing dried up and I was back to lifting heavy shit for a living. This time on an illegal building site with a bunch of Bulgarians who were putting up allegedly soundproof rehearsal spaces for hipster bands in Williamsburg.

Prior to leaving Chicago, I'd had a steady crew of pals. A couple were writers, but most were guys from the truck yard who I drank with. That was my social life—going to the Pumping Company after we brought the trucks in and finishing the night at Standee's, an all-night diner next to a shabby gay bar and an Afrocentric bookstore on Granville. We all lived in the neighborhood, some of us in the same building.

But in New York, once my girlfriend and I broke up, I was entirely alone. So I went to an AA meeting. I never really got the hang of the meetings, but I did stop drinking easily enough that I sometimes wondered whether I'd had to quit. One guy from the meetings, Greg, a cook in a Manhattan restaurant who had already lost a kidney to his own drinking, offered to be my sponsor. We hung out and were ambivalent about working on the AA steps. Usually, Greg just made a nice dinner, and I ate with him and his girlfriend.

One night Greg showed a video of an old kinescope film of his father's one professional boxing match. The guy had been mobbed up and the whole thing was a fix. Greg pointed out how his father, between a middle round, was handed a water bottle marked with a big black X.

"It's liquid speed," Greg said.

His father went wild during the next round, windmilling his arms and chasing his opponent around the ring. It was an awful fight but hysterical at the same time. I didn't know if there was supposed to be some kind of AA message somewhere in there.

Greg and I left a lot unsaid, and I think one of the last conversations we had before I decided to go back to Chicago was pretty grim. At one point I told him, "No, I don't think people can really change."

I didn't know what I was talking about. I didn't even know how little I knew. I remember how sad Greg looked when I said it. We were on a subway platform and an arriving train cut off our conversation. I don't know what happened to Greg once I left New York, but I suspect we each thought the other was headed for dark days.

I desperately wanted to change my pattern of working like a dog and barely scraping by, but I was stumbling back to Chicago with no plans, other than getting back on a moving truck to make some money.

7

Tinley Park Mental Hospital discharged Rachel two weeks after the police found her walking along 159th Street in the middle of the night. She had told the cops she was going to commit suicide, so they had brought her to the hospital. The discharge workers eventually decided it would be counterproductive to release Rachel back to her family due to the ongoing abuse, violence, and chaos happening across the three generations crammed into a two-bedroom apartment. She had no Social Security disability benefits and no public aid, so the hospital provided bus fare and a referral to a homeless shelter on Lawrence Avenue—as if being homeless two hundred blocks away was more therapeutic than being homeless on the South Side. Rachel cried silently through most of the intake interview. Her nose ran and her eyes leaked, but she fought to keep talking calmly. She had no work history and a couple of recent hospitalizations. She had spent most of the nineties in Dwight Correctional Center, a maximum-security prison, after stabbing her husband of ten years.

"I was just trying to shut him up," she said. "We were going on about something, back and forth, and I was trying to walk away but he just got to pick, pick, pick. I grabbed a knife. I just wanted to poke him to get his attention. I guess I hit an artery, but I didn't kill him."

Her next boyfriend had OD'd after Rachel got out of prison, so she moved in with her mother. At fifty years old, Rachel had three daughters, one in Cook County Jail, another in a federal prison, and the third who lived with the grandmother.

"So, why were you in the hospital?"

"I wanted to kill myself."

"How were you thinking of doing it?"

This sounded cold, but if the subject of suicide came up, I had to keep digging. If someone says, "I have ten guns at home and I'm going to blow my brains out if my husband stays out all night," the risk of suicide is much higher than the person who says, "I want to travel back in time and go down with the Titanic."

"I was going to smoke crack," Rachel said.

"You were trying to overdose?"

"No," she said. But it'll kill me eventually."

That didn't really count as suicidal ideation. While walking along the expressway might attract the police, I didn't see any obvious symptoms. No word salad, no paranoid delusions, and no reactions to conversations I couldn't hear. She cried a lot, and I tested her, ticking off possible reasons for her claims of depression.

"Maybe you should be depressed. You have no money, you're homeless, you can't go back to your family, and you're trying to stay sober. Those are actually healthy reasons to be very sad. What do you want to do about it?"

She started crying again, saying she had never been on her own before. While she met the criteria for a depressive disorder, Rachel's inability to sleep could also have been attributed to trying to do it on a basement floor with thirty other homeless women. Her inability to make decisions or enjoy things she used to enjoy could stem from her lack of options and distant proximity to anyone she knew. And she didn't want to get sober.

"I don't like it," she said. "I can feel all this stuff I don't like. It's just hopeless. I'm stuck here and nothing I can do."

She felt better drunk and high. She wanted money, an apartment, and a disability check. Logical enough. I told Rachel if she was willing to do the necessary work to get to the life she wanted, I'd help her carry the load until she decided she could carry it all. Or until she decided it wasn't worth the bother. She dismissed options that didn't include substance use and violence. She had leaned heavily on both for most of her life and had grown comfortable with them. She eventually agreed to try to minimize—if not eliminate—her violent responses.

"Sometimes you can't help doing it," she said. "You have to defend yourself sometimes."

This was true. I suggested we start looking at how to determine when a physical, defensive response would be effective.

"I'm not sure I know what you mean," Rachel said.

"What do you do if someone says they're going to mess you up bad at midnight?"

"Be gone at midnight."

"Okay. What if they say it again the next night?"

"Oh. Now, that changes things."

"It does."

"So, what's the answer?"

"It depends, doesn't it? That's how we're going to start looking at things. What are all the options? Unless you can say getting violent has worked, has gotten you what you wanted every time without costing you too much, then we have to look at other options."

She agreed that violent responses hadn't worked every time. "When they didn't work, those are the situations we'll look at," I said.

"Why?"

"So we can see what does work."

"If you say so. But what if someone puts their hands on me?"

"You want to find ways to keep out of those situations?"

"That'd be fine with me."

"Then that's what we'll do."

"But what if someone does it anyway?"

"Protect yourself. You carrying anything now?"

"No."

"Good. If someone has a gun, the odds of them using it go way up."

"You sound crazy. I don't got no gun."

"Then you won't go back in for shooting someone."

Still dubious of one another, we changed directions and began inching forward through the Social Security disability application. I warned her that her odds of getting disability weren't good. She'd had few hospitalizations, no work record, and her only documented years were in prison. But Rachel dragged us back to our previous topic—violence.

"So what if I know someone is gonna fuck me up at midnight? Guaranteed they gonna and there's nowhere to run to?"

"Then you have to get them first. But that doesn't mean stab and choke 'em. Is anyone threatening you right now?"

"No. But what do I do?"

"You mean no one's ever called the cops on someone for something they didn't do? Wouldn't that get rid of the problem, too?"

"They could arrest you for that."

"They arrest you for stabbing people, too. Where are the odds better for you? Going to prison for making an anonymous call or going to prison for stabbing someone?"

Rachel stayed at the shelter, where she would remain a candidate for their housing program as long as she adhered to all the requirements of attendance and sobriety. Then she could move into a subsidized flophouse room as long as she continued attending AA or NA meetings every day and provided attendance signatures to her case manager at the shelter. She already hated the meetings and got back to drinking as soon as she could get out of sight. Rachel didn't miss one counseling session once we started, even if she had to walk a mile up Broadway. She wasn't mandated to see me, but she kept making the effort. She was honest about her drinking, as well as her proclivity to use violence to solve problems, but I think that was because I had no leverage. I wasn't trying to force her to quit drinking. I just didn't want her to stab anyone.

"I just snap," Rachel said as we were trying to navigate some melodrama involving a crackhead named Levitra. "That's how I am. I snap. Nothing I can do about it."

"Then you're going to keep going to jail. Or get kicked out of your place, right? Like what happened when you were at your mom's."

Rachel's eyes got watery at the mention of her mother, and I wanted to kick myself. I'd walked her down the wrong aisle and then tried to pull her away. I ignored her tears and kept my voice just this side of hard to keep her attention. I didn't want her getting stuck in a crying jag. Rachel said she was willing to do something but didn't know what. The case manager at the shelter had suggested she try anger management therapy.

"Anger management therapy is just silly," I told Rachel. "People who really do have an anger management problem aren't going to have the patience to sit through therapy sessions. They're going to say, 'Fuck this shit,' and walk, right?"

Rachel repeated her mantra: "I can't help it; I just snap."

"How many times have you snapped on the cops?"

"Never. I'm not that crazy."

"Why? What would happen?"

"They'll kill you!"

"You ever been mad when they grabbed you?"

"Yeah!"

"So why didn't you go off on them?"

"Because they would have beat my ass."

"So you sorta decide that beforehand?"

"I guess."

I told Rachel she didn't need to control her anger, just find a new set of tricks to deal with other people. I needed her to buy into the idea that she could make changes in her life. If she could choose not to attack Chicago cops, maybe she could also choose not to attack other kinds of people. "What does it feel like when you get angry?" I asked.

"When someone else does—"

"No. I don't care what anyone else does. What does it feel like to you? How do you know you're getting angry?"

Rachel described the physical reactions of a flushed face, trembling hands, and shallow breath that told her when she was getting pissed. She was able to describe other cues, too, like myopic vision, where all she wanted was to erase someone from her sight, when violence became the only item left on the menu.

"How does all that feel?"

"What?"

"Does it feel good when you're angry?"

"No." She didn't know where I was leading her. "Feels good when it's over," she said, "and it's over when I choke someone a little."

"If there were another way to feel like that—without choking someone—would you try it?"

"Maybe."

"If it kept you out of jail?"

"Oh, yeah, then."

So Rachel began anger management therapy, which she informally titled, *How to Deal with Assholes without Going to Jail.*

• • •

I had that vague feeling I had done something stupid. I hadn't seen Rachel in a couple of days and had imagined her maybe sober and relaxed, and attending her group sessions, thereby relieving me of some duties.

When I got to the office, the secretaries stopped me at the front desk.

"Where you been?" one of them asked. Dr. Blauer wanted people to go hospitalize your client."

"Who?"

"Rachel."

I'd forgotten about her appointment. "For what?"

"She was suicidal."

"No," I said. "She's more homicidal than suicidal. What happened?"

"I don't know. She ran out of here."

I went upstairs to see if anyone knew what was going on. I found two of my coworkers stepping out of the office.

"Oh, here he is," one said. "We were just going to look for your client."

"What happened?" I asked.

"The doctor said your client is suicidal. He wants people to go look for her." Rachel wasn't some Olympian who could run a four-minute mile down Broadway. She walked like she had broken glass in her shoes and anyone in the office could have caught her at the corner behind a ten-minute head start. I found Rachel on the corner of Lawrence and Sheridan with a crowd of women in the J. J. Peppers parking lot, a central meeting place for people in the neighborhood. The convenience store sold liquor, chips, and single cigarettes, and was right between a bunch of social service agencies, SROs, and homeless shelters. The side streets of Winthrop and Kenmore were dotted, block by block, with old limestone three-flat apartment buildings for property owners, courtyard apartment buildings for lease renters, and transient hotels with august names, such as the Chatelaine, the Lorali, the Glenn, and the Aragon Arms.

Rachel and her girls were all leaning in close and giggling like high schoolers, even though they were probably pooling resources for crack and some wine to chase it. One of the girls tapped Rachel on the shoulder as I came up.

"Oh, look who decided to stop by," Rachel said, not angry yet but testing the water.

"What happened?" I said. "I heard you were suicidal."

Rachel's girls drifted back to give her some privacy. "I don't want to go to no hospital," she said. "You try and take me to the hospital, I'll start screaming."

"I won't, yet, but why'd the doctor think you were suicidal?"

"I told him the medicine wasn't working and he told me it should be. I told him to try me a new medicine and maybe that'll work. He told me the medicine works and I told him I didn't want to take it anymore. Then, he asks me if I ever think about hurting myself. I told him I did sometimes, you know. So maybe he should give me more medicine."

During my first interview with Rachel I had asked her the standard questions about suicidal ideation. She gave a more generalized answer

I suspect was encouraged by the correctional system's substance abuse programming: "Crack is killing me and if I keep smoking crack it'll kill me eventually." Rachel didn't really want to kill herself, but she knew what social service providers wanted to hear: "Crack is bad."

Of course she knew crack was not healthy and involved risky behavior that threatened her life, but she also knew that crack felt good, which is why people smoke it. So when the doctor asked her if she was thinking about hurting herself, her answer meant she was thinking about smoking a lot of crack.

"He asked me if I wanted to go to the hospital. I said no. He said he thinks I should. I said, 'Can I go tomorrow?' He said no. So, I said I had to go to the bathroom, and I got the hell out of there." She mimed a cartoonish running start, one leg high in the air. "I'm not going to no hospital."

I started laughing. "Did you run?"

"I'd have a damn heart attack if I ran."

"If you didn't want a heart attack, then you're not suicidal."

"Quit making fun of me," she said and slapped at my arm. Her gang was behind me somewhere, catcalling Rachel for talking to some White guy on the corner. I assured her no one was going to come looking to put her in the hospital. We made another appointment since she still didn't have any meds. I made a note to write that appointment down.

• • •

Jails and prisons had reinforced the set of responses Rachel reverted to when facing off against social service folks. She offered an amiable deference and mechanical compliance regarding matters that didn't present an immediate threat to her freedom or her ego. She had decided years ago that doing time wasn't much of a cost but, getting older, she saw that cost rising. She had little to show for forty-some years on Earth, a thought that panicked her and prompted more drinking. She had no reference points for how to navigate the world without the support of a man or her family or her drugs. Prison had provided a restricted life, where the damage she could accrue was limited.

• • •

Later in the week I had to find Rachel for her psych appointment. She wasn't at the corner where we had agreed to meet, and she never hung out in her room. I cruised up and down the blocks, making figure-eights of the side streets between Lawrence and Argyle, until I caught her walking from the park with two guys. She handed her forty-ouncer to one of them as I waved her over to the car. "You got a doctor's appointment," I said. "Jump in."

Rachel stank of beer, so I pulled over at a convenience store and gave her a dollar for gum. "Gimme another for peanuts," she said. "It soaks up the alcohol."

In the waiting room she stuffed her mouth full of gum and hot peanuts. "Can you still smell it?"

"Yeah, a little."

Now she smelled of gum, hot peanuts, and beer. I told her to talk as little as possible in front of the doctor. Maybe he wouldn't notice.

"Is he going to want to put me in the hospital 'cause he couldn't last time?" she asked.

"The doctor sees about thirty people a day. He's probably not even going to remember you."

The doctor was a pleasant, soft-spoken guy with a fluffy, white afro and jowls like a basset hound. On the previous visit he had been quick to pull the hospital trigger.

"You say you want to kill yourself, then you should be in the hospital," he had said. "So now you go."

In the waiting room, Rachel and I discussed the best angle to take with the doctor: during the last appointment she hadn't meant she wanted to kill herself. She was just so sad that she wanted to numb herself and she hadn't taken any antidepressants since her previous visit.

I also coached her on how to most effectively ask for a refill of her meds: lacking antidepressants, she had been unable to sleep more than a couple hours a night and now felt worse than before.

After we choreographed the interview, I told Rachel not to worry. Maybe the doctor was in a rush and would just crank out a script so he could go home. The secretary called Rachel's name and we went down the hall. Without any greeting, the doctor inhaled once and snapped at Rachel.

"Have you been drinking?" Rachel glared at me like I had dared her to down a couple of forties before the session.

The doctor shifted into scolding mode: alcohol was not good when combined with antidepressants. Alcohol was not good in general. Why was she drinking? Did she consider herself addicted? Did she not care about herself? Rachel didn't answer, but the tears began to flow. She tried to blink them back but didn't wipe them down. The doctor didn't remember Rachel until he looked at her chart. I could read his notations: *s/i—hosp. rec*, which means that, due to the patient's suicidal ideation, the doctor recommended psychiatric hospitalization. "Did you go to the hospital?" the doctor asked, trying to refresh his own memory. Rachel shook her head. "Why are you crying?"

"I don't know."

"You don't know? That's not a very good answer. There must be some reason." The script we had planned out in the waiting room went down the toilet. Rachel simply cried and told the doctor she was scared and didn't want to die like this. She was so sad she couldn't sleep. So tired her eyes felt "crackly." Her family didn't want her anymore. Drinking had caused all of her problems, and she didn't know what to do.

"You have to stop drinking," the doctor ordered.

Rachel let the tears roll to her jaw as if they were someone else's problem. The doctor wrote a new prescription and told Rachel she would die if she didn't stop drinking. Walking out, Rachel pushed at her eyes with wadded Kleenex and said, "Damn, that was the real thing. Crying back there."

"I know."

"How you know?"

"'Cause you're not that good."

She gave a mock-offended gasp and slapped at my arm. "You saying I'd lie to the doctor?"

"I'm saying you're not good at faking it." Maybe I had underestimated Rachel, thinking she could shuck the psychiatrist. I know she had no reason to trust him. He had already enforced the might-makes-right maxim by threatening to hospitalize her and telling her she will literally die if she does not follow his advice. Rachel wasn't faking anything, but I didn't think she'd take her meds later, either. I dropped her off on the corner near her apartment and watched her carry the paper bag of Lexapro samples around the corner as if it was a sack of baby snakes. I wanted Rachel to find some modicum of success that she could attribute to her efforts. All she had been able to do so far was avoid further restrictions of her life. She got by, but she had been able to do that without me. I felt like I was stumbling, trying to instill a sense of power that Rachel didn't even recognize. For Rachel, power was the ability to say I want, and to have that want satisfied. What Rachel wanted was to not feel bad. She only knew a few ways to do that, and those ways kept making her life worse. She knew she didn't have any power.

8

Working with clients was a crash course in pharmaceuticals and psychotic symptoms. I walked into the job with maybe one semester of abnormal psych and one year of experience in Cook County Jail, where a hefty amount of meds was either sold or spit into the toilet. It's the rare person—jailed or not, psychotic symptoms or not—who enjoys taking meds, whether they are antibiotics or antipsychotics.

Bobby didn't want to take his meds because life was better with the delusions—full of sex and entertaining conspiracy plots. Most people detested their delusions and hallucinations. But his were pleasant enough and a distraction from the reality of his life. Leonard didn't like his meds, and I can't say why he was willing to try them for a period of time. But the effects were clear within two weeks. We could speak and I was even able to use some logic on him. But over time, as the medications built to an appropriate level in his bloodstream, the more he realized he didn't like them. He complained that the Risperdal slowed his thoughts and that the spiritual connections, which had seemed so clear before, became blocked. With his meds in the way, God had stopped passing notes.

"I'll keep trying for a while, but things better get better," he said, prying a pill from an aluminum sample pack and placing it on his tongue like a communion host. Leonard had been diagnosed with schizoaffective disorder, meaning the symptoms of schizophrenia and the mood swings of bipolar disorder occurred simultaneously. Both LeFlore and Bobby had been diagnosed with schizophrenia, paranoid type because of their delusions, prominent hallucinations, and disorganized speech or thought. Bobby would go catatonic, watching and listening to the hallucinations. LeFlore would gesture and scream at them. The *Diagnostic and Statistical Manual of Mental Disorders* charts all of this out for clinicians, categorizing symptoms and behaviors under sets, subtypes, and specifiers of diagnoses. The main diagnoses I saw in my clients were schizophrenia and bipolar disorder, not because they are the most common across the entire population but because they become most problematic when untreated. Combined with poverty, substance abuse, and limited social support, both disorders can leave those who suffer from them homeless, hospitalized, or incarcerated.

Depression can become prevalent, interfere with basic needs—such as relationships, housing, and employment—and exacerbate a predisposition for alcoholism or depression. The cycle becomes a blur for the person suffering, as each symptom fuels the next.

• • •

Leonard and I had planned to prepare for his upcoming court case, but he disappeared for two weeks prior to the summons. I expected he was either in jail or on a crack binge, but he showed up bright and early on the right day. "You look good," I told him.

He did, dressed in thrift-store funereal black—a dress shirt unbuttoned past his sternum and only the bulge of his Bible ruining the lay of his sport coat. He had shaved his scraggly beard into a van dyke that accented his sharp cheekbones and greased his hair into a thick wavy pompadour that was usually hidden under hoodies or dirty baseball caps. Leonard hadn't taken any meds in a week.

"I been spitting them out, bro," he told me. "I admit it. I'm only taking them today because I want to be sharp for court in case I have to give a speech."

"You won't have to," I said, thinking about the last time I could verify that he had taken his meds. "In fact, let me do the talking. That's what I'm going for anyway, yeah?"

"Sure. You can be my counselor."

He whistled along with the radio as we drove downtown, pleased to be, for once, accomplishing a task of his own choosing. Going to court, Leonard believed, would eliminate some of his guilt, and then God would approve of him. On some days Leonard was God's messenger. On other days, he was His whipping boy. Either way, the combination of psych meds and sobriety had brought the parameters of his life—$674 a month, no friends, little family, no skills, no job opportunities, and a hard aching for crack cocaine—into focus.

"I want to get right with God," Leonard said, "and I don't know if this is the way."

"Maybe this is the price," I told him. "Whoever said getting right with God didn't cost something? If it didn't cost, more people would try it. You're in the elite here."

The idea that any setback determined a failure scared Leonard most. If he was sober four days and drank on the fifth, he saw himself as a lost cause. But Leonard justified his setbacks as signs from God—and he would follow His illuminated path.

"God will decide," Leonard said, not appreciating my suggestion that the cops who busted him could have also been a message from God to cut down on crack. I figured I had some time before the psychotic symptoms returned. Even after missing his meds for a week, Leonard would go through the honeymoon period now, where everything felt good, his brain was limber, and all the synapses were clicking. When the symptoms came back Leonard would see the world again through fractured filters. The trick would be getting him to take his meds.

• • •

Metal detectors beeped as Leonard walked through the courthouse gate. Security guards ambled up, ordering him to empty his pockets. Along with his Bible, he had a couple of permanent markers and a sharpened screwdriver inside his jacket.

"You never know, man," Leonard told the guards. We found the courtroom designated for misdemeanor fines gone into collections and I handed the summons to the judge's assistant, a young guy with little no-frame glasses. I explained that Leonard had been cited for sleeping on the El train. He couldn't pay the ticket because he was homeless and had missed his previous court summons because the letter went to an address where he no longer lived.

"Are you his translator?" the assistant asked.

I said I was a social worker with a community mental health program, hoping the assistant would catch on. I could feel Leonard behind my shoulder, bouncing on his toes while the assistant told me how there really wasn't much he could do just because I alleged a defendant was mentally ill.

Leonard started pulling on my sleeve and I expected him to erupt. Instead, Leonard announced, "Hey. They were talking about me on the radio. They were talking about this case."

"Not now," I said over my shoulder.

"They were. During the Cubs and Sox game last night. Everyone knows about it now."

"Who won last night?" I asked.

"Sox."

"Good. Give me one second here, Leonard."

"No, tell him I commune with the spirits too, which is how I know. I was sitting on the sidewalk the other day and this pigeon walked right up to me because he wanted to be consoled. So I tried to put him in my bag and, boy, did he get mad. He didn't like that."

The assistant whispered to me. "I'll suggest to the judge that he drop this one. Wait here."

We did, then made a perfunctory appearance in the courtroom. The judge told Leonard to stop sleeping on the El and we were dismissed. "One down," I said.

"Pretty good, counselor."

Leonard had more court dates lined up. On the way home we made a celebratory stop at Starbucks. Walking out with our coffees, I noticed that Leonard had cleared the cinnamon, cocoa, and sugar shakers, as well as the little honey bear, off the table and into the pockets of his sport coat.

• • •

After three days of homelessness, I expected Standish to be on his way to a meltdown, but he was in our waiting room, dressed for a nice day on the tennis court in a polo shirt and khaki shorts, his homemade tattoos poking out from his sleeves and cuffs.

"I'm as happy as a sissy in a work camp," he said, winking at the secretary as we walked past. Standish had found himself among old acquaintances in the church shelter on Bryn Mawr.

"I knew them from the nursing home and one guy was at the Wilson's the same time as me."

They passed Standish extra smokes and brought leftovers from the church dinners, figuring he would repay them when he was on his feet again. Standish held together like that until a long weekend knocked his confidence. The building was undergoing a rehab, with scaffolds erected and gang boxes chained up in the lot.

"Everybody's going to be gone," he said. "The shelter is going to be closed for four days." The calm that radiated from Standish while flirting with the office staff now dissipated. He had that cornered look, all watery eyes and jittery limbs, sucking in quick and shallow breaths. He had stopped taking his Seroquel because he didn't want to be sedated, which was actually one of the reasons doctors prescribed Seroquel—the sedation could keep people from "acting up."

"I don't think I can do it," he said, imagining himself on the street while the shelter was closed. "I can't walk around all day and night. Some motherfucker's going to say something and I'm going to go off. Cook County would be better than staying under a viaduct."

Standish and I had already discussed a contingency plan where, if he had to, he could wait for his next Social Security check while in the hospital. He had seen enough psych units to know the magic words: I'm gonna kill myself. He didn't like the idea. The last time he had gone to the hospital, they sent him to a nursing home and drugged him into zombie-hood.

"You've been in the hospital before," I said, setting the stage.

As softly as I tried to broach the subject, Standish got riled immediately, defending the tiny bit of territory he had left. Pulling up to his full height in his chair, he clearly and profanely expressed his wishes to avoid the hospital. I wanted to scoot back, away from the barrage, but I leaned forward over the desk so he had to focus on me. He told me to fuck off a few times and I talked over him slowly and carefully. I had already suggested he move into a shelter, and now I was telling him to try the hospital.

I thought I should at least look confident when it sounded like I was wrecking his life.

"You know what you have to say to get hospitalized," I said. "You've had to do it before when things were bad. You've done it and you survived. When you had no one to argue your case, they moved you to a nursing home. That's not going to happen again. But right now, this time, you might walk out of the hospital with a place to stay. You know there's a certain emergency fund for someone who's homeless and gets hospitalized?"

"No. How the fuck would I know that?"

"Because I'm telling you. There is and it's enough for a month's rent somewhere. You think I think you can't handle yourself on the street? All I'm saying is why should you have to when we're trying to minimize risks?"

"And I have to go to the hospital?"

He asked about the money again to make sure it was real and whether I would show up to take him in.

"Unless you were so wild I had to call the cops," I told him.

"I don't think I need to do that."

"Good. So, are you coming by tomorrow?"

"How's about noon? I want to catch breakfast at the shelter."

• • •

Dressed summer-sharp again, Standish showed up ready to go, a shaving kit and a change of clothes packed in a gym bag. On some days he seemed to have his act so together I thought he might be hustling me. Standish followed me quietly through the ER and knew exactly what to say, but the intake worker's blunt ambivalence pushed his buttons. She seemed to doubt his sincerity that he saw suicide as a solution to his problems, his ability to find a gun within an hour, and his ability to provoke a cop into shooting him. She told us to go back to the lobby without saying whether Standish would be admitted.

"What's with that fucking bitch?" he said. "She don't think I'm suicidal. Maybe she wants to see if I'm homicidal."

I said something soothing, reminding Standish of his goal here, ignoring the fact he was annoying me with his shitty attitude. We waited and flipped through some of issues of *Sports Illustrated* and discussed the update on Leon Spinks. Standish was of the opinion the guy had wasted his life because he was now a proud YMCA janitor. I posed, just to be contrary, that Spinks was lucky he even had a job. Passing the time, Standish told tales about his third ex-wife, then moved along to grossly inappropriate stories about women. With his blood up, he began flirting with every female orderly passing by, and his laugh bellowed through the lobby and probably down the hall to the intake office. I whispered, "Hey, I thought you were suicidal."

He splayed his big hand over his face and leaned forward and let out a low groan approximating some agony or another. I waited for the two of us to be kicked out for malingering. The intake staff surprised both of us by admitting Standish to the acute unit. We shook hands and I said I'd check in on Monday.

• • •

Leonard continued to receive instructions from God. He decided to quit his meds for good and I suspected he had backdated this announcement and had been off of his antipsychotics for some time.

"I don't like how it makes me feel," he said. "I'm just not there. I can't communicate with Him. Makes me feel heavy or something."

The doctor knew more than we did about meds, I proposed. Maybe we should talk to her. In response, Leonard put his headphones over his ears to block out my voice and await further instructions.

God, Leonard said, sometimes used the Mark Levin radio show to pass him messages. "I need vitamins," he said. "I need more energy, not your medicine. I'm writing a book, and He is directing me."

God wanted Leonard to be a man of valor, one filled with "love and brotherhood," and Leonard wasn't going to need medications for that. All he needed was money.

"I shouldn't be wasting my time with this," he said. "I have bigger things to. I'm special. God is talking to me."

I had missed an opportunity by not praising Leonard more fervently to underline the changes in his life since he had started the meds—no arrests, safe housing, contact with his mother again. Even the delusions had waned while he was sober, though sobriety was painful for him. I had praised him on this last bit, acknowledging that sobriety was truly the hard part, but Leonard had started drinking again and the mania and delusions were peeking through the surface.

"I'm going to leave town," he announced. "The hell with this."

"You got one more court date. You want to blow it off?"

"I don't care, man."

"I thought you wanted to get straight with God, and this was how you were going to do it."

"I did tell Him," Leonard admitted, remembering his promise. "Okay, one more day in court. But if I don't feel better after, then fuck it."

"We'll do our best."

"You did good before," he told me. "Do it again. God is with me."

• • •

LeFlore kept demanding a new state ID and his case manager couldn't put it off anymore. The case manager, Max, a younger guy with more seniority than me, was nearing the end of his rope with LeFlore. While riding in Max's car, LeFlore would stick his whole upper body out the window to scream hello at a woman or grab a woman's shoulders and yell in her face, "You're my cousin!"

During a psychiatrist appointment, LeFlore had tried to protect Max from his delusions. "Don't!" he yelled. "No! I won't let you kill the White boy!"

Max appeared to be near the end of his rope with the agency as well. During his second probation for the kind of work-related issues that generally accompany alcoholism, the rest of us began helping him with his caseload in a last-ditch hope that he would straighten out. A young guy in his twenties shouldn't have any trouble partying on the weekends, but his Mondays started hours later than most everybody else's and he routinely came in wearing the usual drunk injuries—scraped palms, grass-stained knees, dirty elbows. Some days he exuded a thicker sour-booze smell than the homeless people walking in from beneath the viaducts. I offered to help Max get LeFlore through the DMV as quickly as possible so he could get his ID. Max would hold our spot in line and negotiate with the state employees, who would likely threaten to call security on LeFlore. I'd take LeFlore outside for a cigarette if he started to get wild. On the drive out, between bouts of screaming at imaginary adversaries, LeFlore broke into a soaring falsetto, a note-perfect "You don't bring me flowers anymore . . ."

The crowd inside the DMV stepped aside to let LeFlore cut to the front of the line with us in tow. We tried to explain the situation to the state drone manning a desk.

"What are you two, his caretakers?" the clerk asked. "I need to talk to him, not you. How do I know what he's here for? You can't just say what he's here for."

"Fine," Max said, pushing LeFlore forward.

"What do you want?" The clerk asked LeFlore.

"I gotta start going to the gym."

"State ID or driver's license today?" the clerk said.

We all answered in unison.

Me and Max: "State ID."

LeFlore: "Driver's license."

"Gentlemen, pick one."

"'Flore, tell him you need your ID," Max said. "You gotta tell him."

"I'll kick you all out of here," the clerk threatened.

"Not a driver's license," LeFlore gestured with a splayed hand to punctuate the sentence. "I need my ID. It expired. The address is wrong."

"I need proof of where you live."

"Tell him where I live," LeFlore told Max.

"From you, I need it," the clerk said. "I need proof of your ID. This one is expired."

"That's why I need a new one."

The Abbott and Costello routine cycled through three more times before the clerk accepted that this wasn't some scam to rip off the Department of Motor Vehicles.

We moved to the first set of ropes corralling citizens to the numbered stations around the room. While waiting in line, LeFlore gave instructions to the air.

"Martin Luther King, Jesse Jackson, Chaka Khan. I want all you motherfuckers to go back to where you motherfucking came from."

Max and I took turns whispering reminders to LeFlore that he had to keep the volume down. Eventually he reigned his voice in, spouting off at a conversational level so only those in the immediate vicinity could hear him accusing Hitler and Tony Danza of the same unknown crime before changing the subject.

"I'm going to start going to the gym," he said. "I used to play basketball. Look at me." He lifted the back of his shirt. "I got no ass. I used to have a ass. All I do is sit on it now."

While we reserved the right to laugh about some of LeFlore's more disruptive symptoms, we believed that right was earned with the responsibility of providing clinical services to the man. But he was a pleasant guy—never complained, didn't argue with nondelusional people—and we were on his side. So we shot dirty looks at any person who appeared to be on the verge of snickering at him. At the final DMV desk, LeFlore got his new ID. He checked his picture against his name, address, and physical description and then asked the DMV lady why his ID didn't expire for ten years.

"It's usually only good for five," he said. "Why ten?"

"Because you're handicapped," she said.

He snapped back. "I'm handicapped?" He turned to us, standing behind him, and shrugged. "I guess I am."

• • •

Over the next year we watched LeFlore's symptoms get worse. He howled at people on the street, believing they somehow played a role in his delusions. The police grabbed him from a grocery store. He took a swing at someone in front of his hotel. He growled and howled, sang and danced, and scared the hell out of anyone who didn't know him.

His psychiatrist increased his medications until LeFlore was at the human limit for daily Clozaril intake. He had to have his blood tested every other week and when his white blood cell count got low, we'd have to convince him to go to the ER for a check-up. Psychiatrists were hesitant to adjust his meds, even though we could chart that he had become less and less able to care for himself. Even if he was taking all his meds, he was still screaming at his hallucinations.

The problem with meds for most other people is that most of them have to build up to an appropriate level in a person's body. Some antidepressants take four to six weeks before their efficacy can be fully gauged. Each person responds differently to medications. Finding the best combination is a long and aggravating process. At the end of a trial period a doctor has the option to prescribe a different antidepressant, which can take another two months to take effect. A year can pass, which in itself can scare a client into rejecting all medications. Most of the clients I worked with were prescribed some combination of Haldol, Risperdal, or Invega for psychotic symptoms. Geodon, Seroquel, Lamictal, Lithium, and Depakote were prescribed for clients with mood disorders. The side effects—weight gain, diabetes, high blood pressure, insomnia, impotence, constipation, dizziness, slowed motor skills—were unpleasant. Convincing a client to take their medications without implicitly threatening them—*You'll end up in the hospital if you don't*—explicitly threatening them—*Your money will be sent back to Social Security if you don't*—or treating them like children by threatening punishment via hospitalization was the tough part. You couldn't force them. And telling a client that meds work for most people is not much of an argument. When people hear statistics regarding success rates of any intervention they do not like, they assume they are in the minority that will see no noticeable benefits. If the statistics show a health risk to a pleasurable habit, like smoking, people tell themselves they are in the safe minority. If it's pleasurable, it won't hurt me. If it doesn't feel good, there's no benefit. Often, when our clients got hospitalized, the staff gave them an ultimatum: *if you don't take your meds, you don't get to leave*. That put another hurdle in front of us when the client was discharged thinking, *Now that I'm out, I'm not taking any meds.*

• • •

LeFlore trusted us. He had been in hospitals and nursing homes most of his adult life and he wanted to stay out. Either Max or I brought LeFlore his meds every day. We had to tear open the pill envelopes for him because his hands shook uncontrollably, and the pills would fall into the mulch of cigarette ash and garbage on his floor. LeFlore would try to clean his room, but he wasn't very skilled at it. He would knock the coffee can of cigarette butts into the mop water, for example, and continue swabbing black water across the linoleum. Any new clothes eventually became coated with grime and smelled of cheap cigars. We would hire cleaning crews to attack his room, but they either grossly overestimated the price in order to avoid the job or cleaned once and never came back. The idea of a nursing home frightened the hell out of LeFlore. It threatened the little bit of freedom he fought to hold onto, and he was able to determine this was a good enough reason to take his meds. We marked progress in tiny increments, noting trips to the store that didn't end with him attracting security. We would track the hours that passed without him screaming at the top of his lungs.

LeFlore wanted to live without incident. He wanted to go back to college someday, but his goals depended on his medications, so his progress was unsteady. He would forget to take his meds on weekends when no staff could get to him. Or he would tell Max I had stopped by with the days' medications and then tell me that Max had done the same. It took us a few days to realize neither of us had given him any meds. One day, since neither of us believed LeFlore's self-reporting, both of us gave him his meds. We had to bring him to the hospital to assess whether he needed his stomach pumped due to the double dose. We tightened up our system and LeFlore wasn't too pleased. I would end up taking his case again when I took over the program no one wanted.

9

Leonard and I went for his last court date. He left the Scarface outfit at home this time and wore his carpenter's jeans and tank top. He had shaved his head since I'd seen him last. He packed his pockets with his reading glasses, sunglasses, a neon outliner pen, and a magnifying glass—everything he needed for his Bible studies. "They should just throw me in jail," Leonard said as we drove up the ramp onto Lake Shore Drive. "I'm tired of this. I hope they throw away the key."

"Knock it off. This is a misdemeanor."

"Can you turn on the radio?"

For the rest of the ride, he heard messages from God explaining how he should live. "See," he said, pointing to the radio during a Van Halen two-fer. "God's telling me to dance. I should dance all night."

"No," I said. "That's David Lee Roth hitting on an underage girl."

"Oh."

He flipped through the stations and found some Cat Stevens. "Wow-how. I haven't heard that since I was a kid."

"How old were you?"

"Fourteen. I lived right on Lawrence Avenue. I grew up here."

"What was the neighborhood like then?"

"Primitive, bro."

• • •

Inside the courtroom, Leonard waited for his case to be called with the other defendants—owners of cab companies that ignored citations, old ladies who never got their dogs vaccinated, and shop owners who cut corners by doing their own building repairs without permits.

He killed time reading his battered, personally annotated Bible. "I learn more from this than I will in stupid court," he said, holding up his Bible. "This is the law."

Every defendant before us lost. We were going to be sunk, too. The only criteria for getting a case tossed seemed to be if the court notice was not dated or was not sent to an address the city had on file. That Leonard had been in jail for six months, then homeless for another six, was not going to win us any points.

Before we were called up, I went the psychiatric-disability route and asked the clerk how they expected a homeless schizophrenic to respond to a court summons or pay five hundred dollars. The attorney listening in gave a little smile of pity.

"I understand," she said. "We'll see what we can do. But I am going to have to ask your client some questions."

"Is it okay if I answer?" I asked, hoping to cut some of Leonard's agitation from the proceedings.

"Fine with me."

When Leonard's case was called, I stood with him in front of the judge. When asked, "Do you swear to God, to tell the truth?" Leonard immediately copped an attitude. They were on his turf now. "I won't swear to God," he said. "That's not right."

"Just raise your hand," I said.

"I won't do it. It's blasphemy."

"I'll give you a chance to affirm," the judge said. "Would you rather do that?"

"Okay."

"Do you affirm to tell the truth in this court of law?"

"Yeah. Okay."

I tried to explain Leonard's situation to the judge, and she didn't seem pleased. Ignoring me, she questioned Leonard. "Do you live at this address?" she asked.

"He hasn't lived there in over a year, judge."

"I asked him," she said, then asked Leonard, "Can you speak?"

"Yes."

"What's your name?"

"Leonard."

"Can you tell me what happened when you got the citation?"

"He can tell you." Leonard pointed to me.

"I need you to tell me, sir."

"Fine. I was sleeping on the El when I was homeless."

"Where do you live now?"

He gave the approximate cross streets, and the judge requested a specific building number. Housing was so transitory for Leonard that recalling specific addresses seemed pointless. Like people who live in the country, their geographic directions are designated by landmarks rather than building numbers.

"I don't remember," Leonard said. "I just moved in there. I used to be sleeping in abandoned buildings. I wasn't living right—"

The judge cut him off. "Did you live at that address before?" she asked, referring to the summons.

Leonard said he had, adding that his mother still lived there. But she hadn't given the summons to him because they hadn't been speaking due to the order of protection against him.

"I wanted to square things with God and tell the truth, no matter the consequences," Leonard said. "I only care about God, not no judge."

I tried again. "Judge, if my client hasn't lived at that address for a year, and could not be in contact with the people who lived there, and there was no place to forward his mail, how was he supposed to respond to his mail?"

The prosecutor jumped in. "Did Leonard have a driver's license?"

"All I had was a county ID from jail," Leonard said.

"No, you must have had a driver's license," the prosecutor said. "That's how they got your address."

I wanted to ask the attorney where the hell this was coming from. She had said she'd back off since Leonard had mental health issues.

"I lost my driver's license a long time before jail," Leonard said. The judge and prosecutor placed the blame upon Leonard for not keeping his license updated.

"What am I supposed to do, change my address to homeless?" He turned to me. "This is bullshit, let's just go. Let them throw me in jail."

As the judge announced the decision—a three-hundred-dollar fine—Leonard started distractedly kicking the podium, rocking the whole thing back and forth. "Fuck this," he said. "Let's go."

"We're almost done," I told him.

"They gonna arrest me?"

"No."

"Then fuck her."

"Will you shut up?" I suggested.

The judge made some comments about the client's right to appeal but recommended he not bother.

We walked to a coffee shop and had a little case management session under a green umbrella. Leonard still had plans—to write madly, all day, every day, with expectations of revolutionary outcomes. But first he wanted to copyright a few things.

"The slogan and the logo," he said. "What's the difference?"

I explained the difference between a copyright and a trademark.

"But what if it's both together? The slogan is the logo. It's a *slogo*. I can copyright that, yeah?"

The court, the alcohol, the meds, and his direct line to God had all become secondary priorities for the moment. He was writing a book. "What I need now," he told me, "is a publisher."

• • •

It often felt like everyone on my caseload was spiraling down and I had no control over anything. I had voluntarily stepped into a surreal corner of the world, where chaos was amplified and every time I looked around the scenery seemed to have changed. The world is chaotic in general, and anxiety is a response to that, even on a quiet day. I was amping up my own chaos. That's what can happen when you spend all of your time with people who can't see past their delusions or have learned to lean hard on deception to protect their perceived sense of well-being. I did my best to ignore my anxiety and just worked harder to prove my worth—to clients and to myself.

When Standish called from the hospital, he was ready to go. He had even found a boarding house on the South Side he could move into. This didn't sound right. I should have looked into it further because it sounded like too good of a deal, but things were getting hectic, and my caseload kept filling up. I figured Standish was an adult and had capably handled himself so far, with or without his meds. A week later, Rachel disappeared. I went to her hotel and found that cops had swept a crowd in front of the building one evening and she had been picked up for possession. I convinced the desk clerk I had to do a wellness check on her because she wasn't answering her door. I had to make certain she wasn't dead in her room.

The edge of her nightstand was burned from crack pipes. The carpet was scarred with long burn marks from the crack torches she made by wrapping toilet paper or cloth around a coat hanger. She did that because lighting crack pipes over and over destroyed cheap cigarette lighters.

Her med box was full. Only a couple days out of her month's supply of Abilify were missing. I doubted the lack of medications running through Rachel's system had much to do with the decisions she was making. While antidepressants, mood stabilizers, and antipsychotic meds can do amazing things, they don't fix everything. Of all of the reasons clients might or might not take their meds, one is pretty simple to figure out: the rush of street drugs usually beats out the gradual decrease of psychotic symptoms that comes with a regular medication regimen. That usually convinces someone the meds weren't worth the bother. A thirty-second crack blast feels more effective than five hundred milligrams of Depakote.

I suspected both Standish and Rachel were not being honest about their drug intake. I was angry at them for playing me and had to let go of the idea that I had any control over their choices. I wouldn't realize until much later that I was knocking myself out trying to contain their chaos and to prove I was too strong to be terrorized by it. Leonard's choices lately were testing my sunny disposition, too. His mother called every other day, complaining that I had to do something about her boy. Even though he had his own place, he was spending all his days in her apartment, lying on the floor like a little kid with a coloring book writing his manifesto.

"And he's drinking all my damn beer," she complained. When I did see Leonard, his fingers were blistered, burnt and newly callused. His eyes were a bloodshot grayish-yellow.

"I'm curious," I said. "How come you started smoking crack again?"

"It makes me stop crying like a fucking baby."

10

SUMMER 2006

"If this doesn't work, I'm just going to do it," Marco said.

"Do what?" I asked.

"You know."

"Well, I have an idea what you mean, but I really have to ask: do you mean you're going to kill yourself?"

The words came awkwardly. I had a professional responsibility to check for suicidal ideation. I knew mentioning suicide didn't put the idea in a person's head, but to mention it felt too intimate. This was our first meeting.

"Right now, I'm not saying I'm going to do it," Marco said. "But I will if things don't get better. I've done everything and there's nothing else left to try."

He eyed the institutional baby-blue walls as if we were in the Greyhound station toilet.

"This place is the last stop. I never thought I'd be going to a place like this."

My first reaction was a creeping sort of dislike for Marco. I could feel his grief radiating from him. My caseload was already swamped, and I couldn't help thinking my life would be easier if I wasn't involved in Marco's.

"I had to swallow my pride to come in here," he said. "I never thought I would be in a community mental health center." Then he flipped from entitlement to humility. "I see some of those people out in the lobby and think they have it so much worse than me. I should be grateful."

Marco was referred to me because I was one of the few therapists who provided "intensive" case management—meaning I might need to leave the office to help him find a job or an apartment. Unemployed, middle-class, midthirties, and Cuban three generations removed, Marco had been married twice before everything fell apart. As he described all the external problems in his life, his depression made me feel like we were trapped together beneath a lead blanket. He already had years of therapy under his belt and his last therapist had refused to work with him unless he quit drinking. Marco flitted between self-effacing disclosures and sighing irritation when faced with questions about his life. He wasn't beyond trying suicide again. In fact the possibility seemed like a relief. He was broke and needed money, but believed he could never hold a job, and was certain his only recourse was a disability check. He thought he was too weak to support or protect himself but demanded I refrain from any "positive mental attitude" speeches on him. That was good advice. The urge to tell a distraught client that things will be okay is tempting. But as soon as you say it—in a therapy session or not—the client will announce they have been diagnosed with pancreatic cancer or some other catastrophic condition. And even if they don't have cancer, what if things don't get better eventually? You promised they would. I wanted to offer Marco some sense of control. Whether he grabbed for it was up to him.

He seemed as fragile as spun glass. "I want to know what to do next," he whispered. "I don't even know if there is anything I *can* do next."

Marco whispered a lot. I had to gently insert questions like, "By 'them' you mean . . .?" or "'It' refers to . . .?" as if I were intruding upon a conversation that had been going on in his head for a long time, which was exactly what I was doing. I got the basics. Marco was broke and had been for the last year. His unemployment had run out and his Social Security disability claims had been denied. His parents in Miami were paying his bills and barely keeping him above water. He minimized his needs in order to appease them and hated himself for being dependent. Marco had lost a series of middle management sales jobs because he drank too much and for other reasons he didn't want to explain. He had been dragged out of step with the life he knew. The weight of depression and the acute pressure of anxiety terrified him. Suicidal thoughts kept popping up and they were beginning to seem appropriate. Marco whispered and snarled throughout our first hour and tentatively agreed to another appointment.

The therapist who initially interviewed Marco had suggested he go to a day labor office. "What is day labor?" he asked me.

"It's where people line up outside a storefront for the opportunity to do manual labor at less than minimum wage," I said. "I don't know if that's going to be the key here." Marco's hands were thin and his tapered fingers uncalloused. His bleached Mohawk, a style too youthful for his age, wouldn't go over well on the shape-up line.

"I still don't know what day labor is."

"If you were to do day labor, you'd be waiting in line at six a.m. with a lot of ex-cons. The pay is allegedly minimum wage, but the brokers take chunks of it for transporting the crews, for their employment services, for providing the uniforms, mops, or shovels, and most people walk away with about three-twenty an hour. Eight hours minus lunch and that doesn't count the couple hours travel time to the suburbs."

"No," Marco said. "I don't think so."

"It's not much of a plan," I agreed.

• • •

I called a pay phone in the Three South Unit at Chicago Read, one of the state psychiatric hospitals. A new client had disappeared right after our intake interview. "Is Leontis there?" I asked.

"Who's calling?"

"Tell him it's Zak."

"Oh, hey dude. This is me."

"What are you doing, screening your calls?"

"Well, you never know. I'm hanging out at the payphone."

"I got your message. What happened?"

"I called the hotline and said I was going to hang myself."

"Okay. What happened?"

"I was arguing with my dad, and he was drunk, telling me I was a piece of shit."

"How's it going at the hospital?"

"It's pretty relaxing, actually. I'm starting to get bored." The kid had the motivation of algae, but I didn't learn that until I figured out that he used the state hospitals as a means to avoid the usual stresses of life—employment, family, bills. It was his choice, but one that only became clear as I continued offering a wide range of other choices. He eliminated all options that involved effort of any kind. He didn't have Medicaid and was sent to the state hospital whenever he visited an ER claiming he was going to kill himself. Leontis got dumped in my lap for intensive case management and job skills training. I was told I'd be working his case in tandem with a veteran case manager, Thomas, who would meet with Leontis for therapy.

Weeks before he went into the hospital, Leontis had said he wanted a job, so Thomas brought him to meet with me. During the interview, Leontis would only take me in tangentially, looking at the edges of my desk whenever I spoke. If I caught his eyes, he glanced away and jostled in his seat. I asked the basic questions for a first meeting: where he stayed, who he stayed with, what he did all day. He lived with his dad and wanted to get his own place. He wanted to get a job and be on his own. Twenty-five years old and he had never done any of that.

"You want to move out of your dad's place?" I asked.

"Yeah, actually I hate him—"

"Aw, c'mon. You can't say that," Thomas interrupted.

"I do."

"That's your pops," Thomas said. "You have to love him."

The kid was hesitant to stand up for himself. His case manager was telling him how he was supposed to feel.

"Well, I want my own place," he said.

"Okay," I said to end the family-values talk. "First step then is getting some money."

The kid agreed.

"Lee has low self-esteem," Thomas said.

Telling the kid he has to love a person he says he hates is pretty much guaranteed not to raise his self-esteem. Thomas—wearing his therapist's hat—was essentially telling Leontis his emotions could be vetoed. The kid sat with a mixture of optimistic expectation and cringing dread, trying to read everything as a sign of what would come next. Between those two extremes, he aimed to look detached, his head covered in a do-rag and baseball cap, oversized shirt hanging to his knees, rubber bands keeping him from tripping over pant cuffs that dragged beneath his feet. The oversized clothes were meant to give off a menacing vibe, but Leontis looked like he just hoped he would someday grow into his thug gear. I went back to the topic of getting money. The kid had already applied for disability and was waiting for a decision. Social Security paid two types of benefits for people unable to work because of disabilities. Supplemental Security Income (SSI) went to people who had not paid income taxes for a minimum period of time. If a person had paid into the system, they were eligible for SSDI, calibrated to include a percentage of the previous income the person potentially lost due to their disability. But for psychiatric disabilities, the means by which a person was approved seemed to be more of a crap shoot determined by diagnoses, frequency of hospitalizations, and psychiatrists at the Social Security Administration. I didn't even know Leontis's diagnosis, but he had been hospitalized four times this year, each following an argument with his father. He would walk himself into the ER, claiming he wanted to kill himself but had yet to make an attempt.

"What kind of job do you think you want?" I asked.

"A good one."

"Well, what's that mean?"

"I don't know."

"Carrying pianos? Being an accountant?"

"I don't know."

We agreed he would think about it. I told him to bring newspapers when he came in the next week, and we'd look at job postings. I didn't know yet what had kept Leontis from finding work.

• • •

Begrudgingly, Marco pointed out that he couldn't leave his apartment except for his weekly appointment with me. He looked as if he were in physical pain, ashen-faced and cringing at the sound of my voice.

"I just want to stay in bed and wait for this to go away," he said. "This," I learned later, was a crushing depression exacerbated by the external pressures of the world. He had attempted to apply a third time for Social Security benefits, as was suggested by his intake worker.

"I can't do it," he said, showing me the uncompleted applications, which he described as both an insurmountable task and an outrageous insult.

He held both positions simultaneously, creating for himself—and me—the double-bind of being wrong either way we jumped. He wanted help but wouldn't accept it. He wanted money but couldn't apply for a job. He wanted disability benefits but was offended by the questionnaire. He was personally hurt by offers of financial loans from friends, but he took them anyway. Any suggestions I made he batted down.

"So what do you want to do?" I asked.

"Duh. I need money. I'm being evicted."

"That's what you want. How do you want to get it?"

"I. Don't. Know."

"What are the possibilities, then?"

Marco turned away and stood up. "Can we just end it for the day? I can't do this." He walked out and I looked at my watch. Fifteen minutes.

• • •

The next week, Leontis decided he could try landscaping but had never really applied for a job before. I threw ideas at him but kept getting "Yeah, but . . ." answers that illuminated every possible negative consequence of the application process. When he finally couldn't think of any more doomsday scenarios, he admitted, "I don't know how to do this." We started with the job-hunting basics.

"No one can get hurt over the phone," I said. "The worst they can do is hang up on you." Leontis agreed to start cold-calling. I explained the first things he'd want to say, like his full name before quickly mentioning that he's looking for work, to show he wasn't a salesman. We ran through several opening pitches until Leontis felt ready. With the first call, Leontis hesitated and stumbled a bit during the introduction. He recovered quickly and the secretary responded politely before putting him on hold. When she returned to the line and said the company wasn't hiring, Leontis snapped back.

"C'mon, bitch, I need a fucking job!" then looked at me for a cue, the phone still to his ear.

I motioned that he should hang up.

"Hey, that was okay," I said. "First try. But you want to keep the conversation going a bit. Like ask, maybe, 'Do you know when you would be hiring?'"

"Oh, okay."

"You wanna try again?"

By the end of the hour, the kid sounded warmer, less panicked. He still didn't want to go knocking on doors looking for jobs and I couldn't tell if he was anxious, lazy, or both. Leontis left with a homework assignment to bring in every job listing he considered a possibility. He could circle notices in the want ads, print them from a library computer, whatever, but I wanted proof he was working on this. We were going to operate just like people did in the real world—no one knocks on your door offering you a job. The following week, Leontis said he'd found a few places where he could apply but hadn't yet. I told him I'd seen a help-wanted sign at a thrift store. He walked over there, got the job the same day, put in two days of work and walked out again.

"The bitch was treating me like shit," he said. "Do this, do that! She didn't like how I did anything!" Leontis could work but hadn't yet figured that people got paid for following instructions and doing things they didn't want to do.

He had cash in his pockets—his dad provided some funds from his bartending shifts—but couldn't or wouldn't pay the bills for his therapist, psychiatrist, and case management. I checked his chart and found a soupy diagnosis of major depression, anxiety disorder, and agoraphobia, as well as a provisional suggestion to rule out borderline personality disorder. He was under little pressure to become independent. He offered no resistance to any suggestions I made but wouldn't say specifically what he wanted from the world. The kid couldn't perceive what his life might be like in five years. I continued testing Leontis to see if he could devise any plans for himself. We hit coffee shops, talked to a martial arts dojo manager, and browsed a used bookstore. He picked up a true crime pulp and a week later was able to report back on the book. He showed no anxiety about crowds and could handle a night out at Dave and Buster's with his cousin. He could navigate public transportation, the internet, and department stores. We talked about books, girls, television, and exercise as a means to cut the edge of his depression. He said he had seven job applications floating around the neighborhood. I tried to find some leverage I could use to engage him, but he responded to everything with a feigning agreement, often attempting gross and unskilled flattery regarding my intelligence. The immediate goal was to get him to stop calling the crisis hotline whenever he was mad at his father. He had never attempted suicide, but the threat propelled people into action—the crisis workers would send an ambulance and his psychiatrist would demand more support from the agency.

"I always tell them I'm going to hang myself," he said, proud of this one coping skill. "Sometimes I just take the bus to the hospital."

If his dad said he was a piece of crap, Leontis would try to get some other assessment and the hospital offered the only option for him. For

Leontis—and for a lot of people—it was better to be considered insane by licensed professionals than worthless by your own parents. I didn't see any Axis I symptoms—delusions, depression, manic phases. Only a combination of personality disorders, which can be just as crippling as auditory hallucinations. The agoraphobia diagnosis was nonsense. Without the Axis I diagnosis, though, Leontis didn't have a chance of getting a disability check. Personality disorders were not considered disabilities by Social Security. Leontis could have benefited from participating in—rather than merely attending—some serious therapy. I had no clue what he was getting from his sessions. The therapist's notes were cut-and-paste jobs, summarized each week by two vague sentences describing the hour: "The clinician assisted the client by discussing the client's presenting issues and emotional responses to stressors in order to develop coping skills. The client and clinician scheduled next appointment."

Whatever Leontis heard in therapy was a mystery, but I suspected he shrugged and okey-doked his way through. He didn't know what he was supposed to be and had never been taught to measure the world for himself. He didn't acknowledge any long-term goals that weren't fantasies and he couldn't differentiate between the results of a single attempt to complete a task and his entire self-view. He was a tangle of wants that refused to be focused in a single direction. I'd failed so far to drag his attention to the benefits of taking responsibility for his own life. But he kept seeking help and all I could assume was that he knew his life was not what he wanted it to be. There was a wall between us, and I think we both expected the other to work harder to knock it down.

11

Marco found the treatment rooms in our building even more depressing than the rest of his life, so we met at a coffee shop that never had any customers.

"I feel bad for those other people," he said, meaning the clients back in our waiting room. "It reminds me I don't have it so bad. People have it worse than me."

"You said that before. So what?" I said. "A lot of people have it better than you. How does either change things?"

Marco cringed at the reminder of his fragile status. He didn't want to look at other people in relation to himself unless the comparison matched his current mood. This was one aspect of Marco I was able to track over the first several weeks. In a given moment, his emotions defined his self-image and the world. His view depended solely on his feelings, rather than logic, and, more often than not, he refused to accept any positive assessments of himself. That combination shoved him back and forth between contrary views that reflected the double-bind he placed on just about everything: he didn't deserve a good life because others had it worse—and that other people had better lives proved his was worthless. Marco's external problems—his parents, alcohol, drug-possession busts, suicide attempts, unemployment, the landlord—had become so emotionally entangled for him that whenever he attempted to decipher one problem, the others encroached and twisted together into an impossible, unchangeable mess. When the ruminating became too much for Marco, his mind skipped from one topic to the next, tapping into little points of anxiety and engaging all of his worries without working toward any answers. The entire mess floated in the air over Marco. Each piece was manageable by itself, most likely, but together their weight became impossible to carry. Each point he touched upon was painful, so he jumped to the next. The speed of this process would increase with the anxiety of the next unsolved issue. His breathing would grow shallow as panic tightened around him like a metal band around his chest. We tried to imagine a way for him to recognize the anxiety in real time, to find some cue—specific phrases, physical responses, anything—that he could use as a demarcation point to warn himself before the pace quickened beyond his control. He rejected every idea.

"Is there a solution to this?" Marco asked after we both sat quietly for a few minutes.

Weeks earlier, he'd wanted to know whether any hope existed, and my supportive response had made him cringe, so now I told him, "I don't know."

"Thank God," he said. "If you told me there was, I would have walked away."

Throughout his life Marco had been told by others what he was supposed to think. Marco described himself as "the good boy," who did everything he was told, even after a family friend, Uncle Jim, had sexually assaulted him. Marco still felt like an adolescent trying to make sense of the world. He knew something was wrong; something was missing. The instructions for living he had been raised with were not working. And the fault was his; he swore on that. He'd lived his life in deference to other people, who he believed understood how the world worked. But he felt doomed because life wasn't what he had been told to expect.

His Uncle Jim knew all the answers. His parents knew all the answers. He could see their words didn't fit their actions, but it didn't compute that the other people could be to blame for what he'd been through. Nothing they'd told him had come true—not as a child, not as an adult. Blaming himself had been his defense, a way to make sense of the world. The weight Marco placed on his own shoulders to protect his ideal of the adults in his life had grown too heavy over the years, and that weight distorted all of his interactions. Marco couldn't see any of this. According to him, the connection between his past and present was his own weakness and nothing else. His automatic reaction to any type of authority was a cringing defiance that propelled people away from him, proving his silent assessment that the problem was within himself.

That had been the pattern of his life. All of the people who knew better betrayed him or didn't support him when he needed them most. Even so, he was dependent on them for support and for his sense of self. After his first suicide attempt, Marco told his parents about his uncle and what had happened twenty years earlier. He started with his father, who apologized and told him to not upset his mother. When he told his mother, she locked herself in her bedroom. When his father came back home, he cursed out Marco for upsetting her.

When Marco had tried to kill himself with a second overdose, his parents said, "We love you, anyway," and, "You're too old for this kind of behavior."

When Marco told me about the assault I was, dumbly, surprised by what he said of the uncle who had raped him. "I don't understand why he did it. He was really, truly, a nice guy." I poked a bit at the statement, but Marco wasn't going to let go of that perception. The fault was his. He just knew it, even if he couldn't explain why. I let the subject drop. He wasn't going to let go of his guilty narrative willingly and we didn't yet have a relationship where I could make any sort of challenge.

Marco thought he knew of all sorts of things he could do to make his life better; he just couldn't bring himself to do them. No matter how many times he said he knew he should go to the Social Security office, or to the doctor, or out to get a job, he would always report back the same thing. "There's no point. It's hopeless."

Marco had to discover a reason to get out of bed before he could discover a reason to do anything else. And I didn't know where to look for the first small success we could build on. He refused to acknowledge that drinking coffee instead of vodka was an improvement. He also refused to accept the possibility that his depression, which kept him in bed nearly eighteen hours a day, was not some immovable force that had seeped into his being at a submicroscopic level, recoding his genes and determining the path of his life.

• • •

I got a call from Leontis's psychiatrist, Dr. Ensler, who wanted to know what was going on with the kid's disability application. She was a fleshy, overflowing earth mother, trying to hold all of her young clients to her bosom.

"His previous case manager did all the paperwork and we're waiting for an answer," I said.

"He needs to be on SSI," she said. "He cannot work. Can't you do something about this?"

"Not really," I said. "I've been working with him because he says he wants a job. We're waiting for an answer."

"Well, he can't work," she said. "He really needs the disability. He has agoraphobia on top of his depression. He can't work."

"He was playing video games at Dave and Buster's last week."

"Oh, good for him."

I explained that Leontis actually had been looking for work and had gotten a couple of jobs for a couple days each. There was nothing I could do about the Social Security decision except prepare him for an answer he wouldn't like and continue to train him on interviews and basic job skills. I know there are altruistic doctors-without-borders who fly to third-world countries to provide medical aid, but this doctor had her own program: doctors-without-boundaries. She would call case managers and leave voice messages laced with concern and pressure them to do something because she had already made promises to their clients that no one could guarantee. When the promises never materialized, she blamed the case managers.

The next day I met Leontis at the coffee shop and he plopped down a letter from the Social Security Administration rejecting his disability claims. This wasn't unusual. Most people got rejected the first time around. If Leontis walked into a Social Security office wearing nothing but a hospital gown and a tin-foil hat and howling about alien implants, there would still be no guarantees. The appeal process could easily take six months, but Leontis was in a better position than most. He had a roof over his head and was able to look for work during the interim. Some folks had to wait for a decision while sleeping in a shelter.

"How could they turn me down?" he said, laughing nervously. "I can't work. I needed that. I was counting on that."

He didn't want to hear that I had no control over Social Security decisions.

"Just get it done," he demanded. "What the hell? Have you even been doing this long enough? Who else could I have do this?"

I suggested maybe he should be the one to write a letter of protest, and still be prepared to wait months for an answer. "But in the meantime," I said. "We're going to have to find some sort of backup plan."

"Fuck that, dude."

"Okay. If you can live with your dad, that's okay with you, right?"

"No, c'mon. They owe me. I been doing all this for nothing!"

I showed no response, but I wanted to choke him. For two months he had been practicing job interviews, filling out resumes, halfheartedly looking for work, and occasionally getting hired for a day or two before stomping off the job. Either the whole thing was a shuck, or he had somehow convinced himself his benefits would be granted without question and he would never have to work again. His outrage told me more about him than I had learned in two months.

"They can't do this," he said. "I won't accept it. They have to give me money. This is America. There are other people who get it; why can't I? I deserve it as much as they do."

"This is America," I said. "And some people have to work for a living."

"But I can't! The doctor said so. You have to send them the record from the last time I went to the hospital. You have to get everything you can. Get a letter from someone. You write a letter saying I can't work."

"Two days ago, you wanted to work," I said. "That's what we've been talking about all this time."

"I meant maybe a part-time job, maybe."

"Were you just yeah-yeahing me?"

"No . . . I don't know . . . I should go to the hospital again. I'm gonna call. I'll keep doing it until they see I'm right." I had hoped this kid could get a job and start a life. It annoyed me that he was ready to settle for a disability check and willing to threaten suicide in order to better his odds. Now he had a cause to battle for. He had decided he would remain with the agency until he received something to show for his pain. A twenty-five-year-old man diagnosed with agoraphobia and depression who lived with his father was not a likely candidate for a disability check. The diagnosis was too mushy. Agoraphobia couldn't be specified to only potential workplaces. And his depression wasn't triggered by contact with a lawn mower or a fast food deep fryer. Leontis wasn't faking his inability to maintain his life, but calling a suicide hotline whenever his dad got on his case did not qualify him for disability benefits. Most of his life he had been minimally provided for by the Department of Children and Family Services, foster care, and group homes before returning to his father, and the system had failed to prepare him to navigate the adult world. Like the kid who put in a semester of college, failed every class, and lost his debit card at the campus bar, he now wanted to come back home. The system hadn't taught him anything except that he was dependent upon it. I suspected Leontis also had internalized a good bit of the pimp-player work ethic, where "getting over" was considered a respectable accomplishment. Regardless, I had to accept that employment was no longer an option because Leontis had made up his mind. I told him we would appeal the Social Security decision as he requested.

"If you get me this money, I'll buy you dinner," he said. "I swear I'll give you ten percent."

I waited a second to gather my thoughts. "You ever say anything like that again, I'll report it and close your case immediately. You want to hire a lawyer? Go ahead. They'll take your money."

"No, I don't want no lawyer. They'd probably take too much." At that point, I stopped soft-shoeing Leontis's choices. I suggested he start preparing himself for the possibility he would have to work at some point in his life. He disagreed. Leontis had always worked his ass off to provide other people with the answers he thought they wanted. And in return he would only accept the answers that he wanted. To his mind, that was how the world worked. Leontis and Marco were both in pain. Marco blamed himself. Leontis blamed everyone but himself. Marco wanted to know what he had done to deserve his pain. Leontis tried to figure how to make others relieve his pain.

Both Leontis and Marco were repeatedly denied disability entitlements, but while Leontis felt he was owed something, Marco attributed the denials to his own faulty character and lousy luck. I thought I might be able to convince Marco to consider the possibility that he was a decent human. I wasn't sure how to convince Leontis that the world didn't owe him anything.

Leontis started taking art therapy courses because he needed "day structure." He was still bent on being paid for his psychiatric diagnosis and hospitalized himself a couple of more times to prove his point. He eventually decided to close his case with our agency after we agreed to waive his two years' worth of bills for therapy, medications, and psychiatric appointments. Leontis considered this a success. He had finally gotten something for his efforts.

• • •

Marco and I continued to go around and around in search of new coping skills to help manage his depression. After demanding we keep suicide on the table as a potential solution, he asked me, "So, what do you think my state is?"

I didn't know what he meant. An assessment of his progress? A guess at his current mood? Marco would snarl and snap during sessions and, in the next breath, ask not to be confronted. He said there was no point continuing therapy because he saw no progress. Just three days earlier, he had been giddy with the realization that his depression wasn't his fault, but now he perceived that small high as a false hope, just another cruelty. The endless black depression he felt was his destiny and he didn't deserve the happiness other people enjoyed.

"I know this is terrible, but the bed is safe," he said. "The depression comes, and I want to go to bed."

Challenging Marco seemed to propel him further away, so I asked a question. "The bed feels better?"

"Yes!" he said, as if I was finally catching on.

"Okay," I said. "So we count that as a coping skill—staying in bed. It works, for whatever reason. When things get to be too much, you should get in bed."

This approach might have been prescribing the symptom, but it was also a way to start validating his feelings. His psychiatrist had told him to stay out of bed. His mother and his former therapists all told him the same. The only maxim I was working from at this point was that Marco had to be able to recognize he had enough skills to minimize some of his pain, and if previous interventions truly weren't doing the job, then we shouldn't keep trying those. I helped him take stock: "You have two coping skills, three actually, you can count on. Suicide—which might not be terribly effective except to end the pain—staying in bed, and drinking."

Marco thought I was being sarcastic. "How are those *skills*?"

"All of them stop the pain from getting worse," I said. "At least a little bit, and for a little bit. Suicide is your last resort. You asked to keep it on the table, so we will. But the other two skills feel good in the moment. They reduce the immediate pain, right?"

"Sure. I guess."

"Down the line we have to start looking for skills that reduce pain on a more long-term basis. Staying in bed reduces the immediate pain and makes life tolerable enough to get through the day, but the other stuff—rent, a job—still hangs there. Staying in bed isn't the same as paying the rent, but it's good enough for now. Does that sound fair?"

"It does, but what do you think my state is?"

I gave the most basic answer I could. "You're depressed."

I waited for him to lash out at me. "What do you mean?"

"This is depression. The fatigue is a normal symptom."

His face turned red, and his eyes began to water. I thought I had screwed up. "You mean this is how it's supposed to be?" Marco asked.

"Supposed to be? I don't know."

"But what I'm going through is valid?"

"Other people suffer the same way," I said. "That's how it got a name."

"My therapist used to tell me I was a borderline personality."

"Could be you fit those criteria. I don't know. I don't think the diagnosis matters much."

The constant pain of dealing with the world through the lens of borderline personality symptoms easily led to depression. We talked about borderline characteristics and Marco ticked off those he recognized in himself. Meeting two diagnoses, he seemed to perk up. We agreed that during our next session we would go through the fourth edition of the *Diagnostic and Statistical Manual of Mental Disorders* to look up major depressive and borderline personality disorders. I had wrongly assumed that Marco's previous therapists had covered this ground with him. He had walked away from them with one crushing statement reverberating in his head.

"My last therapist, all she ever told me was that I had the worst case of self-loathing she'd ever seen."

12

With a couple paychecks under my belt, I was able to move out of my roommate situation. It had been useful for getting through school since I literally had saved just enough to live on through graduation. But I wanted my own place, where me and my blockhead pit bull, Minnie, could stretch out.

I found an old storefront in the neighborhood, four blocks from the office. This felt like a perfect setup for me and Minnie, a rescue who had been starving when I took her home. Now she had room to run. And I had a desk, bookshelves, and a bed. A buddy from my old moving company gifted me a pool table he picked up on the job. I took it and considered the decorating done.

My back door opened into the rear hallway of a tavern run by a sweet little old lady named Ollie. The option to enter my apartment through the bar added a welcome bit of privacy. My place was between a pair of side streets known, at least at our agency, as the "client corridor." It ran all through Uptown just east of Broadway. The blocks were crammed with SROs and flophouse hotels that housed the majority of my clients.

Over time, some of them noticed me walking the dog or smoking cigarettes out on the sidewalk in the morning, but they never hassled me.

Coworkers suggested I shouldn't live in the neighborhood in order to keep some distance from clients. But I wanted to be in the middle of all of this. I had spent so many years working jobs I fucking hated. Now that I had a job with some social responsibility, a job I valued, I decided I would do nothing but work. I would push and pull and coax people—who were deeply isolated, if not segregated from the world themselves—into living better lives, unconstricted by psychosis, trauma, and substance abuse. And in the process, without even noticing, I would ignore my own needs until an almost austere and isolated personal life became the norm. My exile would prove my dedication to others, and therefore my strength of character, even if it didn't actually do a damn thing for anybody.

13

At 290 pounds, Simone was nearly twice my size, with hands that looked like they could rip a phonebook in half. She was manic-powerful and somehow all the weight she had piled on as a side effect of her medications didn't seem to physically slow her down. Her head was like a softball on top of a beer keg. One side of her neck displayed a tattoo with cursive letters: *Crazy Bitch*. Another on her breast bragged, *Product of Italy*. I drove and Simone sat in the passenger seat, juking to dance music on the radio, rocking the entire van as we rolled up Lincoln Avenue into the north suburbs. We were going to see a state-appointed psychiatrist for her Social Security evaluation. If the psychiatrist found her disabled, then Simone would get $674 a month.

Six months earlier, she had been hospitalized for a suicide attempt after her three-month-old baby died. Simone carried a snapshot of the baby, shriveled and malnourished, with bony arms sticking out of a little pink and blue outfit. The baby's little arms and legs extended unnaturally. She swore the baby was still alive in the picture.

"I didn't do anything wrong," she said.

Child protective services had investigated the death and found that Simone was not responsible, but she seemed to still doubt this, and I wondered about it also. She seemed to have little to no support from any sort of family. It was a tragedy she was carrying alone. In the waiting room of the Social Security office, Simone and I watched some TV on the flat screen there and flipped through gossip magazines. Plaster busts of some dead Greeks and similarly themed wall hangings were positioned around the room.

"Damn, is those real?" she asked. "They must be making sick money here."

By explaining to Simone what kind of information the doctor

would need, I gathered as much as I could for myself. She lived with her ex-con boyfriend who she met when they were both working the third shift at an industrial laundromat. She had been raped at age twelve by her brother and his friends. A schoolteacher had called Child Protective Services one day when Simone started bleeding in class as a result of the assault. Her family abandoned her to an emergency shelter and, subsequently, the foster care system for snitching.

Simone had been prostituted by an older man when she was sixteen. She became addicted to heroin at seventeen and spent two years locked up in Cook County Jail and Dwight Correctional Center. She had already had three abortions. During the next four years she carried three babies to term. The Department of Children and Family Services took the children. Simone described her babies with a chilling possessiveness that cast the tiny humans as inanimate dolls meant to satisfy their mother's needs. Simone couldn't explain why her babies were all born brain-damaged but swore drugs were not the cause, even though she'd been shooting heroin and smoking crack while she was pregnant on the street.

Simone felt cheated because her former boyfriend, pimp, and father of the kids had scored a bit part in a cable television documentary. The pimp's mother was now taking care of the children.

"Should I show the doctor that I sort of cut myself?" Simone asked me. I looked at her wrists and forearms. They were clean. "No, here," she said and pulled up her quadruple-XL T-shirt and spandex shorts to display rows of raised, white slashes on the insides of her thighs. "I was just sad. I wanted to kill myself, but not really."

A little old lady across the waiting room visibly recoiled as Simone's story sprayed out of her mouth like water gushing from a firehose. She came off like a mash-up of a traumatized little girl and an experienced street menace who wasn't putting up with any shit. I told her to pull her shirt back down. The doctor, a White guy in a tweed jacket and oxford shirt, called us to his office. Simone continued her monologue on the way in, not bothering to say hello or introduce herself. The doctor's eyes widened as Simone skipped through her history without any chronology, just providing snapshots of horrific images: full leather restraints in the hospital, a .22 under her pillow, and a child's legitimate terror that kept the lights on all night because someone might break in. The doctor tried to step in with the standard psychiatric evaluation questions—checking whether Simone was oriented to time and place, could describe her psychiatric symptoms, and could relate how her life has been impeded by those symptoms.

"Do you ever hear voices?" the doctor asked.

"I can hear those people outside," Simone whispered. "The noises I hear at night sound like that."

"You hear people outside this window?" the doctor asked, dubious.

I interrupted. "There are people sitting there."

Two cleaning women were on a smoke break. The doctor peeked through the blinds and Simone clapped, happy to be proved correct. She showed the doctor the picture of her dead baby and the doctor almost leapt from his chair. He tried to ask questions about Simone's home life and the baby's father. Simone jumped around, unable to follow the questions for more than a couple of seconds before slipping over to what she wanted to talk about.

"She's never been on disability before?" the doctor asked me.

"She's only twenty-one."

The meeting concluded with the doctor saying he would recommend Social Security entitlements. He might as well have twirled his finger around his temple and made chirping noises. We thanked the doctor and headed back to the agency. Simone had an appointment with one of our psychiatrists, whom she had met several times before. The doctor, who also had seen Leontis, greeted Simone as if she were an old girlfriend coming over for coffee. Simone rolled right into a monologue about the boyfriend who hadn't paid rent the last couple months. The apartment lease and all the utilities were in her name, and she worried the cable would get shut off. The doctor made some vague groans of empathy.

"Oh, Simone."

The doctor, the same one who had advocated for Leontis, told me I had to help her pay the rent somehow. No suggestion the boyfriend get a job to cover that. Simone agreed to meet me once a week for therapy. She needed to start learning how to take care of basic things like SSI and public aid, medical check-ups, psychiatric appointments, and counseling sessions that might help her find ways to sleep through the night.

I walked her out to the boyfriend's car and met the guy, a steroid-pumped young man with waxed eyebrows and long hair cut straight across the shoulders. He gave me a dead fish handshake and I started telling him about the schedule to which Simone had agreed. "I don't know," he said. "I can't be driving her around everywhere. I work during the day."

He called over to Simone, "C'mon!" then ducked back into the car as Simone climbed in the passenger side head-first like a little kid. Boyfriend did a U-turn and Simone stuck her entire upper body out the window to wave as they drove off.

• • •

While Simone was born with the whole world against her, other people have their lives turned upside-down seemingly overnight. The most torturous aspect of chronic mental illness might be for the sufferer to understand the loss of potential and the disrupted life path. Some people can recall the exact point where the psychosis upended their lives, marking where the "normal" route had been destroyed. They know their life as "before" and "after." How do you tell someone to be satisfied with their lot when they saw the first twenty-some years of their life negated by a psychotic break that let loose a flood of voices, tactile hallucinations, and the suspicion that thoughts that once were private were actually on display? When that person says they've been cheated, you can't disagree.

Tyson had been cheated. He knew it and hated the world for it. Safely on the middle-class college track in his third year of undergraduate work, he got hit by a psychotic break with the force of a tsunami. "I was in the library late before closing studying for a biology test," he told me. All of a sudden ten-thousand people started screaming at me, calling me a nigger bitch."

He ran across campus breaking windows until he arrived at his dorm room and hid in bed until the police came. Tyson and his parents hoped for a while that the psychotic behavior was just a response to marijuana—which is a hope many parents hold onto—but the voices wouldn't stop. They criticized Tyson's every move and spoke vile epithets about him. He swore this was not paranoid schizophrenia as the doctors had said. Instead, he believed he was telepathic and could hear the thoughts of people walking past him on the streets. Some days he would sprint through his neighborhood, trying to outrun the barrage of unwanted psychic transmissions. Other days he couldn't bring himself to leave his attic apartment. Tyson spent most of his time in a simmering rage. Angry that people thought he was crazy. Angry that people thought he was gay. Angry that people were shoving their accusations into his head. But mostly he was pissed off because he knew how smart he was and could feel his opportunities slipping away along with his sanity. He felt bugs crawling up his arms. Voices told him he was a trick baby.

"You know what a trick baby is, don't you?" he asked. "I'm supposed to be in college. Not living like this."

Most of Tyson's friends were finishing college and getting jobs out in the suburbs while he was living in a flop, trading sex for drugs and rent. He could see where he wanted to go in life but couldn't see how to get there. Tyson caught me in the hall after an appointment with his psychiatrist and case manager and asked if I had a couple of minutes. We sat down and he got straight to the point.

"How am I supposed to live like this?"

I asked what he wanted to change, and his answers devolved into psychotic talk and disjointed stories. I had clients piling up in the waiting room. I was tired and unfocused. I caught myself trying to rein him in, but I was too late.

"Okay," I said. "What is it you want to accomplish here?"

The kid's eyes welled up. "You can't kick me out. Not like this."

"I'm not kicking you out. I'm trying—"

"I can't leave like this," he said, slapping his own face. "Fucking crying. I won't leave like this, okay? Someone has to hear this shit! Fine. We'll do this like therapy. My first childhood memory was of me standing in the room. I was three years old, watching my mother with one of her friends."

It was like his delusions had gone on strike. His recollections were sharp and clear—names, places, schools, candy bars, toys, brand-name clothing. All the little stuff that gets imprinted on a kid's memory was marbled in with the memories of being a prostitute's child. It was the history he had not told me.

When Tyson was six years old, he and his mother had bounced around the outskirts of Chicago, between Aurora and Peoria, living in hotel rooms whenever Mom got them evicted from short-term lease apartments for missing the rent. Child Protective Services eventually took him away from her and sent him off to a series of foster homes, the kind of places where the adults prepared for caseworker visits by letting the kids out of the basement for proper meals.

At thirteen, a family in the north suburbs adopted Tyson. He managed his way onto the middle-class college track and never spoke of his previous life. He had walled those memories off, even from himself. During college Tyson went to his biological mother's funeral. The only people there were from her AA group.

"I chanted 'I'm sorry,' over and over and nothing happened," Tyson said. "I didn't feel any different. What do I have to do?"

Tyson worked himself into a volcanic state as he told me all of this. He side-kicked the office wall hard enough to crack the sheetrock and screamed that his life was unfair. He had been cheated. He had done everything he was supposed to "and fucking God took it all away! I was in college! I want to kill her for making me crazy! She did it, didn't she? You can't do that shit to a kid and not have him be crazy, right? You can't let people touch me for money!"

At that point, a secretary who could hear Tyson's howling called a code yellow. Codes were announced to alert clinicians and clients about fires, medical emergencies, and potentially violent incidents. Hearing the announcement over the intercom, all staff members—from the tiniest waif on up—were to come immediately.

Tyson heard the announcement and could hear people collecting in the hallway outside our door. He called out, "You better have the biggest nigger cops you can to drag me out of here! I'll fuck up anyone who tries!"

"No one's dragging you anywhere," I told him.

I went into the hall and told the staff the code was a false alarm. But it had at least broken the kid's momentum so I could start talking to him. I tried to direct him toward the various ways to measure the lives of humans, and I posed the possibility that a person is not merely the sum of his accomplishments but what they have to overcome.

"Look at Paris Hilton," I said. "What's the biggest problem she has to overcome? Which club to go to? If she were dropped onto the corner of Argyle and Broadway without her money, fame, and contacts, how long would she last?"

This seemed to appease Tyson enough that he could consider the possibility that carrying a heavier burden didn't make him a loser. I kept shifting the discussion as he kept trying to spiral himself into a fit. Like aikido, I was trying to slip under the verbal shots while preventing him from building momentum again. "Let's go have a cigarette," I said.

Out back in the alley, I pitched the idea to Tyson that we can't be responsible for where we came from. Some people might judge us by the burdens we've had to carry, and that's not fair. But carrying the burden is a show of strength. Tyson did get a raw deal, born into circumstances that turn some kids into monsters. We talked about how childhood trauma can cripple one's ability to develop empathy and shatter the basic human need for an emotional connection to others—a connection most people fight for. Tyson said he wanted a normal life and people to care about. I told him this was where his strength was. He rejected that, claiming he was weak. If he had any strength, he said, his brain wouldn't be so fucked up.

"I'm talking about character, not brain chemicals," I said. "Your character is a combination of all the choices you make. Those choices you make, just like anyone else, are influenced by the life you've lived. And that you're still fighting for the life you want, against the crap you've had to go through, says how strong your character is. Other people who've been through the same as you wouldn't survive, right?"

"I know they wouldn't," he said.

"What do you think they do?"

"They become serial killers."

I hesitated, a little concerned he knew that.

"I'd still like to go back and make my mother pay," he said. "I don't love her. It's a lie that I said I did. I wanted to love her, but there was nothing there. I wish I could kill her for this."

"You know what the problem is with revenge killing?" I said. That caught his attention, and he smiled a bit.

"What?"

"You can only kill the person once."

"Yeah, but . . . I don't get it."

"If you could kill the person you hated the most, would all your problems be fixed?"

He thought about this, and I hoped I hadn't walked myself into an ugly corner. "No."

"Why not?"

"I'd still live in a shithole. I'd still have no money."

I drove him home and we agreed to meet again the next week. He never made the appointed days or times we agreed upon, but if Tyson came in and I was around we would find time to talk. The rest of our sessions weren't as explosive as the first. He refused to take his prescribed medications, but he kept coming in, hoping for something to turn his life around. Until, one day, he stopped.

I saw him in a hospital a couple years later. He had set a fire at a group home. Tyson didn't even live there; he'd been visiting a pal who regularly bought Tyson's meds. But he was an adult now, and a danger, so they'd sent him off to the state hospital.

• • •

Simone's boyfriend, Johnny, hated me. She and I had made note cards with daily reminders about her meds and food and tips on how to get to sleep at a decent hour. The next week she said she had to quit.

"I can't do this anymore. Johnny got mad when he saw the cards you made. He said, 'What are these, from your boyfriend?' and took them away."

The front desk called right then. Johnny was there to pick Simone up and had said he was leaving if she didn't get out there immediately. On her way out she said, "He's going to kill me."

Simone started crying when the psychiatrist suggested Johnny sit in for some impromptu family counseling. "No, no, no," she said, wiping her nose with a chubby fist. "He'll get so mad. He hates Zak."

I had gone out to their apartment a couple of times after Simone had missed appointments and medication pick-ups. Johnny wouldn't let me in, saying she wasn't home and whining that I had woken him up at three in the afternoon. One time, I caught him dragging Simone out the back door as they saw me coming up the front. "Sammy's got to come to work with me," Johnny said, pulling her by the hand down the sidewalk.

"This will only take a minute," I said.

Johnny shrugged. He said he was going to go start the car and that it was good to see me again. Handshake. Pals.

"He didn't want me to see you," Simone whispered. I gave her a filled prescription and a bus card in case she ever had to travel to the office on her own. If she wanted to leave the guy she needed the means to do so. She acted like I had saved her life by handing her the bus card, but she still never came to the office alone. Johnny was respectful toward the doctor and polite with me, but he barked at our secretaries and terrorized Simone. I would have had more respect for him if he had taken a swing at me. He was operating from the belief that Simone would leave him as soon as she had her own financial resources. And he was right

"He tells me I got no say because it's not my money," Simone told me, "and when I have money I can have some say. I sorta agree with him, but I'm not staying when I got my own money. He says he's going to be my payee, but I said you said this place was going to be my payee. He got mad about that, but nothing he could do."

According to Simone, Johnny usually held onto her cell phone, wouldn't let her out of the house unescorted, didn't let her cook, didn't let her take the bus, and took her with him to work rather than leave her to her own devices at home. Johnny said he would help her get her psychotropic meds but nothing else related to her treatment. What she needed was tough love, and he was happy to provide it. Johnny clearly benefited from keeping Simone medicated, but if she had access to other people, she might start listening to them. Maintaining his control of her depended on limiting her options, not expanding them. Simone's doctor continued to insist that couples counseling was a fine idea. I thought the session would be nothing but navigating lies and letting Simone deal with the fallout when she got home. No matter what she said, she was terrified of Johnny.

"Do you want us all to sit down with him," the doctor asked Simone, "or would you two want to sit down with Zak and come to an understanding?"

"No, no. He'll get mad."

"I think we can find a way to talk to him so he won't get mad," the doctor said, as if she had the power to keep the guy from slapping Simone when they got home. Simone shook her head frantically, snot and tears flowing. The doctor looked at me to back her up on this homicidal idea. No chance.

I asked Simone if she felt safe at home.

"We have fights," she said. "He hits me, but sometimes I hit him first." She pushed a dry giggle.

I asked if she wanted to stay.

"I got nowhere else to go."

"What if you did?"

"I don't have any money."

"What if you didn't need any?"

"I don't know. I'm okay for now."

Johnny picked her up after the appointment, all smiles and handshakes. Once Simone left, the doctor told me, "I think he is doing her some good. He picked her up out of the gutter. He's keeping her off drugs."

Just because a guy "helps" a woman out of the gutter, it doesn't mean he's not a vicious, self-centered bastard. You don't give someone like Johnny an MVP award for pulling his girlfriend from a burning building then tamping out her flaming clothes with an aluminum bat.

Simone would have to decide whether she wanted to leave Johnny, and that goal would have to outweigh any comforts he provided. She had to believe she could live on her own. A few minutes after she left with Johnny, Simone ran back into the office and caught me in the hallway.

"I told him I forgot something," she said. "But I wanted to tell you when I get my own money, I'm gone. I want my own place."

• • •

At her next appointment, Simone came in and cheered to the doctor.

"You won't believe it, nigger, I'm not pregnant! Isn't that great, dog?"

"Simone," I said. "You do not call a doctor 'dog'—or 'nigger.'"

"Oh. I didn't mean nothing."

"Oh, it's okay," the doctor said. "We have a special relationship."

Simone said she didn't want to leave Johnny anymore. She said he was being nice.

• • •

Tyson had been pulled from the foster care system into a stable and safe environment, but after the psychotic break in college, any emotional gains he had made slipped away again. His family had informally disowned him after he had gone after his aunt with a steak knife. He knew the life of normalcy he dreamed of was no longer possible. But he'd had a taste of it. Simone had never even set foot in that zip code. She had never been taught to look forward, and there was not much behind her she wanted to remember.

14

Bobby's psychiatrist held a passionate grudge against caffeine and sugar. She told every client to stop drinking pop, coffee, and tea. Generally this was good advice, but not exactly a triage approach to dealing with severe mental health disorders. Bobby announced during his first appointment with the doctor that he enjoyed two two-liters of Coca-Cola every day. Clearly entertaining himself, he giggled when she warned him that his soda habit was going to kill him.

"Is there anything else?" the doctor asked, hoping to conclude an appointment where Bobby had listed every physical ache and pain but denied any psychotic symptoms.

"Hmm, my upstairs neighbors are sorta loud."

"Bobby," I said, hoping to put the brakes on him.

"I think they're lifting weights."

I tried again. "Bobby, everyone in your building is eighty years old."

"Well, these ones are strong."

Bobby didn't give a damn what the doctor thought of his diet or what he should do about it. He was aggressively lazy, almost protective of his laziness as a lifestyle choice. And he wouldn't be held to any obligations that weren't on his terms. Bobby's progress was evident, though. He no longer stared through concrete walls and his delusions had quieted down as he continued his medication regimen. He was not exactly building a full life for himself, but he was suffering less. One afternoon, Bobby and I won an argument with a public aid worker over a disputed payment and thought we'd celebrate with some Burger King. At the drive-thru he called out for four Whoppers but protested when I pulled money out of my pocket. Even though I had agency cash he demanded we go Dutch. He would pay his own way and eat what he wanted. Okay with me. He had done enough inpatient time where no choices were available to him.

We had been discussing the possibility of a little exercise, just walking a couple of blocks in the mornings. He had put on a few pounds every month since we'd started working together, but eating was the only joy he had. Handing the bag of grease over, I said, "You know, you may want to take a nice walk after all those."

"True," Bobby said. "But I may want to lay in bed all day."

The man didn't want any free food or free advice. I gave him points for that.

• • •

Even though Marco continued to claim he was damned to failure, he eventually began to apply problem-solving skills. He finally realized that no angel of mercy was coming. I had said so a hundred times, and he had held out against the idea for as long as he could, so this was progress. Marco's problem, at its base, was not a lack of money but a belief that he didn't possess the ability to hold a job. He needed validation that his problems were psychiatric and not characteristic of his entire being. He needed someone to believe him that he was not at fault. One day he told me, "I would rather know what to do next instead of why I do what I do. I can know why, but that doesn't help me anymore."

Even with years of psychotherapy under his belt, he hadn't seen his life improve. The world was still having its way with him, and his parents had stopped sending money every month. We focused on the immediate: how to not commit suicide, how to get out of bed, and how to pay the rent. Marco knew intellectually that he had to first change his responses to the world in order to feel any relief emotionally. But he always assessed his efforts as worthless. In fact, he did that for months, even when there was no evidence he had made any effort. He knew he would fail, so no point trying.

• • •

The case management stuff got easier. I figured out how to get sample psychiatric meds and how to find a public aid worker on the telephone. The front desk folks at the hotels knew me by sight. When I would introduce myself to the little woman behind the counter at the Wilson Men's Club, she would cut me off: "I know who you are. Go on up."

When Standish got out of the hospital, he slid right into a rooming house in Canaryville. After a month, the rooming house closed down. No power, no water. The owner disappeared. That's when Standish told me why the room had been so cheap. The owner was one of the floor staffers at the psychiatric unit where Standish had crashed.

"I didn't tell you because you'd have been suspicious," Standish said, frustrated and running his hands through his hair. "Now I can't find this fucking guy. People call him Sally. I can't remember his real name at the hospital."

I called and asked for the guy by his nickname. When he picked up, I started, "Hey, Sally. I'm working with Standish, who you met while you were on the clock at the hospital. I heard you're closing your place."

"That's not exactly true," he said. "But he does owe me some rent money."

"I don't see how he owes any rent without water or electricity."

"There's water. There's lights."

"Excellent, because it would look really bad if you were recruiting tenants from the hospital and not providing the basic needs."

"But when do I get the rent? He can't just stay for free."

"He says you're all paid up. He says he paid a couple months in advance."

"He's not."

"Maybe you should take him to court. He says he's paid up."

Standish went back to the shelter where he had been a month earlier. I stashed his stuff in our garage again and we applied for the shelter's housing program.

● ● ●

To Marco, constant depression felt safer than false hope, and we both knew that was a problem. "You need to push me more," he would tell me. "I don't want to be fragile."

I thought maybe Marco wanted me to push him so that eventually he could push back and say, "It's too much. I quit." I suspected that on one hand he wanted to chase me away, but on the other he wanted to make sure I wasn't going anywhere, even if he threatened suicide. "If you feel this is a total waste of time, let me know and we'll end sessions or find you a new therapist," I told him.

Marco wanted me to make the decision to tell him he was a waste of time and that we were through. So I backed off and left his threats—suicide, quitting therapy—on the table for him to choose. I hoped to show him he had control of how this relationship would flow.

15

"What's going on with the landlady?" I asked Marco.

"I don't know," he said.

He knew the eviction was coming. He hadn't paid rent since his parents had cut him off.

"So, right now, what do you think is going to happen?"

"I don't care. I can't deal with it. Whatever happens happens."

Marco could wall off his distressing feelings for brief periods, but he couldn't stall an eviction. He could try to ignore the internal, but external events invaded without his permission. When that happened, anxiety seized his chest, clamped down, and stopped him cold.

"It feels like when a car engine just locks up and you can feel nothing's moving," he said. With Marco, the slightest change in behavior counted as progress, especially when it resulted in relief from depression and anxiety. Describing his concerns in concrete terms counted, too. We had to be able to describe problems before we could do anything about them. We had to be able to describe emotions before we assessed whether they were helpful or not. We had to define anxiety before we could chase it away.

Marco hated being asked to be specific. He hated compliments or any demarcation of progress. If anyone praised his behavior, he feared they would expect him to repeat it. He wanted others to believe he was good. But he didn't want to be held accountable and he didn't want to fail at anything ever again. He didn't want to be bullied and he didn't want to stand up for himself. He hoped his anxiety would go away if he just ignored it, like a sort of mutual nonaggression pact. Some days, Marco's anxiety and depression would break like a fever. He would enjoy a brief spell of confidence and giddiness before fear rushed back in and demolished the illusion of well-being. Still, he viewed the moments of temporary relief as proof he wasn't so bad off that he needed therapy. None of it changed his belief that he was just a bad person at his core. Marco's landlord was about to send the sheriffs to clear him out of the apartment. All he needed to do was take a step in some direction.

He refused to act. "I don't care what happens," he said.

He felt certain he couldn't get a job. Social security had ruled itself out. He wasn't going to move back in with his parents, not even to their summer house in the Florida Keys. So he asked his ex-wife for a loan. Not a permanent solution, but Marco didn't want to hear about that.

"I've gone as far as I can go," he said. "There's no point. If she doesn't loan me the money, I'm done."

• • •

At the next session, Marco arrived with a voice message from the ex-wife waiting for him. He refused to listen to it. "I know what she's going to say," he said. "I don't have to hear it. I've played out all my options and I'm done. I have to say that suicide is an option right now because I don't see anything else."

"You haven't even heard the message yet."

"I don't have to. I know what she's going to say."

"How?"

"I don't know, but I'm pretty sure. Even so, I can't take her money. It would ruin our friendship."

"At least check your messages before you plan to kill yourself," I suggested. "If she says no, then suicide moves one step up on the option list."

"What's the point of bothering?" he asked.

"What if she's saying no problem? What if she's saying nothing other than to call me back? If she's saying no, then we'll deal with that."

"I really hate it when you get like this, all logical."

The message said, "Call me back."

Marco stepped out onto the sidewalk to make his call. I stood back and lit a cigarette.

"Hi, darling," he said smoothly, the quivering whisper gone from his voice. I wanted to ask why he couldn't do more of that. I let myself get lost in my own thoughts to avoid the temptation of eavesdropping. Marco turned away and drifted down the block, one finger in his ear to block out street traffic. When he hung up, the panic returned to his voice.

"Christ, she wants me to come over tonight and we'll talk about this," he said. "I don't know if I can."

"Why not?"

"She's asking me if this is really going to solve the problem. I don't know. I don't know if I can do this. I'm torturing her. I can't put her through this."

"From everything you said, she doesn't sound too tortured."

"Fine. I'm using her as an excuse, okay?"

"If you don't want to meet her, then you shouldn't."

"I will, okay?"

"Just listen to what she has to say tonight."

"I might."

"Fine."

I didn't know if he understood how close he was walking to the edge of actually being homeless. Or whether he understood that no one was going to break down his door and save him.

• • •

Marco's ex offered the loan and he hated himself for accepting the money. He promised to pay it all back but cringed at the thought that he would be held to his promise. He immediately wanted to offer everything he'd borrowed to his landlady, who had already started eviction proceedings. I explained the most likely result: he would be able to pay the back rent but would still owe the current rent and the eviction process would continue.

"She's a nice person," Marco said. "She's been very sweet."

"I'm sure she is, but she's still a landlord. She wants to know the money will keep coming in."

"But it would be so much easier if she would take this money."

"Easier for who?"

"Me and her."

"Will she take the money?"

"I want her to."

"You want her to. Does that translate to what she will do? What has her behavior been so far?"

"I don't know. I don't care. I think she will."

Marco wanted to force his desired reality. "I'm going to allow myself to feel good and not think about it. I made a decision and I think the landlady will go along with it."

I made sure Marco understood that he had to ask the landlady whether she would accept his terms before giving her the money.

"Don't just hand her a wad of cash," I said. "The important thing is you have the money and that changes things. You have enough there to get a studio apartment along with a couple months' breathing room. I want to tell you—it sounds like you're attributing your own empathy to this woman. If she says no, do you want to go to plan B?"

"A new apartment?"

"It's a possibility."

"God, I don't want to think about it."

• • •

By the next week, Marco had received a fervent no from the landlady.

"How dare she turn me down?" he asked, truly outraged.

"You still have a couple grand in your pocket," I said.

"So what."

"Well, that's how you get a new apartment."

"I wanted to stay in mine."

"I know you did."

"She said she wanted to work this out."

"She did say that, but she wanted it to work out for herself."

"She was just cold on the phone," Marco said. "Didn't even want to hear what I had to say. The sheriffs will throw me out in two weeks."

"She's a landlord. Their two main concerns are getting the rent and protecting their property. She gave you some breaks, but eventually she'll prove out that she's a landlord."

"So, she's not a nice person?"

"She might be in her personal life. Maybe she is when the rent comes regularly. Who knows? All we know is that we have her answer. This is just business to her. Her goals are different than yours, that's all."

"Then she's a bitch, you think?"

"I don't know her. But generally, landlords are the enemy. They want the most money for the least amount of effort. But, right now, you need an apartment."

"What if I just don't fucking bother?"

"Don't bother looking for an apartment? Then, yeah, this is where you can end up at the point you feared—being homeless, living under viaducts. Not having a place to live is the first step. And you're pretty much at the eleventh hour here."

• • •

I tried to visualize my conversations with Marco as some sort of balancing act as he slammed from one side of his continuum to the other: The world should protect him—the world should go on without him. He deserved better—he deserved nothing. If one thing went wrong, he was a bad person and shouldn't be helped because he couldn't do things right. And because he couldn't do things right, there was no point in trying or in even asking for help. I knew he was in pain, but there were days I wanted to walk away from him. To hell with it. Good luck, pal. The longer we worked together, the more I could see where to push an idea and where to lie back and wait for him to come around. I had to anchor Marco and keep him away from the extremes.

• • •

Marco began our next session with passionate certainty.

"I can't take the rejection anymore."

The sole apartment application he had completed had been denied.

"Oh, I'm pathetic. It's not going to happen. I might as well face it. I'm going to be homeless."

"You've only looked at one building," I said. "The rejection you're talking about is a reflection only of your financial situation, not of your character or morals."

"That's a load of crap."

"It's not."

"Prove it."

"I will. If an apartment was any reflection of a person's character or ethics or moral worth as a human, then I would have a much better apartment."

This got half a snort out of him, and he told me to go fuck myself, but a tiny window opened.

"I'm going to be homeless," Marco said. "It's my worst fear come true, finally."

"Okay, listen. You just said, 'I'm going to be homeless,' as if that's the only possible outcome in this."

I listed the other possibilities. He could get a studio and have two months' rent. He could sleep on someone's couch. He could get a flop hotel room in the neighborhood. He could move back in with his parents. He could hospitalize himself. He could even kill himself. Throwing that last option out there still raised my hackles, but I saw Marco shake off that option immediately.

"This isn't optimism," I said. "You're right when you say all that self-awareness is worthless if you can't act on it. Now's when you have to act.

You have a week to get these things done. Not all of them, just the ones that will provide an apartment for you. If you don't, then yes, you will be homeless. The world will continue without you no matter what you do. It's your call now. This is the area where you do have some control."

In his black mood he truly couldn't see his options. Like anyone else, he wanted proof that relief was in sight before letting go of his faith that life would crush him. Sometimes faith, even faith in something awful, is all someone feels they can count on. The black feeling, the emotional spiral, the weight in the center of Marco's chest were solid. His belief that he was damned and doomed was as concrete as the building he was getting kicked out of. Later in the week Marco left a petulant message on my voicemail. He had found an apartment. He would be safe for three months.

"Now I have to pack," he said. "It never ends, does it?"

He still saw this all as a loss rather than progress. He stayed in bed for the next week and didn't return any of my calls. I didn't know if I would hear from him again. After a couple of weeks, he called to see if I was still available at our usual time. I was and we kept going.

PART TWO

16

FALL 2006

My director called me in for a talk. Conversations with him were soothing. He could announce an in-house Ebola outbreak without anyone getting too terribly upset.

Every five years or so, he said, a major restructuring sent ripples throughout the entire agency and a year would pass before routines would settle again. Around the offices I had already heard anxious grumblings about coming changes, shifting job titles, programs transferred to new buildings, and supervisors shoved into new programs.

The agency needed a supervisor for the Assertive Community Treatment program that handled the clients who were more "intensive" than my current caseload. I said I was interested. The director said he would mark me as a candidate. I realized later that this promotion was like answering the call, "Whoever's not paying attention, step forward." No one in the agency wanted the job of ACT supervisor. No one else even applied.

Clients in the ACT program suffered through multiple psychiatric hospitalizations, frequent homelessness, severe substance abuse and medical issues, inappropriate behavior in public, a history of nonadherence to medication regimens and post-hospitalization referrals and presented with little motivation to work toward recovery. None of the clients I had worked with so far would meet the criteria for ACT. Like Olympic diving, there were points for "degree of difficulty" in the community mental health system. Basically, any client the rest of the agency could not or would not hold onto was shunted to the ACT caseload. ACT clinicians' duties were to keep the clients out of the hospitals, jails, nursing homes, shelters—and off the local news.

I had already seen the subterfuge of dumping "difficult" clients into other programs. Having been at the agency for only five months, I had been the recipient of the dump jobs. I did not want to continue that, but I didn't know ACT was considered the bottom of the mental health barrel.

I had a month to get organized. In the director's office, I started thinking about which clients I could take with me to ACT and which I would have to pass off to other case managers.

• • •

I was proud of the promotion. Took it as a sign that my work was valued. I had earned a reputation for taking on tough clients and was proud of that, too. But I also began to resent the expectation once I realized other people saw my willingness to step up as naivete. It wasn't exactly that, but I operated under the self-imposed belief that I had to prove my worth by working longer hours and taking on the cases that scared other people. Back in the truck yard, if someone else carried one piece of sheetrock at a time I had grabbed for two. I didn't earn respect in the same manner here. I had wanted praise from clinicians easing their caseloads, but now I suspected they saw me as an easy mark for doing so.

Once, a client threatened to shoot his therapist. Rather than close the case, the therapist's supervisor asked me to determine whether the client had a gun. I readily agreed. The young man had no interest in working with me. I understood that threatening to shoot me might be less satisfying than threatening to shoot the therapist. I spent enough time with the client to learn he didn't have any weapons, and rather than processing his feelings, I explained what would happen clinically—and legally—if he continued his threats. The client avoided me after that.

Another client they sent my way spent his intake session describing to me his desire to rape his previous psychologist. He justified this discussion as a means of working through a fantasy. Talking to me, though, was not enough of an outlet. He wanted a female therapist with whom he could "process" his fantasies.

I had been warned by my pop, "You're not a bouncer anymore. You don't have to police the whole place."

Without being accusatory, he explained to me why I thought the way I did. That I thought I was being righteous but was actually fostering the limitations of other clinicians. That they would never have to do the hard work if I kept volunteering to do it for them. I was also creating a shunt valve for clients our agency was not equipped to help. If I kept this up, the unwritten rule would be that clinicians could dump inappropriate clients on me, saying, "I can't take this guy. Let what's-his-name take the case."

This had already become a clear pattern, and I'd perpetuated it. I wanted to prove I deserved the job, even though no one but me had bothered to doubt it.

My skewed self-assessments went back to my internships, where I could never tell whether I was doing a decent job or not. Attempting to generate self-approval through the acceptance of strangers was a toxic formula. That might be fine if I were surrounded by people I could trust, steady as a metronome. But I wasn't.

• • •

I didn't want to believe I had been played by Standish, but I suspected I had been. I can note the times I found his stories illogical, and I avoided confronting him on the discrepancies. I hesitated, checking whether his physical and psychological distress were PTSD symptoms or just malingering mixed with some crack urges. Over time, I noticed gaps between Standish's levels of functioning. He could capably negotiate a subsidized apartment for himself, but he would also fall apart every couple of years and end up back in a nursing home or a homeless shelter.

When he and I were almost done working together I got his test results from a recent blood draw. He'd come up positive for cocaine.

He explained he had been intimate with a prostitute and she must have been using crack.

It was a hell of an excuse that felt more like an insult than anything else. He was free to smoke crack for breakfast if he wanted to. We both knew I couldn't stop him. But I berated myself for missing the signs. Either he was a premiere hustler, or I had to sharpen up. I wasn't the morality police, but this was a major barrier to his progress, and I'd missed it. Even smoking crack, though, Standish was doing well enough that he wouldn't qualify for the ACT program anyway. I'd miss him. Personally, I liked the man.

17

I moved my few personal items and files to a desk downstairs just as a work crew began tearing apart the ACT office. New offices were being built, but my team would be working in the hallway until construction was completed. Tarps covered our desks and files. The team had one wall phone to share in the kitchen.

One of my staff members handed in her resignation immediately after I took over. I learned later, through the billing system, that she had done almost nothing in her previous posting over the past several months. Another prospect took one look at the ACT program and applied for a transfer. A third wanted to come in at ten each morning rather than nine because getting up early was difficult. The welcome I had expected was not coming. The group I'd inherited was climbing out the windows while I was still unpacking my desk. I'd hoped for a cohesive unit of clinicians who could truly protect each other and work as a team. Maybe they were—just not with me.

A chief hurdle for any new mental health team looking for cohesion is to close the gaps that allow clients to "split staff." That's when a client makes the same requests or demands to different staff members until they find one who will give them what they want. Or when they tell a new clinician that a former clinician provided perks outside the norm when, in fact, the arrangement is a load of fictitious bullshit. Either way, the client is betting the house that team communication is dysfunctional, which is usually a smart bet.

Some of our clients were ACT lifers—sophisticated staff-splitters accustomed to the parade of case managers that passed through their lives. Many tried to hustle extra cash from new clinicians by claiming special deals that deviated from standard operating procedures: "I always get an extra twenty on Tuesdays!"

Most ACT clients initially came to the program when they were out of money and out of housing. When a person on disability has chronic problems maintaining housing and basic needs, the Social Security Administration will hold their checks until a payee—a family member, friend, or organization—accepts responsibility for the recipient's finances. Most conversations with our clients began, "I want my money!"

Our caseload held the bottom rung of male prostitutes working for crack money. We had clients who panhandled at car windows and El stations or committed smash-and-grabs at retail stores. One tiny woman hid from the cops in a Laundromat dryer. One man had just gotten out of the federal pen for making threats against the president.

Over time, I would develop protocols for handling potentially violent clients. Since the team worked with clients in the neighborhood rather than the office, standard workplace safety precautions didn't apply to us: we didn't have panic buttons, we didn't have a security guard, and we weren't allowed to carry weapons. Even if we were armed, no one on the team was paid enough to deal with the kind of choices that come with armed confrontation.

None of our clients, if I performed my intake assessments correctly, would be linked to gangs. Not because we excluded them per se, but because most people who would qualify for ACT services would be useless to a gang. Those with the weaponry and the willingness needed to commit the kind of coordinated crimes that would benefit a gang rarely came to an ACT program asking for housing.

The entire caseload wasn't criminal, but they all suffered from severe and chronic psychotic symptoms. The world was an antagonistic place for our clients. They struggled to manage their business while hearing voices and seeing phantoms. For many, isolating in a hotel room felt like the only option. No one ever came to the office complaining, "I need to improve my functioning in the world." They hadn't volunteered for schizophrenia, hepatitis C, and crack addiction all at the same time either, but that was often the load they brought to our program. And they didn't usually show up intending to deal with those problems. The only assistance most of them wanted was a bed and a Social Security check.

• • •

I scrambled those first few weeks, trying to remember clients' names, medications, symptoms, drugs of choice, budgets, addresses, landlords, schedules for the week, and appointments for each day. Every day, one clinician covered the action around the office: meds, money, psych appointments, general complaints. Everyone else ran around the neighborhood looking for their clients and administering treatment wherever they found them.

At the office, clients flooded the waiting room. It bugged the hell out of the secretaries. Clients wandered into therapy sessions, let themselves into the team office, audited group sessions down the hall, and helped themselves to available phones. Some clients, including a man who had swung an axe at a garbage collector back home in Puerto Rico, would wait patiently for services all day, napping quietly in the waiting room.

LeFlore was the only holdover from my old caseload to follow me to the ACT program. One day he surprised everyone in the office by bursting into a pitch-perfect version of "Someday" from West Side Story. He was a good fit for ACT, as our new clients were a formidable crew.

Maggie was fixated on getting to Youngstown, Ohio, to see a mysterious boyfriend who she said called her each night and invaded her thoughts. She didn't have a phone in her apartment.

Harry had been hospitalized after trashing our waiting room. Upon his return, he called the crisis line to complain that when he had decided to kill himself by stepping in front of a bus, his case manager had the nerve to suggest he take the bus to the hospital. Mackie, a towering man, came to the ACT team fresh off a fight with a liquor store clerk. The clerk had knocked Mackie on his ass and crammed a garbage can over his head and shoulders. Mackie had run out into traffic like that and was hit by a car. Evan was a Sudanese cabbie who couldn't distinguish between his passengers and his auditory hallucinations, which he believed came from the backseat. The confusion led to fights and fender benders. He wanted to quit ACT from the word go, he said, because it interfered with his work, and he had rent to pay. Clarisse had one bad leg and one wandering eye. Her fingers were stained black and orange from little cigars. When angry, she hissed. When asked about her meds or psychotic symptoms, she mimicked the doctor's questions. She swore her husband, who had died years ago, was waiting for her outside the office. Her grandmother spoke to her through the smoke detector in her apartment. She required no medication, she said, "because I'm psychic. You are, too. And you knew that."

• • •

One morning in the office, Clarisse dragged me from about six hundred other crises I was managing to ask me a question.

"It's important," she said.

"Okay, what?"

"Are you starting to lose your hair?"

"I think so."

She hissed, pleased with her observation. "I think so, too. You shouldn't wear a hat. It makes it go faster."

I actually enjoyed working with Clarisse, but progress was difficult to measure. Sometimes she would introduce me to her psychiatrist—who I already knew—by saying, "This is my brother. He's been watching me since I was a little baby." One morning Clarisse slipped into my car, followed by the sharp, unmistakable stench of urine, powerful enough that I wanted to punch myself in the face. I broached the subject as delicately as I could. "Did you shower today?"

Clarisse exploded, pointing her nicotine-orange finger between my eyes.

"You don't talk to me like that! That's not your business. I know what you all do in that office. You disgust me! Let me out here! I'll walk!"

I had to hospitalize Clarisse once when her neighbors complained that she was knocking her head against a wall. Each step of the hospitalization was a balancing act to convince her she was not being tricked, that I was not shipping her to Mexico, or even saying she was mentally ill. It was time, though, for an emergency check-up.

In the ER I had to convince her to provide a urine sample in the bathroom instead of the hallway.

"There's an idea," she said.

Once the nurses got her into a gown, we waited in an exam room. Clarisse sat up on the exam table, swinging her legs and holding her urine sample like a cocktail.

"What can I say? I'm an unpredictable girl."

• • •

I was sure Evan would eventually kill someone on Lake Shore Drive while doing battle with his hallucinations from behind the wheel. So we made a deal. ACT would subsidize his rent only if he gave up driving his cab, took his meds, met with clinicians every day, made it to his monthly psychiatrist appointment, and saw me for therapy once a week. Two months later, I missed an appointment with Evan because I was busy hospitalizing someone else. Evan left me a bludgeoning voicemail.

"You say be there at four o'clock! I am there at four o'clock! You are not there! You are a liar! You are no good! You say four o'clock and I am there, Mr. fucking American cool guy! You do not do this to me! You show me your balls and I show you my balls! Thank you. Bye-bye."

He left another message the next morning. "I want to apologize for Tuesday. I was having some negative feelings. I will see you next Tuesday. Thank you. Bye-bye."

Evan had never seemed terribly invested in our sessions, so I hadn't figured he would mind missing one. But I was wrong. Just because he was an ACT client didn't mean he didn't deserve the same respect as someone paying two hundred dollars an hour for their therapy. I began to see the ACT team through the eyes of our clients. For most of them, we were the only humans on the planet who were safe. That status was our only real advantage, and maintaining it meant we had to be predictable. Our clients' lives were chaotic and disappointing enough. Our job had to be to reduce both of those factors as much as possible. Everyone—regardless of their station—wants to feel safe and be heard. Whether in the office, our cars, or some hotel room, we had to be able to keep our word. And if we couldn't keep it, we should make up for it.

18

WINTER/SPRING 2007

I thought about quitting a lot that first year. I had never aspired to supervise a bunch of social workers. The ACT team was designed to truly function as a unit, with every clinician responsible for working with every client. We designed it that way precisely because every client had so many pressing needs that the only way to avoid burnout was to spread the intensity of the caseload across the team.

I didn't particularly like being the boss. Clinicians cried, had temper tantrums, and passively refused to do the work. The team didn't like having a new boss and the first year was pretty miserable. I blamed myself, thinking my duty was to keep them happy with their jobs. I made a deal with myself to start looking for new work if things didn't turn around. I didn't like how it felt. I did not want to be chased out of a job. I had to conquer my anxiety about running the unit. That meant no more trying to appease the personal wishes of clinicians unless their personal wishes were specifically to work with ACT clients.

One clinician, who had been with the team for years, bemoaned every change to protocol by citing how much better things used to be. He was almost a month behind on his clinical notes and the administration was hounding me about his productivity. When I gave him a written warning, he said, "Before, this wasn't how we settled issues."

"Yeah," I agreed, thinking back on my days in the truck yard. "At my last job we settled them out in the alley."

Over the next few months, everyone on the team left the agency or transferred to a different program. I had been told when I started running the unit that the typical stay for an ACT staff member was about eighteen months. Each opening, though, offered the chance to hire someone new.

The first therapist I hired, Shannon, was the benevolent social-work equivalent of the bad guy in *Terminator 2: Judgment Day*. You could crush him between semitrucks or blow him away with a shotgun and he would merely reform, seemingly stronger than before. Shannon was a former college football player who had long ago given up on cardio. Nothing chased him away from clients or deterred him from his job. And he wasn't squeamish. Cockroach and bedbug infestations didn't bother him. He would personally teach a client how to wash her feet. In the few instances where a client had family in the picture, Shannon would meet with them over a weekend to get more background information. He became my gold standard for new hires.

Another core staffer, Mariella, was a veteran of the worst inpatient mental health unit in the city. That and the United States Army. Neither had burned her out. During hiring interviews with Mariella and Shannon I remember thinking I'd have to get my shit together if I wanted to keep them around. The previous team would have resented these two, which was reassuring to me.

While I was learning how to hire staff, we added a program assistant. I was so unaccustomed to office work I didn't know that "program assistant" used to be synonymous with "secretary." Stella was a soft-voiced, punk-rock Latina with a Bettie hairdo and one rose tattooed on the back of each calf. She was the youngest of all the agency's program assistants but proved adept at squeezing emergency psych appointments into doctors' schedules, keeping our med stash full and up to date, and bending agency policies in order to waive fees for clients who lacked insurance. At first, Stella didn't have the confidence to hit the button to apply for the ACT job. So I cajoled and hounded her to the point of crank-calling the front desk and telling her, "Hit the button already," before hanging up.

I also had to hire a nurse, more case managers, a substance abuse specialist, and a peer specialist in order to meet state requirements and receive funding. Finally the team was starting to feel like more than a random collection of newbie case managers.

• • •

The general perception that our clinicians and our clients comprised the trash heap of the agency became a point of pride for our team. We didn't have the same status as the "sit-down therapists." We weren't going to change the perspective of outsiders who didn't recognize that someone had to work with these people. And before long we didn't care. We were only the trash heap to those who would avoid our clients at all costs. A pal of mine who had learned how to tattoo by practicing on his own body painted our team banner: *If you can't be counted on, you can't be counted in.*

When a therapist from another program suggested a summit at a local tavern where representatives from each agency program could air their suggestions to promote unity—"Like in the UN"—I suggested our team would take Israel's role. Anyone who wasn't us was a potential enemy.

Our nurse, Yvonne, was fresh out of school but not exactly born yesterday. She was a new grandma who had raised three kids and looked twenty years younger than she actually was. When a client tested her with some inappropriate comments, her eyes flattened: "If you ever disrespect me, you are going to the hospital—but not the psych unit."

My new core staff agreed on one thing—the clients came first. The only factor that could trump that rule was our own safety. We couldn't provide clinical services to anyone who was looking to hurt us. As long as we kept our clients safe from the world, and the world safe from our clients, we were completing the paramount requirements of the job. Our expectations for clients differed greatly from other programs, where if clients missed three appointments, their cases could be closed. We didn't have that luxury because our clients were legitimately unable to make most scheduled appointments. If they could, they wouldn't be with us. We had to know our clients well enough to find them out in the world, even when they didn't want to be found. If they didn't want to work with us, they had to actively run and hide. One young man on our caseload who was certain the water system in Chicago was poisoned figured out how to call the head of the Department of Mental Health and asked, "Can you get the ACT team to leave me alone? If they come to my apartment one more time, I'll get a lawyer."

Our interventions went against the typical recovery model of "client-directed services" precisely because our clients' choices often posed threats to themselves and those around them.

• • •

Otis came to us from a state hospital. During his intake interview I had trouble piecing together the words he was attempting to say, much less a full narrative. Words just popped out of the toothless garble: "Obama," "Mississippi," "jail," "police," "downtown." Naturally we took his case.

Otis was worried about being jumped in his sleep. At night he would push his dresser up against the door of his SRO room and he kept a broomstick with the word *MASTER* written along the handle by his nightstand. We came to a sort of compromise.

"You keep it for when someone breaks in," I told him. "Not for when you break out."

"Hah, Obama," he said.

Frustrated by his unconventional communication skills, Otis started writing messages on paper bags and passing them to clinicians. We gave him a stack of legal pads and a handful of pens. One day I heard the case manager across the hall from my office trying to convince Otis to take his meds. He barked, "Nah!" and went back to scribbling his messages. After a moment, he asked, "How you spell 'Nah'?"

"No?"

"Nah!"

"N-O?"

"I say 'Nah!'"

"You have to take your meds here, Otis."

"Nah!"

Otis went on with a rambling, bellowing complaint that could not be deciphered.

"I don't know what you just said," the case manager admitted.

"Quit acting crazy, bitch. You know what I said!"

I walked into the treatment room as Otis started scribbling again. He only knew me as the guy who ran the program.

"What's wrong, Mr. Johnson?" I asked from the doorway.

I always used his last name, hoping he would feel respected by the formality. Maybe because he was from the South.

"Oh, hey, boss," Otis said.

"There a problem?"

"Nah."

"Good."

I pointed to his med box.

"All you have to do is take these two pills. Can you do that or is there a problem?"

"Okay."

He threw a contemptuous glance at the case manager and swallowed his meds.

Complaints from Otis's hotel managers were frequent. He scared the housekeeper every morning by stepping out the door in his boxers and swinging his MASTER broomstick.

One night he threw his refrigerator out the eighth-floor window of his room and ran away. Shannon deduced this the next morning when he found a refrigerator in the street with Otis's weekly medication box inside. The room was empty, and the MASTER stick was gone. Otis was undermedicated and in the wind.

Four months later, Stella walked into the team office.

"Otis is back!"

Unsure whether to be happy or annoyed, we sat in a collective state of deep ambivalence as Otis handed over a crumpled bunch of hospital discharge papers and a business card from a nursing home. While away, he had been hospitalized several times, each time brought into the ER by the police then discharged to a nursing home from which he would then escape. It was a hell of a cycle. During each hospital stay, Otis wound up restrained and drugged for shoving staff, knocking nurses to the floor, or grabbing orderlies by the hair.

Somehow during his time away, Otis's speech had improved. We could now pick out some of his words, like "sleeping outside" and "Haldol shot."

Some of the women on the team, following Mariella's lead, lightly scolded the big man: "Where you been? We were worried about you, dammit."

Otis got a little teary-eyed at the welcome, smiling and nodding, but the sentimental reunion didn't last long. We set him up in a new residence and he disappeared again. He returned a month later to accuse me of stealing his money. I didn't have his money, so he cursed me out and left again.

• • •

Evan, the former cab driver, lived at the Wilson Men's Club because he had been kicked out of every other place in the neighborhood. He was totally undocumented except for a Xerox of someone else's Social Security card and remained dependent on our program's rent subsidies. Our deal to subsidize his rent kept him and others safe from his driving, but the result was a sense of entitlement that, in time, became a raging tsunami of unrealistic demands. Raised in an upper-middle-class family composed of doctors and other degreed professionals who sent him to the US for college, Evan was accustomed to a much higher standard of living than we could provide. The housing subsidy opened the floodgates to all sorts of requests, including special shampoo to prevent baldness, dry cleaning services, and money for "meeting women." His cousin called the office once a week to tell Evan's case manager, Phillip—a former Jesuit seminarian who had a thing for jam bands and jazz—what the man needed. The cousin always made sure to add that Evan should stay far from his family members living in the Chicago suburbs. They had dropped him like first-period science and continued to send him small amounts of money to keep him at a distance.

For us, there was no end to Evan's requests.

"I need a computer. I need a chair and a desk. You have to buy me glasses. I cannot get a job without glasses. I need clothes for a job interview."

The requests themselves were not unreasonable, but there were basic issues Evan needed to address before he was ready to be fitted for a power suit. Psychotic symptoms, for example, like throwing flurries of punches into the air like a drunken shadow boxer and screaming bloody murder at no one in particular. Meanwhile, he had grown accustomed to our financial support and liked to remind us we needed to up our game.

"You have to buy me food."

"Where'd you get the money for cigarettes?" I said.

"But I bought these with my money!"

"Use your money for food."

"But I would be able to save money if you people bought me food."

"I would be able to save money if someone bought my food, too."

Evan would throw his hands up in disgust. "What has changed? The other supervisor would give me money all the time! I am not lying! He would!"

I didn't know if he was lying, but I sensed I was getting the new-guy treatment.

The Wilson, where Evan stayed, was pretty accommodating. Drinking, crack smoking, brawling, stealing, trading sex for money, and extortion were not necessarily causes for eviction. But somehow he found ways to piss off the managers there. We got called out one night after he launched into a racist diatribe in the lobby.

"You got to get him out of here," the clerk said. "Even the White guys want to kill him. The motherfucker told me if we were back in his country, I'd be dead. Motherfucker isn't getting out of this one alive!" After the cops hauled Evan to the psych unit, the night clerk dragged Evan's belongings from his bunk and into the basement. I negotiated to keep Evan's cubicle reserved since the rent was paid. The night clerk kicked back hard.

"He ain't right! There's something wrong with him! He pulled a knife on the guy at the taco stand. He's yelling about his powers and how he's gonna kill all his enemies! Fuck him! I don't like him and someone's gonna kill his ass. I can't do much about it, neither."

The other desk clerk stood silently, fondling a sword that tucked into the shaft of his walking cane by sliding the blade out and letting it drop, clicking the handle against the shaft. A flophouse rent negotiation technique. I successfully bargained for one more chance and, upon his return, gave Evan strict instructions.

"Do not speak to anyone in the hotel."

Without question, Evan drove me and Phillip nuts. One afternoon, Phillip came into my office not knowing whether to laugh or scream.

"Zak, he wants the doctor to prescribe Viagra for stress relief. He doesn't have a girlfriend."

Phillip was a kind-hearted guy who had seen little of the world other than the seminary, a few Phish concerts, and maybe the back of the turnip truck. He was an easy touch for Evan.

Despite the possibility that Evan might one day drive us insane, we had to remember the pain and confusion he was living with. Working with clients who exhibit severe psychotic symptoms provokes a frustrating mix of sympathy and annoyance. They break your heart and piss you off. You train yourself to understand who they are and what they're going through but ultimately there is a gaping chasm between your two realities. Evan felt strangers reaching into his body and grabbing his ribs and lungs. He would wake up in the middle of the night certain some other human had been fused onto his back. His ancestors were inside his body, scolding him by sending messages up through his bones. He couldn't explain how or why but refused to accept it as psychosis. Instead, he believed his symptoms were punishment for displeasing his family. He believed he was cursed. In fact, he was tortured.

That kind of stuff can leave a case manager or therapist feeling isolated from a client, like they're not even people in the relationship. The psychosis is the barrier to a client's ability to recognize that there is a relationship at all.

"I am waiting," Evan said during one of our therapy sessions. "Someday I will have my powers. I am like the Batman, who, when he gets all his power from his home planet, can kill all, all of his enemies. That is what I am waiting for. I will get the kiss from the girl I love, and she will wake me up. I was to be married to this girl. Her family ruined it. I have to suffer until then."

Evan scared a lot of people. Once, he slugged his sister during a psychiatrist appointment. I heard she went down like a falling tree. No shocker that people kept their distance, and Evan was desperate for some human connection. His family had forced him to move out after his second suicide attempt. He was another reminder that most of our clients had no one to count on.

My therapy sessions with Evan at that time were really just thinly veiled safety checks. He would ask me how many times a day a man should masturbate, and what it meant if he thought of several different women at once. Some days he became so guilelessly graphic that I walked out with a nerve jumping under my eyelid.

Still, that he could continue to walk around applying for jobs at liquor stores and property rental agencies—his goal was to get in on the dying real estate boom—was a testimony to his resilience. I kept meeting with him out of fear he would eventually give up and commit suicide. I kept an eye out for signs that he was planning to use his special powers against his enemies or to quiet the voices in his head for good. The goal for Evan's therapy wasn't to explore the psychodynamics behind his delusions but to keep him off the local news.

• • •

I had to assign Phillip the extra duties of a supportive employment specialist—another requirement of the state. The position was simply a case manager who helped clients find jobs in the community. The last guy had handed in his resignation the week I started and going through his documentation, I couldn't really discern what he had spent his time doing. A lot of his billing hours were "job development" and "building community resources." We knew we didn't have any employed clients to show for his efforts. The theory behind supportive employment went like this: we offered an employee who would have a support system of clinicians to address any problems in the workplace that might be caused by severe psychotic symptoms. I didn't understand how this benefited any employer at all. If I were running a hardware store and had to choose between applicants—one who showed up on time and did his job and another who needed a team of clinicians to keep him from howling at the moon—I'd go with the one who wasn't prone to psychotic episodes, every time.

I did, however, understand the therapeutic aspects of work. Some of us are like dogs. We need responsibilities, something to do, something to define our value and purpose. But not all job searches were therapeutic, especially when the odds of success were frustratingly minimal. What our clients needed was intensive job and life-skills training as they attempted to find work. If they met the requirements to receive ACT services—frequent hospitalizations, incarcerations, substance use, homelessness, and chronic psychotic symptoms—they were, more often than not, unqualified for most jobs. But if they kept fighting to gain employment, despite setbacks and letdowns, we marked that as success. Too often the process was a crushing disappointment. We had to get clients to a point in their treatment where a job search held a higher possibility of success.

That wouldn't be easy. Joseph was a longtime client and old sad sack who had wandered the neighborhood for years without ever contributing a word to any conversation unless forced. Out of nowhere, at sixty, he decided he wanted to start working. During a mock job interview, Phillip said, "I noticed you have a few gaps in your resume. Is there anything you might want to say about that?"

Joseph answered carefully. "Yes. I've had a lot of hernias. And I don't have any friends because people are scared I'm going to kick them in the balls."

• • •

Some referrals came to us specifically because we had a registered nurse on our team. The side effects of a lifetime of poverty and medication left a lot of clients with chronic high blood pressure and cholesterol, and full-blown diabetes. Add to that HIV, hep C, incontinence, cirrhosis, and STDs, and Yvonne was basically running a one-woman MASH unit.

Miss Jin, a tiny, restrained woman who spoke no English, lived her days with blood pressure hovering at near-hospitalization levels. Yvonne increased, then doubled, her blood pressure meds, then increased them a little more. Nothing helped. Exasperated, Yvonne stormed into the team office.

"What does this woman do? Drink soy sauce every morning?"

We commissioned a translator to help solve the mystery but that was a bust.

"She makes no sense," the translator told us.

Miss Jin wouldn't answer any questions but would point at Yvonne and declare that they were sisters from Vietnam. Sisterhood aside, Miss Jin wouldn't allow Yvonne into her apartment to look for clues, like a saltlick or stockpiles of injectable MSG. After months of haggling, Miss Jin relented. Turned out she ate handfuls of pickles for breakfast, the fridge stocked with rations that would last weeks.

Yvonne got a lot of mileage out of her mothering skills. She was a pro at setting hard boundaries for people while also showing them they were accepted. Clients didn't enjoy the order she imposed, but they did believe in the safety that came with her rules.

Clyde was fifty-something, sallow and chronically disoriented, with a memory that flickered like a candle. The only exceptions to this condition were bursts of laser focus that guided his pursuit of alcohol and the money to buy it. While we could stabilize his hypomania and depression, we suspected brain damage from a lifetime of heavy drinking would continue to limit his potential to manage his life. The hep C could be minimized, and the liver damage could be curtailed only if he quit drinking—immediately. His feet were turning black from lack of circulation, his bladder was unreliable, and his hygiene nonexistent. Clyde rarely knew what day it was unless it was payday from his payee account.

"He will die," Yvonne said after working with Clyde for a couple months. "Lectures do not work. He doesn't understand."

The soft talks went out the window and Yvonne crowded Clyde like a drill instructor.

"The doctors will cut off your feet if you do not take your medications!"

We had to be careful of "forcing" people to participate in treatment. We could not say, "If you don't see the doctor, you will not get money for groceries." We could, however, assess whether a person could make connections between their decisions and the natural consequences, like losing their feet. Our clients regularly made choices that put them at risk of dying. We could have argued that Clyde would be better monitored and in a nursing home. We also knew he would likely walk out of any nursing home we sent him to.

After a year of pounding on Clyde's locked apartment door, arguing over daily meds, and dragging him to the hospital out of fear his toes needed to be amputated, Clyde began to participate in his treatment. Yvonne had continued to see him every day and he seemed to value the relationship.

If Yvonne was heading into public with Clyde, he would get a stern lecture the day before about showers and clean clothes. This was not punishment. If doctors were going to examine you, you had to clean your body—not to be nice, but so they would respect you. Clyde began dressing with more care when he was meeting Yvonne. The clothes weren't spotless, but they were better than the urine-soaked rags he had used to wear. The simple truth was he liked being with his nurse.

After a few months, Clyde began showing up laundry-fresh, in creased jeans and a cardigan sweater. Yvonne even convinced him to replace his old prison-issue glasses with something more elegant.

Whenever he managed to show up clean and sober, the women on the team made sure to treat him like Denzel's twin brother and the guys treated him like he was coming by for a poker game. Clyde smiled at the compliments, a little baffled about what had happened. When Clyde only drank on the weekends, we celebrated his progress. When he began to drink daily again, we had to start over.

19

Food and housing come first. It makes little sense to tell a client to take his meds, quit drinking, and start therapy before they have food to eat a place to sleep. The homeless shelters are Darwinistic nightmares, and antipsychotic medications can guarantee that a person sleeping does not wake up while his roomies are stealing the shoes off his feet.

As supervisor, I conducted all intake interviews and I always had to scramble to find housing for new clients. But housing also had to be part of the sales pitch since almost everyone we worked with was homeless, or close to it.

Dean was a six-foot hulk. When he walked, he led with his chest. I think he would have weighed five hundred pounds if his hypomanic symptoms hadn't burned so many calories. Even sitting still, he vibrated. He had three teeth, a wandering eye, and a Cubs cap that never left his head.

Dean ran away from nursing homes like most people run to the store. More often than not he was immediately picked up on the street and hospitalized. He had lived on his own for all of three months during the previous five years. He screamed at people a lot and did so with me during his intake interview at the hospital.

"I'm JFK. I saved PT Boat 104. Bay of Pigs! Never stood down! I'm Joe Namath and Jay Cutler's my son. I have a Nigerian wife on Wilson Avenue. She'll cut your throat. She's a nurse."

He answered all of my direct questions pretty much the same way.

"None of your fucking business, punk! Your agency, I closed it down when I left. I can destroy the whole world if I want to. I'm Steven Seagal and you're Bruce Willis. Remember when I kicked that gun to you when they kidnapped your daughter?"

I only nodded along. He was a terrified man trying to be terrifying by presenting a bizarre hypermasculinity. I also suspected he was having a laugh somewhere in there, like part of him knew—or at least thought—that he was charming. Whatever he was doing, it must have worked for him somewhere in the past.

Dean eventually signed the papers and agreed to work with us. As I was leaving the room, he called out, "Hey!"

"What?"

"You're Bruce Willis."

"Okay. I'll see you Thursday. By the way, you have money for a place to stay?"

"Yeah."

"You do? You got a bank account?"

"Don't worry about it. It's safe."

Great. I told the hospital staff we would take his case. I also told Dean I couldn't promise we would be helping him for long if he could only communicate by screaming.

"I'll scream when I feel it's necessary," he bellowed back. "Don't worry. I'm a psychiatrist. I'm God!"

On discharge day, Dean greeted me with, "Hey, Bruce Willis! Let's get out of here."

I had to slow him down and get the discharge papers and prescriptions from the staff, who said, "Good luck"—to me more than Dean.

I asked Dean where he wanted to live.

"The Carlos. I lived there before. They'll remember me."

"What if they don't have a room?" I asked.

"They will."

"What if they don't?"

"They will."

"You think we should have a backup plan, in case?"

"No."

I asked if he had money and he said he had more than enough at his friend's apartment. I didn't believe he had a dime.

In my car, he claimed to be Steven Seagal, Sylvester Stallone, JFK, Oliver Stone, Dick Butkus, a psychiatrist, God, Jean Claude Van Damme, Jimi Hendrix, and a Vietnam vet who'd had his feet blown off. Without a radio in the car, he provided a monotone bellowing of classic rock lyrics: "Hey Joe, where you going with that gun in your hand? Bwah blab blab la blah. I'm going to shoot my old lady. Gonna shoot her right in the can. Bwah bwah ba da da . . ." He was clearly having fun, relieved to be out in the world. Between songs, he rattled off an estimated price of every building we passed and screamed when he saw a *For Sale* sign. He bragged that he had already sold most of the properties on every block in the neighborhood.

We met up with one of his friends, a teetering, gentlemanly drunk, who handed over Dean's most recent Social Security check and told me, "Take care of him."

Dean's singing continued as we drove to the only hotel he approved of. The last client I'd brought there had torn the sink out of the wall and left for the day to run errands.

"What if they don't have any rooms available?" I asked again.

"They will."

"I hope."

"You don't need to hope. I'm God."

I began looking for a spot to pull over. His behavior was going to have to change immediately, or no one was going to rent him a room. We got closer to the hotel and turned off Broadway onto a side street. Dean kept singing.

"I'm Jumping Jack Flash! I'm a gas gas gas!"

My temples were throbbing, and I could feel the blood rushing to my hands. I was going to be stuck with this guy all damn day. No way would any flophouse manager rent him a room. I'd have to take him back to the hospital and maybe have the cops drag him out of my car. "Please allow me to introduce mahself! I'm a guy with wealth and taste! I killed all the Kennedys and made tracks to Bombay. Wooo Wooo!"

As we turned onto the block where the hotel was, Dean stopped singing long enough to tell me, under his breath, "I'll shut up when we get there. Don't worry." Reluctantly, the young woman behind the glass at the hotel desk agreed to rent Dean a room, even while he kept singing Bon Jovi through the slot in the window. "You sure he's okay? Is he crazy or something?"

"Everyone's a little crazy," I said, handing over my business card and explaining that she could call if any concerns arose. The ACT emergency number bounced to my cell phone. Three hours later, she called.

"Your friend just got beat up really bad in front of the hotel!" Shannon and I found Dean in the ER, a golf ball over his eye and a broken nose. Behind his curtain, he howled at the nurses that he was Dr. House and would be forced to drink his own urine if they didn't bring him more water.

We walked around the corner, coming into his view as he parted the curtain around his bed.

"Hey! It's Bruce Willis and his Black sidekick!"

They sent Dean upstairs to the psychiatric unit. I lost contact with him because the staff couldn't legally answer any questions about Dean without his permission. I didn't want him to get released again just so he could walk into another beating. After a few days without any responses from the psychiatric unit, I went back to the hospital. Outside the unit, I buzzed at the sally port and waited. A young woman peeked out the security door and asked, "Can I help you?"

"I'm Bruce Willis," I said.

"Oh, thank God. This guy's been saying that his case manager, Bruce Willis, would come and get him out. We thought he was nuts."

• • •

A couple of days later we went back to the Carlos hotel. This time we had to get past the front desk girl and her mother, who was a much tougher gatekeeper.

"There's something wrong with him!" the mom said. "I don't want no crazy people in here causing trouble."

"He didn't cause any trouble," I said. "He got jumped, actually in front of your place. He wasn't even here."

She got the hint, and we moved down the hall to talk further. Dean, his face a rainbow of purple and yellow bruises, stayed at the front desk. "You gotta scare them, Zak!" Dean yelled. "It was better thirty thousand years ago before Eve!"

"Dean, shut up! Go have a cigarette!"

At least he was using my given name. I kept after the mom, assuring her there would be no problems with Dean. He got one more chance. Dean and I picked up more rent money at his pal's apartment. As we walked through Wrigleyville, Dean screamed at people "You must be Mrs. Mayor Daley," he barked in some little old lady's face. "How's the cancer? You'll be fine, I can tell. You look good."

I was getting angry again. These people were not bothering him. In fact, people were making a sincere effort to stay out of his way.

"Helloooo laaa-dies," he cooed to a gaggle of twenty-something women. "Who wants to join a sorority? I'm JFK, you know. I can get you in. Play your cards right."

Dean was simultaneously trying to amuse himself and keep others at bay. He knew he didn't belong, not with these girls, but he refused to be rejected outright. He was not oblivious to the world. His self-defense consisted of yelling bizarre obscenities at people so they wouldn't attack him. He wanted to be a powerful man, so he appropriated caricatures and cliches: JFK, General Patton, Steven Seagal, Sylvester Stallone, a doctor, a Vietnam vet, a psychiatrist. I thought of all of this later. Walking through Wrigleyville that day, I was just annoyed. He was going to get himself stomped again. Crossing Addison and Broadway, I yelled at him, "Why are you yelling at people?"

"Don't you raise your voice to me, pal!"

I had to back up without being obvious. Calmly, I asked, "Or what?"

"Or I'll snap my fingers and destroy everything. Because I was born in a crossfire hurricane and Jumping Jack Flash is my name."

By the next month, Dean had to move again after he began calling every person he saw in the hotel "Mi amigo Pedro," including Mom the manager, for whom he added, "Suck my dick," just for her.

Over the next few months Dean toned the volume of his tirades down to a pressured bark. His dialogue remained inappropriate, but he was no longer constantly screaming. He became more settled with familiar people and only threatened to blow up the world when introduced to new acquaintances. He had not been beaten up or hospitalized for a while and that was significant progress. We may not have been able to eradicate Dean's delusions or disruptive behavior, but we could help him find better ways to cope with them. If he wanted to believe he was Steven Seagal, that was fine—as long as he didn't act like Steven Seagal.

• • •

Whenever Dean and I hit the neighborhood together, he acted as if we were in a buddy-cop movie. Whether this was a conscious fantasy or a delusional coping mechanism to explain his life, I couldn't tell, but I went along with it. Checking him into a hotel one day after yet another eviction, he leaned in close and told me, "You do all the talking. I got your back."

While we waited in the hallway to speak to the manager, other residents stopped to chit-chat with me. Dean whispered, "We're doing government work here. CIA covert ops. You think you should be talking to all these people?"

I whispered back, "If I don't, they're gonna get suspicious, right?"

"Yeah. That's right."

I knew the woman coming out of the manager's office, a caseworker with another agency. As she and I had a couple friendly words, Dean interrupted.

"I do have to find an apartment, you know. We don't have time for you to flirt with every woman you see."

This time, I just looked at him.

He said, "It's a burden, I know. I got the same problem."

Shannon presented to Dean the idea that self-defense didn't always depend on volume and aggression. He cited the Clint Eastwood spaghetti Westerns where the hero hardly spoke. Dean liked the idea and considered incorporating that persona. He didn't do it, but he considered it. He also began attributing pseudomilitary or law enforcement titles to his case manager.

"This guy's a cop. Chicago PD. Watch it."

From Dean, this was a compliment. The safer he felt, the more he clowned around with the team. He knew his responses to anxiety were beyond any normal range. At times, we suspected he was able to judge his own behavior. He knew he was funny, and his outrageous proclamations reduced his anxiety. The ability to define reality usually does.

Sometimes Dean referred to our team psychiatrist as Jackie Kennedy. He began one appointment by trying to put her mind at ease. "I just want you to know the kids are fine, really. They're healthy. Everyone's okay. John-John's parking the car."

20

Deejay was from Sudan, one of the Lost Boys. Beyond that, we didn't know much except that he had been in the US for nine years, had gruesome scars across his back, and was missing both pinky fingers. Deejay never told us what had happened. During his first year with ACT, he didn't say much of anything. Maybe he had been pulled out of his village and made an example of by the South Sudanese soldiers. He had come to the US somehow and we knew he wanted to go back to Egypt. The agency that referred him told us that much. But he had been selectively mute, they said, since a suicide attempt several years earlier. When we started working with Deejay, he made no eye contact and almost no noises or verbal acknowledgment that we were speaking to him. He moved slowly, like he was testing the air around him. When he walked, his center of gravity hung behind his hips; each step reached out in front of him and landed softly to pull him forward. We felt like he would collapse if we made any quick movements.

On a good day, he would answer a question with one word, like "food" or "go," and we had to figure out what he meant. Sometimes he would help with a nod. If he disagreed with a clinician's guess, he would simply look away.

He never took his antipsychotic medications. We learned this while battling a grotesque cockroach infestation in his apartment. Apparently, his previous case managers never saw where he lived. The roaches had established squatter's rights and Deejay was a hands-off landlord. He would fix himself a can of ravioli and put the dirty dish back in the cabinet. Cereal, half-eaten sandwiches, frying pans of rice were all put away dirty or left out in the open. The apartment belonged on the Discovery Channel. Roaches were pouring out of everywhere and flowing down the walls like minuscule herds of cattle.

While his therapist and I bombed, sprayed, and squashed every living thing we saw in the apartment, Deejay crouched in the corner. Only once did he get up to help, grabbing a can of air freshener and spraying the stove top where roaches were scrambling for cover.

"Stop," I said. "That just makes them smell nice."

Beneath the rotted leftovers and nests of roaches, we found packs of Deejay's medications from the past year.

"You're supposed to be taking this stuff," I said, holding up a medication packet dated six months earlier. He looked at me like I was an idiot.

Deejay's case manager, Holly, was a polite, soft-spoken young woman who didn't want to force clients to take their meds. This was a constant rift among the team—do we ask people to take meds in front of us or not? That argument is loaded with all sorts of implications about patient rights vs. patient care. But as I was changing my clothes in the alley and shaking bugs out of my jeans, I didn't really give a shit. It was difficult for me not to silently—and incorrectly—blame Holly in that moment, as if she could force Deejay to take his meds.

• • •

About a year after we began with Deejay, we started to suspect he was becoming more comfortable with the program. Using informal sign language, he offered to share his rum with the female clinicians and invited Holly to join him in bed. Some of the team assessed him as a lost soul, unable to communicate basic needs. Others believed he knew exactly what he was doing.

Mariella once challenged Deejay in the waiting room.

"Don't be eyeing me like that," she said. "You couldn't handle all this."

Then she told the team, "He knows what he's doing."

I had a discussion with him regarding the limitations of the clinical team. He nodded his understanding that we were not his dating service.

As the ACT team grew, we passed Deejay's case to an experienced therapist, a Nigerian man named Martin, who was certain Deejay was more capable than he was letting on. We had already seen some discrepancies in Deejay's behavior. Some mornings, Martin would find him in bed with a woman. Other days, the team would find him waking up in the sand of Foster Avenue Beach. We really didn't know where his abilities stopped and his limitations started or how to assess his needs.

Meanwhile, cockroaches and bedbugs had established another beachhead in Deejay's apartment. After weeks of prompting him to clean up his place, Martin and I had accepted that he would sooner shave his legs with a cheese grater. He wasn't concerned about bringing bedbugs into our office, either, and he deflected any concerns we had about hygiene with two words.

"It's okay."

A year earlier, an answer of any kind would have seemed like huge progress. But now he was treating us like a gang of panicky hypochondriacs. Martin picked a fat bedbug off Deejay's shoulder and showed him.

"This! This is what I mean."

"It's okay."

Expecting a bedbug explosion across our client population, we bought our own fumigation outfits—white paper jumpsuits with booties. Martin and I added rubber gloves and made doo rags from cut-off shirt sleeves. We loaded up on bug spray, bug bombs, garbage bags, and cleaning supplies and went to Deejay's place.

We threw out his old mattress and tossed the rotting food and open beer cans. Deejay protested only the beer. Martin and I agreed we couldn't let a client sleep on the carpeted floor, especially after we had soaked it in insecticide. Deejay had absolutely no money. He had barely enough to buy a couple of packs of $1.25 cigarillos each week. He would go without food in order to buy beer and rum. So we tapped out the petty cash account for a new futon and frame. Deejay didn't like the mattress.

"What don't you like?" Martin asked.

"It's okay."

The next day, Martin went to check on Deejay and found only the metal frame of the futon in the center of the studio apartment.

"What happened to your bed?"

Quietly, Deejay said he'd thrown it out.

"You threw it out? Why?"

"It smelled funny."

"It smelled funny? It smelled funny because it is new. Just from the store. You are not used to new. I don't know what you are going to do. We don't have any extra beds around the office. You can sleep on the floor or on the frame."

"It's okay."

Martin came back to the office and told us the story, concluding with, "That boy is crazy!" Feigning amazement at bizarre behavior was not mocking the client but a way for us to vent some aggravation. It's actually one of the few release valves we had—to laugh at our seemingly futile—and sometimes ridiculous—job duties when we felt like clients were actively working against us. Empathy didn't preclude having a laugh, especially if we were acknowledging the steep slope of the hill we had to climb.

Deejay did not see the insect infestations as any impediment to his life. He had girls over, he had beer to drink. He wanted money to entertain company and we couldn't figure out why he would get incrementally more incensed when, each week, someone would have to go over his budget and explain to him that he only gets $674 a month and his rent costs $450. Repeatedly, Martin did the math with him, and Deejay would swear he was being shortchanged. His communication skills improved greatly when money was involved.

Deejay would sulk in our waiting room, trying to understand what had happened to all the money he thought he had.

"That boy is crazy," Martin said, walking into the team office. "He was pounding his chest, spitting on the floor."

"Did he spit on you?" Yvonne asked.

Martin's smile disappeared.

"He's not *that* crazy."

21

Shannon sat across from me in my office, lightly slapping my desk for emphasis.

"What these folks need," he said, "is exercise. They don't do anything but sit in their rooms and smoke all day. These meds aren't going to help them much either."

He had a plan and already had the Broadway Armory Fitness Center offering free gym memberships to our clients as long as they were supervised. He also found a yoga instructor willing to volunteer her time.

"You going to do this?" I asked.

"I'll do it."

"People in general don't like to exercise. It's going to take forever just to get them to the gym."

"I'll get it done."

"What do you need?"

"Maybe some petty cash."

"Okay."

Shannon got it done. He corralled a gang of floridly psychotic clients into our newly christened Health and Wellness Program. This was a total shock to the systems of clients whose only exercise had been lifting cigarettes to their mouths or running from police. Shannon argued that they were beyond sedentary and that minimal physical exercise, at least, was essential to fighting medical issues exacerbated by heavy antipsychotic meds. None of the staff disagreed with him, but we were all reluctant. We knew how difficult his plan would be.

The Health and Wellness group met five days a week, with a different target exercise every day—yoga, cardio, weightlifting, stretching, or basketball. Shannon spent three hours a day dragging clients to a city gym for a one-hour session. Months passed before clients stopped actively protesting and they still only begrudgingly showed up to work out.

Our clients had trouble staying focused in the gym, often stepping off of stationary bicycles or yoga mats to light cigarettes. They faked upset stomachs, fainting spells, and bad backs. But they couldn't discourage Shannon. This was holistic care, and he wasn't going to quit.

During one session, a client named John swore he couldn't, and wouldn't, touch his toes.

"You were able to yesterday," Shannon said.

"I can't."

"Just try."

"No."

"John, just try."

"I said I can't!"

"If it was a cigarette on the ground, you'd be able to!"

John stomped out, but Shannon brought him back the next day.

Shannon spent months organizing and refining his caseload so no minute of the day would be wasted. Clients stepped into a ready schedule of group sessions, medical appointments, psychiatric appointments, and shopping trips where they would work from a shopping list based on their individualized health needs. Shannon scheduled medical and dental appointments in blocks, bringing six clients into a waiting room all at once, which meant the slower the doctor worked, the longer our clients hung out in his waiting room. This usually sped things up.

Shannon routinely worked ten to twelve hours a day and claimed to never grow tired. At one point, the administration asked, "Isn't he working too hard?"

Shannon was prepared for this question.

"If they want to," he told me, "you tell them to come meet me at six in the morning and they could see what I do every day. I've worked like this all my life. That's how I am. I'm not going to slow down. But if you want me to, say so."

I didn't want him to slow down. I wished I had ten more of him. Our clients, he argued, needed the overtime.

"There's always more to do," he said.

I once saw Shannon dishing out to a sociopathic young kid, twenty years old with a felony record, who had been sent to us from a downtown hospital after he got kicked out of his mother's Cabrini Green apartment.

"My baby momma's momma, she mad at me," the client said, testing the air for some sympathy.

"She call you a bust-down?" Shannon asked.

"How'd you know?"

"Because you are! You got no job, no skills, no education, lay up all day bragging about what a man you are. That ain't no definition of a man. You call taking care of your baby borrowing from your momma to give something to your baby momma, right?"

"How else am I supposed to?" the kid asked sincerely.

Shannon's tactics didn't work all the time. No one's did. Some clients ran like he was the devil incarnate. Others said they would rather be in jail. The guy who refused to touch his toes at the gym referred to the exercise group as "Wealth and Hellness."

As much as Shannon's gang grumbled about the exercise program and his relentless life-skills lessons, his consistency proved to them over time that he actually gave a damn about their lives.

• • •

LeFlore came to the ACT program soon after I did. As his hallucinations had grown more frequent and severe, he couldn't help but respond to them more aggressively. His case manager had left the agency and no clinicians outside of ACT had wanted to deal with his random outbursts of obscenities and chronically miserable hygiene. Before joining us, he had been on Clozaril—a last-chance medication when nothing else is effective—for several years with no discernible improvement.

LeFlore's other medications were Depakote, Risperdal, and Trazodone at a staggering combination of dosages.

His appointments with our psychiatrist only proved how sick he was. If he wasn't yelling at the doctor or signaling to his ten-foot-tall pal who stood behind his shoulder, he was asleep and drooling on the doctor's desk. On his worst days, LeFlore couldn't differentiate between the world and his hallucinations. His outbursts were responses to internal stimuli that coopted the pornos he watched constantly in his room. He would drift into his own world, grabbing women in the hallways of agency buildings and yelling at them, "You're my daughter from Africa!"

The Clozaril wasn't working and LeFlore hated the twice-weekly blood draws. Often his arms shook so badly from the side effects that the phlebotomist dreaded seeing him come down the hall. LeFlore would never take his weekend meds and we couldn't convince the doctor to change his medication schedule to ensure he was taking everything.

After he'd grabbed a woman in the lobby of his building, her boyfriend knocked him to the sidewalk and the landlord followed up with a thirty-day eviction notice.

We considered how long we could hold onto LeFlore before we were totally unable to keep him safe in the neighborhood. He dreaded the idea of a nursing home but didn't seem willing, or able, to do what he had to do to stay out of one. We would find him with a pile of empty beer cans in his room and he would deny they were his.

"My friend just came by. I didn't drink. I haven't drank since 1993!"

"What's your friend's name?"

"Ahhh . . ."

When Leflore drank, his hallucinations intensified exponentially. When his symptoms took over, he would mop the carpet with Pine Sol and leave raw meat on the windowsill.

If a team member found old medications stashed in his room, LeFlore defended himself: "Zak told me not to take those!"

I brought the new clinician, Holly, along to meet with LeFlore one Monday morning. LeFlore sometimes drank through the weekend, so I knocked hard enough to wake him. He stumbled out, a swarm of gnats following him like a little cloud. He looked over my head to Holly behind me. LeFlore growled something about his daughter and tried to shove past me. I stepped in front of him and barely ducked a Three Stooges-style two-fingered eye-poke.

I grabbed his arms and lowered my center of gravity for some leverage once I realized how strong he was. We looked at each other, not knowing what to do. He then recognized me, which was good because I realized he could have easily escalated the violence. He yanked his arms back and ran to his room, slamming the door. Holly and I called the police for assistance with an involuntary hospitalization, but Leflore went peacefully.

The hospital staff placed him in leather restraints. I pulled a chair up next to his bed and sat down.

"Zak, why'd you do this?" Leflore asked. "I thought we were friends."

We were both puzzled and I felt guilty, seeing his wrists strapped to the rails of the bed.

"Do you remember what happened?" I asked.

"I didn't do anything."

I couldn't assess whether he knew what happened or not. Either way, we had to find a way to keep working with him without staff being assaulted.

A new psychiatrist was brave enough to change LeFlore's medication regimen. Shannon made LeFlore a priority, moving him to the top of the hot list, which meant monitored medication visits twice a day. We moved him into a new building, threw out all the filthy clothes and got him a refrigerator. The team took turns visiting him on the weekends to make sure he took his meds.

Shannon spent more time with LeFlore than any clinician had, going to his room with washcloths and a pumice stone to show him how to take care of his horrifically neglected feet and step by step how to scrub his toilet and bathtub. Both had gone long neglected and grown as black as his feet had. All of this threw LeFlore off balance in a good way. He was used to clinicians who kept their distance.

Shannon dragged LeFlore to podiatrists and pedicurists. His feet were mangled from wearing the wrong size shoes for years.

"Who would've thought to check his shoe size?" Shannon said.

Slowly, LeFlore's feet began to heal, and he started attending Shannon's Health and Wellness group. When Shannon added cardio boxing to the exercise regimen, I went along to observe. We set LeFlore up in front of the heavy bag and gave him some rudimentary instructions. Before throwing a single punch, he began to trash-talk the bag.

"Fuck you looking at, huh, motherfucker? I'll kick your fucking ass."

"LeFlore!" I interrupted. "You aren't going to scare the thing. Just hit it."

He did so, reluctantly and grumbling, hitting the bag with the strength of a windshield wiper.

Even though LeFlore's clothes were worn through and chewed up by the springs in his mattress, he resented spending money to fix those problems. Shannon hounded him about his wardrobe until he agreed to set aside some of his budget for new clothes. Eventually he began proudly wearing new polo shirts and fresh jeans. He no longer looked like the ACT prototype under layers of filthy, grayed rags. He flipped the collars up on his golf shirts and started shaving every day. The matted dreads were shorn away.

Part of Shannon's success with LeFlore's hygiene and appearance was attributable to Shannon's strategy of appealing to LeFlore's central ambition: meeting women. For an hour or for life, it didn't matter. On occasion, we had found him in his room with what must have been either the hardest-working or most desperate prostitutes in Chicago. Shannon explained to LeFlore the concept of taking pride in one's appearance like this:

"If there's a woman coming down the street, walking toward you, who do you think she's going to look at, Mr. Target or Mr. Thrift?"

• • •

A weekly group outing to the grocery store became a regularly scheduled part of the ACT routine. We called it Big Shop. Most clients complained about the supervised shopping because they couldn't buy whatever they wanted, like booze and junk food. Instead, we encouraged them to follow a dietary regimen Shannon had worked out with our primary physician and Yvonne, the nurse.

LeFlore joined the Big Shop group, having progressed from being barely cognizant and disruptive in crowds to an acknowledged member of group counseling and skill-building sessions. He didn't appreciate the change as much as we did. The groceries cut into his beer and cigarette money. In the back seat of the ACT van, LeFlore waited to roll with the rest of the gang as last instructions were given out. Shannon asked LeFlore an innocuous question about his Link card. LeFlore caught Shannon's eye in the center rear-view mirror and suggested a deal.

"If you suck me, I'll suck you."

The Big Shop gang burst into laughter.

"That's not appropriate," Shannon said. "I need you to come on back to the conversation here. What did I just ask you?"

LeFlore repeated himself, slowly emphasizing the syllables. "If you suck me . . ."

The other clients howled, and the van became a locker room on wheels. Undaunted, Shannon redirected LeFlore again.

LeFlore repeated his offer, quickly this time.

"If you suck me, I'll suck you!"

LeFlore, who was still pretty unskilled at making his points directly, was trying to make one to Shannon. He felt his budget was unfair and wanted to spend his money without any supervision. The state had long ago decided that LeFlore needed a payee to handle his money for him, but the more coherent he became, the more he bucked that decision.

"If you suck me," he said again, "I'll suck you."

The other clients whooped and barked, choking on laughter and rocking the van back and forth like kids who can't make enough noise to match the joy in their hearts. Shannon ended the stalemate.

"Okay, LeFlore, you're clearly not going to be able to handle yourself in public. I'm dropping you off before we go shopping."

"Aw, goddammit!" LeFlore yelled. "I got nothing at home but cereal and water! You can't do that!"

"Oh, you can hear me now, huh?"

"That's not fair! I want a new case manager! I'm gonna talk to Zak!"

In the morning LeFlore came into my office, sat down calmly, crossed his legs, placed one hand on the opposite elbow and cupped his chin between his thumb and forefinger.

"I need a new case manager," he said. "This isn't working between me and him. Look at me. This is the worst I ever been."

Actually, the worst I had seen LeFlore was when he'd tried to jam my eyes into my brain. This was the longest string of coherent sentences he had given anyone in five years. If LeFlore could fake disorganized thoughts and internal stimuli to screw with his therapist and protest his meager budget, we had to mark this as major progress.

Two days later, LeFlore was over his grudge against Shannon.

"He's okay. I'll keep him for now. I just want more money. It's not fair to live like this."

22

Most of our clients had such dire needs that they required the skills and attention of our entire team. ACT was designed to be a campaign of full press, intensive services aimed at clients who faced steep recovery challenges and were almost certain to progress slowly, if at all. More often than not, they had been failed by every other program, social service agency, and institution in town. By the time they reached us, progress was measured in micrometers and graduation from ACT was rare. I was still new enough to have only seen clients decompensate into psychiatric nursing homes or death. I wanted to see some successes.

Duong appeared to be an exception to the usual ACT endgame. After ten years in our program, he had become stable enough that we thought he would do fine transitioning to a single case manager who would simply check on him once a week. Duong had not been hospitalized in a couple of years and was able to handle his money and his meds with little assistance. We even got his psychiatrist to sign the Social Security forms allowing him to be his own payee. For a time, we thought we had a success story to chart—an ACT graduate.

We had passed Duong to a less intensive program within the agency and hadn't seen much of him for about six months when he started popping into the office wearing strings of beads, sports coats with shorts, and pink tank tops—not his usual garb. We checked with Duong's case manager, who said he hadn't taken his meds in three months. Soon after, the desk clerk from Duong's building brought him to my office. Duong was cackling so hysterically he couldn't speak. The clerk explained that Duong had been laughing nonstop for days and his neighbors were becoming unnerved.

"Duong, what are you laughing about?" I asked.

"I don't know," he gasped, wiping tears with the back of his hand. "I want to stop."

Duong's eyes were red with broken blood vessels, his stomach was cramped, and he would yip with pain if he tried to stand upright. Why the desk clerk had walked Duong seven blocks to our office rather than calling an ambulance, no one in the room could explain.

We got Duong into my car and drove to the hospital. He continued to laugh while fitting himself into a pair of my old running shoes I had left in the front seat.

"Take those off."

"No! I keep 'em!"

When we parked in front of the hospital entrance, I had to rip the shoes off his feet and walk Duong inside barefoot. The visit was the beginning of a series of hospitalizations and weird scenes that went on for months: Duong pulling a stolen stethoscope from his jacket at a currency exchange while trying to pay his rent. Duong sitting in our waiting room in a stolen life preserver and construction helmet. Duong switching his style from Target men's department preppy to a blonde mohawk and leather trench coat. Duong walking into a public aid appointment and screaming at a woman wearing a hijab: "Oh! Hi, Muslim!"

When Duong was manic, there were no restraints on his behavior. He was a slight man who could slip easily into loose-limbed, childlike hypomania, giggling and bouncing around. Most conversations with Duong during these spells began with, "Duong, stop it!"

In one of his many discharges from the hospital, a young female staffer walked me and Duong to the elevator. As soon as the doors closed, Duong introduced me to the woman.

"Zak, this Michelle. Michelle, this Zak. Give him phone number. He fuck you!"

"Duong, shut up!" I said, noticing for the first time he sounded like a Cambodian Chico Marx.

Duong would spend all his money on clothes and forget to buy food. He would dress in a woman's full-length, blood-red trench coat accented with a pink beret and a purse. He would wear a security guard uniform, full camo, or nothing at all except Mardi Gras beads and a pair of shorts.

His fashion choices were not always safe. He had to parade past the drug crews on Winthrop to get to the El station where he liked to shake hands with commuters as if he were running for public office. We suggested he tone down the wardrobe for safety. Sometimes he wore a secondhand police uniform because he believed it was his job to patrol the neighborhood.

Duong knew he was safe enough with us that he could test the boundaries we set for him, much like a child. Boundaries, when presented clearly between parties, keep people safe and allow them to save face. Healthy people learn how to identify and respect boundaries so they don't hurt themselves or others. Duong's psychosis meant the learning curve for him was steep.

Psychosis is the fear of annihilation, the fear that one's physicality and cognitions, which separate them from the rest of the world, are permeable things. It's an essential question: "Where is the dividing line between myself and the rest of the world?" We all ask that question to some degree when assessing relationships and responsibilities, but a person suffering from psychosis may struggle against what feels like a world that is constantly intruding. If a person hears voices in his head, sees things that are not there, or has to fight off intrusive thoughts that are not based on the objective reality the rest of the world shares, then the fear of disappearing, of being crushed by the world, becomes a real and relentless one. With Duong, we had to gauge which behaviors were prompted by psychosis and which were characterological—his personality. This was true of most clients.

• • •

During one of Duong's hospitalizations, the attending psychiatrist decided Duong belonged in a psychiatric nursing home because he had been hospitalized too many times. We argued Duong had a subsidized apartment and was working with an ACT program on a daily basis.

Psychiatric nursing homes are not sunny retirement communities where the whole family visits Grandma every Sunday. In Chicago, the psychiatric nursing homes that ring the Uptown neighborhood have been the targets of local, state, and federal investigations. They have become warehouses for people unable to maintain independent housing due to psychosis, medical issues, substance abuse, or a combination of the three. The homes made headlines after a doctor in Uptown was disciplined for taking kickbacks from drug companies to overprescribe Clozapine to nursing home patients. Autopsy records showed that at least three of his patients died of Clozapine overdoses.

Still, some residents prefer nursing homes to city shelters because they provide food, heat, and at least a modicum of privacy and security. Medicaid and Medicare cover the bills, rent, and three meals a day. The cost is calculated to match each client's monthly Social Security check minus thirty dollars. Whether a client makes six hundred dollars a month or two thousand dollars a month, the nursing home takes all but thirty bucks. The nursing home also becomes the client's payee, which means all SSDI checks go directly to the home. Those checks are rarely, if ever, handed back to the client.

Against our protests, the hospital sent Duong to a psychiatric nursing home. After a couple of days, he punched out a window, angry at being told he couldn't return to his apartment. Eventually, he learned that if he acted up, they would kick him out. They sent him to another nursing home—owned by the same company—where Phenobarbital was added to his medication regimen. That sedated him to the point of mumbling weakness. We couldn't find which nursing home they had shipped him to because the hospital was "protecting the client's privacy." Eventually, I got a slurred phone message from Duong.

When I went to visit him, even the mumbling was gone. His mouth hung slack, and he dragged his feet as he shuffled through the lobby. In fact, it seemed like every client in the place shuffled at the same pace.

Classic rock blared in the day room where a karaoke talent show was underway. At the microphone, one patient muttered his way through "Tiny Dancer," rocking side to side. A small audience of doped-up patients stared blankly.

Duong and I talked to the discharge nurse and explained again that he had his own place, a subsidized apartment. He saw his ACT therapist and case manager every day. She began writing up his discharge.

"I'm gonna get in trouble," she said.

Shannon and I got Duong out the next day. We planned to see him twice daily, even over the weekends to make sure he was back on the right medications and stood a chance of staying out of the hospital.

On Sunday, I couldn't find him.

On Monday morning I got a whispered call from the nursing home staffer who had signed the discharge.

"Duong went back to the hospital," she said. "They went and got him."

"What do you mean?"

"The staff went back to his apartment and told him he forgot to sign something. They brought him back and they had an ambulance here to take him to Lakeshore. Don't tell anyone I told you. I'm going to lose my job."

I went to the psych unit and found Duong. The involuntary commitment papers noted that he had "eloped" from the nursing home. The nursing home claimed to have no paperwork.

We had to wait a day, but we grabbed Duong on discharge from the psych unit and brought him straight home to his apartment. We believed he was better off in our care than he was in theirs, but once we had him, things got worse. He began skipping his meds and the babbling mania returned. He said we were treating him like a baby, and he didn't need our help. He quit our program and stopped paying his rent until the managers in his building wanted to throw him out. They would only agree to let him stay if we handled his rent money. Duong didn't like that arrangement.

"I no baby!" he said.

Way off his meds, he walked into the office one day carrying a stuffed animal and a purse full of bootleg DVDs, giggling and showing off the random trinkets he had blown all of his money on. Then he demanded we cough up some money for food and cigarettes.

One day, he walked out of his apartment and tried to hump the leg of the woman working behind the front desk. She called us and Shannon went out with a hospitalization petition, getting there in time to meet the police, who had also been called.

We wanted to get him in the hospital where, we hoped, a Haldol shot could bring him a little closer to reality. The Haldol injections were oil-based and took a while to sink into the body and flow through the system. We expected more hospitalizations before the Haldol went to work on Duong's symptoms.

As expected, the next doctor wanted Duong shipped back to a nursing home immediately. I visited Duong and said, "You have to tell them no nursing home."

"They say I have to. They make me sign papers."

"Keep saying 'No.'"

I caught the attending psychiatrist on the unit one morning.

"He belongs in a nursing home," he said. "He can't take care of himself. You people aren't doing your jobs. He's not taking his meds."

I wanted to explain that we were working like dogs with Duong but that was a losing argument. I couldn't prove we were doing our jobs. Even if I provided the service notes for every interaction with Duong, the doctor would likely ignore the evidence against his own opinion. The doctor wasn't my boss. He didn't have to listen to me, and I didn't have to listen to him.

I asked the doctor, "What does Duong want to do?"

"He belongs in a nursing home."

"Okay. But is he agreeing to go?"

"He needs to be in a nursing home."

"Did he agree?"

"He will."

"I doubt it. If he doesn't want to go and has somewhere else to live, you can't force him."

"He belongs there. You people aren't doing your jobs! You're colluding with the patient!"

The doctor, purple-faced now, argued that I was incompetent and putting the client at risk by letting him walk around the community.

"He signed an agreement that he would go to a nursing home!" the doctor barked.

"What agreement is that?"

"Just what I said. He's willing to go."

Duong was standing right there. I asked him: "You want to go to a nursing home?"

"No."

They discharged Duong to us the following day. I took this as an act of spite, as he was clearly not ready.

A week later, we had to hospitalize Duong again after he walked out of his building in his underwear. When I went to see him, the same doctor said that Duong had to go to a nursing home. I explained to the staff that he wouldn't go unless he wanted to.

The social worker saddled with the job of talking to me said the doctor wasn't going to budge. I held to our position.

The next social worker said, "The doctor really wants your team to support his decision that Duong go to a nursing home."

"We won't."

"He's going to be mad."

"Have him call me."

The doctor found me at the nurses' station and erupted. His accusations were a flurry of surprisingly coarse invective. Our team was colluding with Duong, we weren't doing our jobs, and we were, overall, "Doing shit! He's going to a nursing home!"

"He doesn't want to."

"He signed an agreement!"

"How do you enforce that?" I asked.

I didn't know what agreement he was talking about, but Duong could have signed the Magna Carta, and it would not have mattered.

"He signed an agreement," the doctor said.

"I don't get it. If he's too psychotic to take care of himself in his own apartment, how is he not too psychotic to sign an agreement?"

"I'll take you to court!"

"Go ahead."

I doubted the doctor would choose to lose a day's pay. They weren't allowed to bill Medicaid for court appearances.

The doctor stomped off and left me with the rest of his staff at the nurse's station. They were cringing, like a family realizing the neighbors had just seen the drunken grandfather ranting in the driveway.

As I waited for the elevator, a staff member slipped me a copy of the agreement Duong signed for the doctor. On hospital letterhead, Duong agreed to voluntarily enter a nursing home if he were hospitalized again. Beneath Duong's signature was that of another hospital social worker. The doctor hadn't signed.

I met with the administrative director of the hospital in their cafeteria. I explained what our team did, what our goals were, and who we served. I explained the disagreement between the attending psychiatrist and my team. Then I slid a copy of the agreement across the table.

"One of your doctors is having patients sign these," I said. "I don't think it's legal, but I'm not sure. And the staff who signed it, she could be in trouble if something happened here."

The administrator and I agreed that, effective immediately, none of the ACT clients, including Duong, would be seen by this doctor again.

Two weeks later, Duong had to be hospitalized again. Apparently, he had kicked out a window in his building on the way out the door. Duong didn't want to go to the hospital voluntarily.

"No! You give me twenty dollars. I sick because no eat healthy. Give me money, I eat healthy. If I go to the hospital, I hurt myself. I start hitting my head against wall if you stay my payee. I be homeless first. I don't care."

I called the police and began filling out a petition. Some cops were wonderfully gentle with our clients. Others complained about being a taxi service for mental patients.

One cop told me, "I don't have to do this, you know!"

"Why you telling me? Go tell your sergeant. I'll tell him if you want."

I'd had enough of people who acted put out whenever they had deal with our clients for five minutes. Like Duong, I wanted to fight everyone, too.

With the police outside the treatment room door, I told Duong again, "You're going to the hospital. You can go with me or with the police. You are not going to a nursing home."

"Police first," Duong said. "I never speak to you now. Goodbye!"

Our only success at that point was we had a new psychiatrist assigned to Duong at the hospital. When Duong was discharged again, no nursing homes were mentioned, and we brought him home. He still argued that he didn't need the agency to handle his money and was offended that we didn't trust him to pay his own rent. Whenever the team got frustrated with the ingratitude of our clients I had to remind them that we would not be thanked for our work. That was just a given. If they wanted grateful clients, they were in the wrong part of town.

After a few months, Duong's symptoms subsided, his behavior became less disruptive, and he joined Shannon's shopping, exercise, and substance abuse groups. Shannon came to my office with an update on Duong one day.

"You know he says he's got a brother in a different nursing home," he said. "Right down the street. I think it's only right he gets the same chance as his brother."

So, we busted him out, too.

23

Deejay was selectively mute and not at all physically imposing. Even when he was off his meds, he didn't act out. Instead he just stopped responding to the external world and sank further into himself. All in all a quiet guy. By coincidence, it seemed like whoever was assigned to Deejay's case wound up moving on to other jobs, so he was always having to get used to a new person interfering in his life every day. I thought it best for clients to have one primary case manager or therapist and a single emergency contact responsible for every aspect of their care, but in our field that wasn't always possible. During one of Deejay's transitions between case managers, he stopped taking his meds again and we didn't notice until I got a call from his landlord.

"Your guy just kicked out the windows in my fucking lobby! I want him in the hospital now!"

"Who?"

"The little quiet guy!"

"Deejay? Get out of here."

"You come here and look. He's up in his room now. I can't have this. You gotta get him out of here or I'm not taking anyone you bring me."

This was a common landlord threat, a cost-saving measure to avoid eviction court: get the mental health team to move the client rather than file a thirty-day notice and fight in court.

I agreed to come to the building. The lobby was a room across from the clerk's desk and all of the windows were broken. The landlord was especially pissed off because he was also the maintenance guy. He wanted Deejay hospitalized and evicted.

"Did you see him break out the windows?" I asked him. "When did it happen?"

"My guy told me someone saw him do it last night. The windows been busted since."

"So, you didn't see him do it. Someone else says they saw him do it. I can't just hospitalize someone because of a secondhand report, what someone says someone else did a day ago."

As I rambled on, feeling righteous for defending our client who had never committed an act of violence or even presented much hostility, there was a slamming noise from the top of the stairs behind me—wood breaking and something crashing into something else, repeatedly.

The landlord and I ran over to find Deejay at the top of the stairs with a two-by-four knocking out the staircase railings. I yelled at him. He dropped the two-by-four and stepped quickly into his room.

The landlord called the cops. I called the team to have someone bring me the involuntary hospitalization paperwork I had neglected to grab. I really wasn't expecting this.

I knocked on Deejay's door and took the silent response as a welcome. He was standing in the middle of the room, in the tiny space between his bed and the sink. The windows were open behind him, letting winter air in. I tried talking but Deejay did not respond or even look up at me.

Holly arrived with the hospitalization paperwork but stayed in the hallway. The police came right after. This was my mistake—I should have called the police to ask specifically for the Crisis Intervention Team, Chicago police officers who were trained to address mental health issues. The basic takeaway from the training was that you do not shoot the person for not responding to your orders.

 A friend of mine who taught de-escalation techniques to police departments had snuck me into one of the Chicago Police trainings for CIT teams. In role plays, some of the cops tried to threaten actors playing suicidal subjects into compliance. One actor stood on top of some gymnasium bleachers as if he were on a bridge over the Chicago River, threatening to jump.

The officer kept commanding, "I want you to come down here

right now. I want you standing right here, now."

"I didn't call you," the actor hollered.

The cop kept repeating himself.

Eventually, the actor tried to give the officer a hint without breaking character.

"I don't like your tone of voice, officer."

"How's this?" the officer asked. "Get the fuck down here now!"

The lieutenant in charge of the training called time-out to explain that a refusal to comply with a directive was the first clue this might be a mental health issue.

This was years before every phone had the capability to video and livestream arrests, and our team would, not infrequently, warn clients not to run from the police. Not to be good citizens but to avoid being shot. Without question, some of the cops in the neighborhood were patient and right on point when we had to call for help with a hospitalization. And sometimes, it would have been better to drag the client to the hospital myself.

I was still trying to talk to Deejay when four cops flowed into the room, past me, and surrounded Deejay. They actually tried their best to tell him calmly that he had to go to the hospital and that everything was okay, but DeeJay responded to nothing until one cop tried to grab his wrist. Deejay fought back, grabbing for their hands and belts. He looked like he was trying to grab a gun and the cops could not get his skinny arms under control.

One cop yelled out, "Taser, taser, taser," and the others stepped away from Deejay. His winter coat blocked one of the needles; the other stuck him in the stomach. Deejay continued flailing and trying to get out of the room. I was stunned he was fighting so fiercely, pushing the cops toward the open windows.

I climbed over the bed and grabbed Deejay by the shoulders, pulling him backward onto the bed. While I tried not to think of the generations of cockroaches and bedbugs we had battled in this room, the cop with the taser disconnected the part of the gun that fired the needles so he could use the "drive stun" component and punched Deejay in the leg with it. Deejay and I were now sharing the electrical jolts. I might have yelled something about the cop's relationship to his mother between shocks.

They got Deejay under control, cuffed his wrists and ankles together, and carried him out of the room like a big suitcase. One of the cops, who I recognized from previous hospitalizations, mumbled as he walked past me.

"You okay, bro?"

I didn't feel bad physically, just a little jittery. When the violence kicked off, my adrenaline had amped me up. I understood I was putting myself in a dangerous position by jumping in but sitting back and watching felt worse. In a fight, there was usually something I could do to control the situation. But back in Deejay's room, I'd seen the cops' batons and knew if he wouldn't be subdued, he was going to get beat. Jumping into the fray was one way to alleviate my anxiety in the moment.

We had plenty of clients for whom the threat of violence was part of the daily routine, and we could prepare, somewhat, for confrontation. But Deejay had never been violent, and it left me wondering how badly we were failing him.

Once we got Deejay into the hospital, I went back to the office and briefed the team. Deejay's case manager would follow up with the hospital the next day, Deejay would be discharged, and we would try to make sure his landlord would take him back.

Around eleven that night, I got a call from the Chicago Police. I thought maybe it was a customer service survey, but it was one of the officers from the afternoon.

"Hey, that guy we took in today? I guess he escaped from the emergency room at Weiss. With the taser, we had to take him there for a medical checkup. Sorry about that. Thought you should know."

I drove over to Deejay's building. He was standing at the front door, in the cold, wearing his hospital gown and bootie slippers. I walked up slowly.

"Deejay, you gotta go back to the hospital."

He didn't answer.

"You don't have keys. I don't have keys. The landlord is mad at you. We have to fix a bunch of stuff before you come back in."

No answer.

"You gotta go back to the hospital. You want to go with me or with the police?"

"You."

So we drove back to Lakeshore and checked Deejay in again.

24

Phillip, the jam-band fan and former seminarian, was growing frustrated with the job. This was a constant risk for all staff, but some were more dependent than others on accolades, and the accolades never really came. During a team meeting Phillip requested to work on a Saturday to help a client get to a food pantry that was, for some reason, only open on the weekends. I advised against it—we did enough during the week and the client was a street-smart man who had survived incarcerations, hospitalizations, and homelessness, at times hustling sex to survive. Phillip believed the client was helpless enough that he needed assistance getting to a food pantry. The team argued that Phillip was being played. Phillip was offended. If Shannon or Mariella had asked to work with a client over the weekend, I would have accepted their assessments without question. But Phillip was a soft touch. I'd had to warn him more than once to not loan his clients money.

Soft touches can grow bitter. This was part of the "good for you" aspect of our field and something I tried to warn new staff about. We were not going to be acknowledged for our work. Thanking clinicians whom they had not invited into their lives was a responsibility that our clients should not be expected to meet. Even when outsiders expressed admiration for the work we did, they always diminished their praise by adding, "I could never do that work."

Phillip was falling behind on his paperwork and asking for exemptions from the basic rules of the agency to meet his personal wants. He wanted to wear shorts and flip-flops at work. He wanted to listen to his boombox in the team office. I didn't care what he wore to work, but the rest of the team definitely did not want to listen to Phish while they were trying to talk on the phone and type up their notes at the end of the day. I had to talk to Phillip about the responsibilities of working in a shared space and told him if he needed music to decompress he would have to wear headphones or listen in his car. I dreaded this nonsense.

Phillip's client interactions had become more oppositional. During our supervision meetings, he complained that a client named Dylan wasn't making any progress and wanted to close his case.

Dylan was raised, at least partially, by parents with unfulfilled artistic aspirations. I had the sense that they blamed Dylan for this due to the demands his behaviors placed on the family. Later, Dylan went through multiple foster placements and residential treatment programs. With us, he had trouble with basic tasks like washing himself and taking his meds, and most of his energy went toward smoking crack. One night, he ripped the carpet from the floor of his hotel room on the off chance a crack rock was hiding underneath. Working with Dylan required tenacity, patience, and the ability to not take his behavior as a personal affront. Phillip gassed out quickly. When he took Dylan grocery shopping at the corner store to make sure he had plenty of food for the week, the kid simply returned the food for cash, fifty cents on the dollar. Phillip went to the store and suggested the cashier not do that again. I gently reminded him that that could be a breach of confidentiality. After Phillip cut off Dylan's corner store connection, the kid began selling his food to his neighbors.

Phillip kept trying to think of ways to control Dylan's "noncompliance." And I wanted to curb Phillip's "noncompliance." Phillip's frustration took over completely, and his treatment approach devolved into thinking of ways to control Dylan and break his noncompliance. In a parallel process, I tried harder to break Phillip's noncompliance. I was as angry at him as he was at Dylan.

• • •

Our team always looked for points where we could intervene with clients without being coercive. We couldn't withhold their money or demand they stop using drugs, but we could make it a lot of work for them to continue to hurt themselves. Sometimes a client would threaten us by using the only real leverage they had besides violence: guilt.

"You're going to make me do what I have to do."

Translation: "If I have to prostitute myself because you won't give me money for drugs, then it's your fault."

Our response: "If you understand that, then you know you have a choice. You are choosing to do something dangerous. No one is making you do that."

We weren't allowed to close a client's case because his drug habit was in full flower or tell him to come back after he got clean. We had to guide him toward the first steps in his recovery and closer to the idea of living without drugs. Or even living with fewer drugs until the idea of no drugs seemed at least a faint possibility.

Our efforts to throw up barriers between Dylan and his crack habit only led to more dangerous behavior. His threats about hustling sex for drug money were not empty. This was not what we wanted.

When Dylan took all the furniture out of his hotel room, piled it up in the hallway and sprayed it down with a fire extinguisher, the front desk called the office demanding he be hospitalized. Mariella happened to be around the corner visiting someone else, so she swung by the hotel where the kid had locked himself back in his room.

I got to the hotel as Mariella was talking to the kid through his barricaded door, the hallways filled with discarded and extinguisher-sprayed furniture.

"Get away from my door or I'll kick your ass!" he yelled.

"All you have to do is talk to me here," Mariella called back. "Open up."

"Get away from my door!"

"Dylan, open this door."

"I said I'm gonna kick your ass if you don't leave!"

"You got to open the door to kick my ass, so come on."

Dylan didn't accept the challenge but continued to make threats.

The hotel had called the police. When four cops arrived, Dylan taunted them: "You got a warrant? Read it to me through the door. Slip it under the door. Slip your badge under the door."

Eventually the police and hotel staff figured out that Dylan shared a bathroom with his next-door neighbor and went in that way. We heard a skirmish before the cops came out with Dylan in cuffs.

Disheveled but proud, Dylan called out, "That was fun!" as the police took him downstairs. We followed the ambulance to the hospital and called his parents.

Dylan had learned the "I'll act up if you don't give me what I want" trick from a childhood spent in residential treatment programs. After he'd aged out of the youth programs, he'd been sent to a nursing home, and from there he was sent to us. He had never lived on his own.

As a kid, he grew up on the point systems and compliance measures that were typical of most group homes: if you make your bed, you get a gold star. If you get enough gold stars, you get to go on an outing off the premises with staff. By twenty his perception of clinical relationships consisted of immediate punishment or immediate reward. He had learned to tell caseworkers and therapists what they wanted to hear and which threats scared them the most. Dylan was the product of institutions where treatment meant coaxing clients to be compliant. Given an ultimatum, clients have only three options: obey, lie, or fight. At best, a clinician might help a client identify with a set of priorities that would keep him safe: take your meds every day, don't drink or use drugs, don't steal, don't fight, don't prostitute yourself, eat healthy, get medical check-ups, get a GED. But if stern lectures were effective, we wouldn't have jobs. The most common response to ultimatums is mechanical compliance, where the client "okeydokes" the clinician and gives them the answers they want to hear. This is subterfuge and clinicians fall for it all the time.

We did hold a lot of leverage over our clients. We had access to their bank accounts, their landlords, their doctors, their money, and their medications. With that kind of power, any suggestion can sound like a threat: if you don't do what I say, then you risk your housing, your mental stability, and your money. The client learns, after many years of receiving services, that there is a set of responses to which clinicians respond favorably. The relationship becomes a series of mutually insincere interactions. The client responds to consequences, but treatment remains superficial and inconsequential. The clients end up training clinicians, and the clinicians learn that this is how it is supposed to work. Another likely result of pushing a client to comply with recovery goals is the client will simply give up: to hell with this—I'm better off on my own. This isn't always a terrible thing. Sometimes clinicians have to set parameters for services early on, defining the boundaries of the relationship and defining the expectations for both the client and clinician. Dylan decided he was better off taking care of his own business, his own responsibilities, rather than having a team of social workers meddling in his life. He was able to find an auntie to be his payee and go to a city clinic for medications and psych appointments every month. A few clients were able to improve their functioning in spite of us after deciding, as one client said, "Anything is better than ACT!"

Before Phillip was assigned to him, Dylan had grown used to the mutual nonaggression pact between himself and his previous case manager: I'll tell you what you want to hear as long as you don't push me too much. But Phillip pushed Dylan too hard with lectures on morality and tried to impose his own goals and values. The problem was, Dylan didn't want to be a social worker.

With Phillip, Dylan couldn't get any leverage through mechanical compliance or with crack-withdrawal-fueled temper tantrums. As Phillip became more restrictive, Dylan retreated to the most easily defendable position: total apathy. Phillip brought his frustration to me during our supervision sessions and couldn't figure out why Dylan had stopped engaging with him. I wanted to walk away from the problem. I didn't want to hear about it. Phillip saw himself as having an authoritarian role with his clients, though he would never say it aloud. He knew what Dylan had to do to stay safe in the community and he was going to make sure he did it. As Dylan became more evasive, Phillip became an enforcer, threatening consequences he could never follow through with, like withholding the kid's money in order to save him.

We had to set basic safety boundaries for any client, but we also had to watch where clinical interventions slipped into ultimatums. Legally and ethically, we had to intervene when a client's behavior presented a danger to himself or others, but Dylan wasn't meeting the criteria for hospitalization, only the criteria for being a kid with minimal self-preservations skills.

Way beyond frustrated, Phillip told me, "He just gets under my skin."

"You can't be taking this personally."

"I'm not."

"If you're mad at him, then you are taking it personally. Has his behavior changed since you started with him?"

"No."

"Does his behavior match what the intake says and what the previous reports said?"

"Yeah, he was smoking pot in front of me, blowing it in my face!"

"So, why are you blaming yourself here?" I could see Phillip's blood rising. His face mottled as he described Dylan's behavior. To Phillip's mind, Dylan was deliberately sabotaging his treatment.

As I explained to Phillip what was going on between him and Dylan, I recognized the same dynamic between me and Phillip. I was sick of hearing about Dylan. I didn't like Phillip, and I didn't want to talk to him anymore. I wanted him to leave and go do his job. I took some deep breaths. Phillip had to stop lecturing the kid. Dylan already had a dad and didn't need another. The kid was annoyed, the case manager was annoyed, and I was annoyed. We were all stepping on each other. I had to back up so Phillip could back up so Dylan could back up. I was proud I'd recognized this—actual psychodynamics at work. To break this chain, I pushed my discussion with Phillip toward our own limitations. We might not ever provoke the kid into making healthy decisions, and if that were the case, the best we might be able to do would be to minimize the damage the kid did to himself. Dylan said he wanted to give up, but he knew he did not have the autonomy to do so, nor, I suspected, did he really want to. The only position he knew in life was subordination to some authority. From that point of view, the only option he saw was to oppose everything.

Our clinicians had the almost impossible duty of determining whether client behaviors were due to psychosis, mood disorders, acute or chronic substance abuse, personality disorders or a total lack of motivation. None of these issues were mutually exclusive. In fact they often overlapped and fed into each other. We had to maintain a balance between providing a therapeutic relationship and intervening in almost every aspect of our clients' lives without chasing them away. We had to be part therapist, part investigator.

I suggested Phillip quit giving orders and just talk to Dylan.

"So, what am I supposed to talk to the kid about?"

"I don't know," I said. "Skateboarding? Girls? Find out what he gives a damn about."

Over the next couple of months, Dylan made minimal progress. Phillip had to manage his anxiety around Dylan's lack of progress, and I had to deal with my own anxiety around dealing with Phillip. I wanted Phillip to be more like an Aikido master—able to deflect any problems with minimal effort or impact, using his own momentum to guide the client toward a solution. I didn't want Phillip to mark every day without progress as a failure on his part. He would never last if he did.

Dylan wanted to move back home with his parents. He told us he had been visiting them every weekend, but we couldn't verify that because he refused to give us permission to speak to them. We didn't actually believe him. We figured he had found somewhere to score drugs outside the neighborhood.

When Dylan's father called to request a meeting with us, I expected the worst. When Dylan and his dad sat down in my office, Phillip and I braced ourselves for a "What have you done to my child" rant.

Instead, the dad expressed his thanks. He and his wife were ready for their boy to move back home, he said. The family actually had been having weekend visits over the last month and they were going well. His parents said they were astonished by the change in their son. We were amazed they saw improvement because we didn't. They moved Dylan back to the south suburbs at the end of the month and we never heard another word from them. We were baffled.

Soon after, Phillip handed in his resignation.

Dylan's seemingly successful reunification with his family was not a common scenario in our program. Most of our clients did not have families waiting eagerly to take them back. For them, we were the lone guardrail between them and the edge of the cliff. Some clinicians leaned into that pressure; others backed away. Mariella leaned in hard and pushed back. She maintained an expectation that the job would be difficult, even confrontational at times, but she didn't expect anyone to thank her for her efforts. She was clearly dedicated to caring for her clients and could be a little intense with them, but sometimes they needed her fierce mothering.

25

I remembered Ronnie from my internship at Cook County Jail. He was a polite, psychotic man who punched people in the face for no apparent reason. He walked with military bearing, like a wind-up toy, his gait interrupted by involuntary facial twitches every dozen steps or so. He marched into my office in the middle of February wearing nothing but a T-shirt and jeans.

"Um hm, Mister Zak?"

I hadn't seen him in nearly three years. "Where're your clothes?" I asked.

"Um hm, I'm okay. I just got off the bus from Georgia. I went down there since we saw each other last. It was okay, but I wanted to come back home."

Ronnie didn't have a place to stay or a dime to his name. After several rounds of open-ended questions that had to be phrased precisely in order to get useful answers, Ronnie explained that he'd been thrown out of a psychiatric nursing home for no reason and had been on the street since.

"They said I attacked them."

"Why would they say that?"

"I don't know. Because they think I did, but they started it. Um hm. I did put my hands on one guy, but he was being mean. Disrespectful. But, really, I wanted to move out anyway."

I introduced Ronnie to Mariella. She explained the rules of our program. First and foremost, no violence.

"Um hm. I agree. That's good."

We opened Ronnie's case and started from scratch: no housing, no meds, no ID, no winter clothes. We hooked him up with a coat and sweater and drove him to a shelter in the neighborhood. The next morning he was waiting outside our office by 7 a.m. Mariella and

Yvonne let him in for a cup of coffee. I came in as Ronnie stepped back outside for a cigarette. Minutes later, another client ran in, telling us to hurry outside: "Some guy's hitting people!" Ronnie was in a boxer's stance, hands up, elbows protecting his ribs. Two pedestrians and their lunch pails were sprawled out on the sidewalk like flipped turtles. As one man struggled to right himself, keeping a hand over his bloody nose, Shannon stepped into his path to coax him away from Ronnie. Mariella and I got in front of Ronnie, talking softly to get him to put his fists down. Ronnie only explained that his opponents had started the fight by disrespecting him. Police and an ambulance came to the office. Ronnie went to the hospital. Over the next month we got Ronnie set up in a hotel room, got his Social Security entitlements active again, and got him a state ID. We learned how severely his crack habit directed his typical day, and we learned the standard prompt for Ronnie's assaults. Generally a friendly man, Ronnie would wave to strangers, expecting a return greeting. He would wave by sticking one arm straight out and wagging his hand side to side at the wrist like a little kid. When the intended recipient of the greeting didn't respond in kind, Ronnie would march forward and smack them in the mouth. To him, "they started it" by not waving back.

Mariella had near-daily battles with Ronnie over his money. The Social Security Administration had rightly decided Ronnie could not be his own payee. Once, Ronnie disassembled the sink in his room and sold it for crack. More than once we found him with nothing but the clothes on his back, marching in just his gym shorts and loafers.

"What happened to all your stuff?" Mariella asked him once.

"Someone stole it."

"Where were you this morning?"

"I was in my room."

"You were not. You left the door open."

"I was, too, there."

"Okay. I'm going to walk out of this room. When I come back, you better give me some different answers. Quit treating me like I'm special."

"Um hm. Yes, ma'am."

Marching the neighborhood in his shorts and attempting to slug people who didn't wave back to him, Ronnie got hospitalized quite a bit. We couldn't catch him every time, and eventually, he was sent to a psychiatric nursing home, still in his boxers. When Mariella located him, the staff hadn't given him any clothes yet.

"You don't leave this room," she told him.

"Um. Yes, ma'am."

"You stay right here. You don't go outside for a cigarette. You don't go outside for a bag of chips."

"Yes, ma'am."

"We're going to be right back with some clothes and then we'll get you out of here. But you do not go outside, you understand?"

"Yes, ma'am."

"You gotta stay right here until I get back. Besides, the world don't need to see all this hot chocolate."

"Yes, ma'am."

Mariella got together a stash of clothes for Ronnie. She told the staff she was taking Ronnie out to do laundry. No one questioned her and she never bothered to bring him back.

• • •

Mariella was determined to advocate for our clients, and if that meant she had to call out her coworkers, she could live with that.

Holly, a new therapist on the team, was fresh out of school and hadn't done much else. For her, ACT was just a stop along the road to becoming a sit-down therapist. She'd said the right things to get hired, but her reticence to engage with our clients was obvious. She didn't like how messy—literally and ideologically—the job could be.

One of her clients was Henry, whose alcoholism and crack addiction gave his bipolar symptoms a run for their money in the comorbidity race. Holly returned from a visit with Henry one day and told the team how horrified she was to learn Henry's "girlfriend" was not exactly that.

"She just lives in the building," Holly said. "He pays her for sex, but he's been paying her in fried chicken. They were in bed when I got there."

Apparently Holly had seen an empty KFC bucket next to the futon mattress. In her sweet-voiced she explained that Henry was taking advantage of a woman who had nothing to sell except for her body and he was wrong to consider this a girlfriend-type relationship. Mariella countered immediately.

"Hold on, now. How do we know Henry's taking advantage of her? Where do you think he's getting all his crack from?"

"We don't know the crack is from his girlfriend," Holly said.

"Well, a lot we don't know. Maybe Henry's being taken advantage of. We don't know this woman is worth a six-piece meal."

"Sex is worth more than fried chicken," Holly said.

"Maybe to you. Depends what you have more of and what you want more. Maybe this woman isn't worth it. Maybe she's only worth a couple wings and our guy is getting ripped off."

The team argued over who was in the right—Henry or his female partner—but Mariella brought up a good point: this is how some people lived and there was little point in criticizing clients for surviving the best they could.

Of course Mariella herself would dress down a client if she felt she was being taken advantage of. I heard her once tell a client, "You say 'I don't know,' again, and we're gonna fist fight." As tough as she was, clients took some pride in a scolding from Mariella. They knew it meant more than the usual social-worker lecture.

26

Dean and I stepped into an elevator once and there was a Black man in there. Dean looked at the man and stage whispered to me. "Look at him. He's not Black. That's ten thousand dollars' worth of makeup. He's got a whole movie crew in his room helping him out. He gets more of everything like that."

Dean believed it was safer to say this kind of crap if I was standing next to him. I told him to shut up in the same blasé tone he'd made his observation in to avoid escalating the situation. The Black man said nothing, but he looked really pissed.

Dean was rough on a lot of the staff. He was rough on his neighbors; he was rough on the neighborhood. He wanted respect. He wanted to be a powerful person. We didn't pretend he was JFK, but we didn't tell him he wasn't. Challenging delusions never worked. Arguing against a person's belief about his own identity only pushed him to hold on to it tighter. With Dean, we could read the of his delusions and respond accordingly.

But Dean's anxiety about who he was and his place in the world would escalate when he was exposed to too much stimulation. The more people around him, the worse his behavior was. The more people he didn't recognize, the more he felt he had to defend himself. The more he and I were together, the more he calmed down. And even if he didn't totally calm down, he at least didn't spiral into wild screaming fits anymore.

Dean's relationship with our staff was enough for him to feel a little less threatened when he was out in the neighborhood. His disturbing declarations of celebrity and power would recede a bit as long as he felt he wasn't alone, like he had some protection. He seemed to be doing better. He would joke around, hoping others would respond in kind.

I thought he was doing well enough that I could pass his case along to the rest of the team and no longer be his partner on his daily patrols.

Dean protested this and, for a while, all the progress he had made seemed to crumble. I should have paid better attention to how important our relationship was to him. What we considered a graduation of sorts, he considered a rejection. In turn, he refused the company offered by other clinicians, at least until they were also able to prove in.

The team would visit Dean in his room to make sure he was managing his medication and report back:

"I told him yesterday that because he's taking Depakote, he should never drink grapefruit juice with it, as it's counteractive. So last night he buys grapefruit juice and is making a point of drinking it the whole time I'm there."

Or: "He's drinking white wine."

Or: "He tore up his treatment plan and threw it in my face."

One female clinician complained: "He asked if he could smell my Georgia peach."

Things weren't going any better with Dean at the office. Stella let me know one day that the janitors were angry because Dean had taken a dump right in front of the building while people were waiting for the doors to open. Apparently he told the janitors, "It's okay. Zak's secretary will clean it up."

During this spell of acting out, Dean threw a chair at someone in the lobby of his building. Building management called the police. It was my turn to deal with Dean again. I drove over to Lakeshore Hospital, where I found him in an intake room, his belt and shoes taken away.

"I'm not talking to you," he said, pulling his cap over his eyes.

I sat down with him, and we waited in silence. Eventually an intake worker arrived. He was young, with elegant full-sleeve tattoos of vines and leaves reaching out from his polo shirt. He started off with the standard and totally appropriate questions, but Dean wasn't having any of it.

"You can talk to my attorney," he said, jerking a thumb toward me and pulling his cap down over his face. The intake worker looked at me. I nodded and explained who I was, marbling in bits of Dean's history and explaining that the recent incident may have sounded more violent than it actually was.

"Okay," the intake worker said. "I'm going to just check his insurance status and see if we have a bed. I believe we do."

As the worker got up, Dean called out to him without removing the hat from his face, "Hey, kid, your parents know you have those tattoos?"

The worker looked pissed. "I'll be right back."

Dean called out again as the guy reached for the doorknob, "Hey, kid."

"Yes?"

"Your father will never be proud of you."

Dean had an uncanny ability to hit a nerve. The guy slipped out and someone else came in to take Dean upstairs.

"You gonna come get me when I'm done here?" Dean asked me.

"Yeah. I'll see you before then, too."

"Stop by, you get a chance."

• • •

On his best days, Dean reminded me of an uncle I had. When I was still in grade school I noticed he had this great ability to make bizarre statements or tell bald-faced lies with a totally straight face, all with a sense that it was a put-on, that maybe *everything* was a put-on. I remember him telling me at some gathering—as I watched the adults doing adult things—"You know this is all bullshit, right?" Dean was able to make observations like that, uncanny and spot-on, cracking himself up with some truth no one else perceived.

Dean was released from the hospital, and we had to do some apologizing and negotiating with his building manager to minimize the threat of eviction. With me as his primary, Dean slipped back into his routine and was able to work less confrontationally with the team.

During some talks we had, usually riding in my car, he began to open little windows into his childhood. I could never be sure how factual anything he said was, but he described some real scenes of terror, like finding his mother after she'd hanged herself and being dressed as a little girl by his grandmother after his father disappeared. There may have been a couple of wives and a daughter. He may have worked construction and attempted to sell cars on Western Avenue. He was clearly a Chicago guy but wouldn't disclose what neighborhood he grew up in. As much as he frustrated me with his delusions and hypermasculine facades, Dean was, at his core, a terrified and traumatized child, playacting in order to find his place in the world. The delusions patched over the trauma, covering what he could not face.

• • •

As Dean slowly warmed to me and the team again, ACT was in the middle of a routine state audit. The auditors examined client files, treatment plans, medical records, and clinical notes. If things weren't in order, or the auditors caught a whiff of anything shady or negligent, the agency could lose money and the team could be subject to a more serious investigation. My worst fear was being accused of cherry-picking clients, taking easy cases, and passing on people who really needed help. I knew this wasn't true, but I was anxious.

On the third and last day of the audit, the boss auditor, Nancy, said, "I would like to interview an ACT client to see what they have to say about the services provided and also just to, you know, make sure you're all working with people at the appropriate level of care."

"When would you want to do this?"

"Now."

It was the afternoon, and the place was pretty empty. The doctor was gone, the payee bank was closed, and staff were busy writing their notes.

I stepped outside and found Dean leaning against the building, straddling the *No Smoking* boundary painted on the sidewalk with a cigarette in his mouth.

"Dean, you got a minute?"

"I guess."

"I have the state here, going through our files and stuff. They want to make sure we're doing our jobs and now they want to talk to someone who works with us. Can you talk to them?"

He shrugged.

"Sure."

Nancy was waiting in the doorway of the treatment room across from my office. I formally introduced her and Dean. He screamed in her face.

"Hi, Aunt Mary!"

She backed into the treatment room and Dean followed her, shutting the door.

I sat down at my desk where I could watch the door. A minute later Nancy came out and I met her in the hallway.

"We're done," she said.

Dean walked past without looking at me.

"I didn't tell her shit."

Our program passed the audit. Later, Nancy pulled me aside.

"That man you brought in for the interview denied knowing who you were or having ever heard of your program. He denied he was a client of the agency at all."

Dean had my back. To him, the meeting with Nancy was a scene in a cop movie, the one where Internal Affairs investigates the hardworking police who do what they have to do to get the job done. Dean wasn't going to snitch.

27

WINTER 2007

Bobby came back to us after I got a phone call from his mother letting me know he was "having problems" at his building. Bobby didn't want to work with the agency again. His case had been closed after I moved to ACT. He vowed to his new case manager he could take care of his own business—taking his meds, going to the doctor, not walking outside naked—without her help.

He took care of none of this, and his mother had called the crisis line to ask if I could go see him in the hospital again. I did and Bobby said he wasn't interested in ACT. Deep into his delusions at that point, he saw no need for meds. He enjoyed his delusions—he was a man of power and wealth and had girlfriends all over the world. He had powers that stemmed from his Native American heritage and his family's military background.

"My dad was in Vietnam," he told me. "He spilled seed over there before he met my mom. It's in the soil. It's a sin. Now I have to take over to make up for what he did wrong."

When symptomatic Bobby would refuse all assistance. He would admit nothing, agree to nothing. When off his meds, he wrote letters to local news stations, announcing to the newscasters an itemized list of the women with whom he wanted to have sexual relations and the policy changes he wanted to see enacted in Southeast Asia. His lawyers would tear the station down brick by brick, he promised. He wrote letters to the FBI, complaining about the pay phone on Lawrence and Sheridan taking his quarters.

He didn't want me reminding him to take his meds, but he didn't mind my negotiations with his landlord, who wanted to kick him out for walking around naked.

Bobby stayed with our team. Each year he would test whether he really needed his meds by not taking them, which led to multiple hospitalizations annually. After each round, he would refuse to work with us again.

Whenever the delusions subsided, he would begrudgingly accept our assistance, but only if it came directly from me—he didn't know anyone else on the team yet. He would tell me the voices got angry, his wives no longer liked him, and he knew the FBI was after him. Once stabilized, he would usually last a good ten months before attempting to go without his medications again.

During Bobby's stable periods we would encourage him to do things other than sit in his room, eat, and watch TV. When his symptoms gathered intensity he would just stay in bed and wait for his wives. At one point, he dragged his refrigerator from the hallway kitchenette to his bedside so he would be there in case one of them showed up. Even as he told us about his wives, he denied having delusions, claiming he moved his fridge bedside simply out of laziness. I took him at his word and began a personal training regimen, picking him up and taking him to the gym twice a week to meet with Shannon and the rest of the Health and Wellness gang.

He rode the bike dutifully, and after a month he had lost a couple of pounds, but he didn't think the result was worth the effort and gave up. He quit taking his meds again, too. Once, he dumped them in the toilet and challenged me: "Now what? Now you go home!" Occasionally, he would end our med standoffs by barricading himself in his room and I'd have to call the cops. They knew him well: "Is this the fat guy again?"

One time, the cops and I waited while the building engineer removed Bobby's door from the hinges. Bobby just stood silently and watched, occupied with whatever delusions were rolling through his head. Only when the cops started cuffing him did Bobby curse everyone out, concluding with, "You're all dead."

The officer cuffing him asked, "You fucking talking to me?"

"No, not you. Just them."

One time, I had to refuse to accept Bobby's discharge from the hospital because, while I was reviewing the paperwork, he was making another list of all the people he would assassinate. The top line read: *People Who Will Be Killed in April Due to Their Offenses Against Nature*. Beneath that was a list of minor celebrities who might consider a death threat a boost to their careers.

When I was tired and dealing with Bobby, I felt like he was purposely trying to chase me away by refusing to accept basic logic, though I knew his delusions trumped logic every time. I liked the man and had occasionally seen him emerge from the fog of his symptoms as a funny and empathetic guy who wanted a normal life. The tragedy was the distance he knew he had to travel to reach what he wanted—a real life with a real wife to come home to at night and a job to go off to in the morning. If he believed his meds would help him find that stuff, I doubt he would have ever returned to the hospital. But he didn't want a job, he didn't want to lose weight, and he didn't want to leave his apartment to find a wife. He felt it was too much, that he would never get there, so he would stay in his psychotic fog.

His delusions defined reality, and everyone else—me, hospital staff, his family, psychiatrists—became interference. He said it was like watching two televisions at once—one was the reality he could see in front of him, the other would creep into his head from behind, the volume drowning out what was real. Then the pictures would start coming and he couldn't hear people like me at all. Sometimes, he would simply choose to ignore me, waiting for the more interesting stories to take over and give him instructions.

When Bobby returned to his nonpsychotic baseline each year and was able to join his family for Sunday dinners, his mother would send the team a box of chocolates and a sweater meant to fit me. We would eat the chocolate and donate the sweater to our emergency clothes closet.

28

Shannon was nothing if not tenacious. After a year of barely perceptible progress with clients in his Health and Wellness program, he remained hyperfocused and determined that it would work. The group had started at ground zero, with Shannon just working to enforce the basic rules about hygiene, not wearing winter jackets while on the treadmill, not leaving yoga for a cigarette break, and not coming to the gym drunk. If a client was able to walk on the treadmill for five minutes, he was praised heavily and encouraged to do more. Now, while no one was threatening to become a four-minute miler, clients began losing the old "Thorazine shuffle" and gaining some awareness of their bodies, adding a confidence to their stride that replaced the foot-clomp stumble and the depressive slide-step. It was amazing to see Shannon's gang starting to walk like they had somewhere to go, even moving down the street with a sense of purpose on some days. Clients who had started out walking five minutes on the treadmill and complaining like they were Guantanamo detainees were, one year later, walking forty minutes.

My confidence in Shannon was unshakable, but I would never have predicted the miraculous results he was having with this gang. We saw blood pressures drop, alcohol intakes decrease, and more pride in hygiene and general appearance.

The only female client who stayed with the group for any length of time entered the program with the aid of a walker and worked her way up to fifteen minutes on the exercise bicycle. The walker was replaced by a cane and the cane was even retired for a time. This was head-spinning progress. But the client's niece, who was also the client's payee, complained that the exercise group was too stressful for her auntie. I began receiving phone calls from the niece threatening to hold us responsible if the woman died. She said we were "forcing" her aunt to exercise.

"Like you running a concentration camp! My auntie sits on that bicycle all day and has to sit on an ice pack at night! That man you hired broke her vagina!"

The niece vowed to sue us if we forced her aunt to march one more step on a treadmill. Eventually she pulled her aunt from the ACT program. Sometimes our clients' families became the biggest barrier to treatment.

As other clients progressed, Shannon added more variety to the workout regimen. Thursdays became rock climbing day. The first few sessions were spent showing clients how to simply climb into the harness gear and assuring them the therapists holding the safety ropes wouldn't let go. After the first client made it to the top—eyes shut, asking, "Am I up?"—the rest of the group wanted to prove themselves. They actually cheered for each other.

Shannon talked with them about progress and how to measure it.

"You are not competing with each other," he said. "You want to do a little more than you did last week."

When one of our three-hundred-pound clients did his first push-up, he got an ovation from his peers. They remembered that just months earlier the man had needed assistance coordinating his limbs on the Universal machines. Two months later he was able to do three push-ups. In four years of work, he slimmed down from 320 pounds to 275 pounds.

But all of his success didn't improve the client's motivation. A clinician had to literally drag him out of his hotel in order to get him to Health and Wellness. We found little difference between the excuses our clients gave for avoiding the gym and the excuses of nonpsychotic people: It's too cold. It's raining. I'm tired. It doesn't make a difference. No one had any bizarre delusions that prevented them from going to the Health and Wellness Group. Psychotic or not, getting to the gym is the hardest part. Emphasizing the benefits of the program, Shannon would tell the exercise crowd, "This is holistic care—you're gonna do it."

29

Some clients could be coaxed and cajoled into doing nothing other than hanging on. Molly spent every day panhandling with her boyfriend. She didn't know how old she was. She didn't know if her parents were on Lawrence Avenue or somewhere in Europe. She said she had kids, but she didn't know where they lived and could only guess how old they were.

Rather than go to the Laundromat, Molly would throw out her clothes and pick up more at the women's shelter, a bridesmaid's dress or a tennis outfit if nothing else were available. She wasn't picky.

Molly routinely commissioned a neighbor to shave her head but complained to us one day that her barber was threatening her over an outstanding balance. He had been charging Molly twenty dollars per buzz. We spoke to him, and Molly was given a waiver on the balance due as well as the cost of any future haircuts.

Figuring that any visit to a doctor would lead to a stay in the hospital, Molly refused all medical treatment, often in spectacular fashion. When stomach pains doubled her over one day, and clinicians had to coax her to an ER, Molly tore an IV out of her arm and ran like she was being chased by a man with an axe. When a psychiatrist told her she might end up in a nursing home if she didn't see the medical doctor, Molly told her, "You're dreaming." She would live on the streets before anyone locked her up.

The team debated whether Molly's diabetes and high blood pressure—she was borderline for hospitalization for both—demanded that she be sent to a nursing home. We agreed a nursing home would be able to take care of her medically, but we also knew Molly would rather be dead. She had jumped out of moving vehicles when she suspected she might be getting hospitalized; she would certainly walk away from any nursing home.

Molly had an apartment, a schedule of friends to visit, and corners to frequent. Her building offered three hot meals a day, so she wouldn't starve, not that she was ever hungry. Every day was new; every day was the same. Left to her own devices, her diabetes and blood pressure would eventually become immediate threats to her health. We couldn't hospitalize her for being suicidal or homicidal because she was neither, but we didn't have to leave her alone, either. Left to her own devices, her health would deteriorate severely and immediately. It would be pointless to send her to a nursing home simply because she wouldn't stay there, and the team decided it would be unethical to close her case.

So Shannon volunteered to chase Molly, who usually left her hotel room before Mariella or anyone else was out in the neighborhood. His mission would be to catch her each day at six in the morning. Any later and she would likely be scouting along her panhandling trail where he would never find her. This was the best part about having a full team available to work a caseload—we could add more support than one person could ever provide.

Shannon found Molly every morning and delivered meds, money, and fresh socks. She began a regimen of basic self-care skills. If she happened to leave her room especially early, Shannon would try to catch her on the street and test her blood sugar wherever they were standing. Molly referred to Shannon as "the man" because she could never remember his name. The man also tested her blood sugar every day.

When Shannon asked her why she never went to the Laundromat, she said guilelessly, "No one ever asked."

Shannon wanted to get her to a doctor for a check-up. She was starting to warm up to him, but she wouldn't go without some coaxing. Shannon had an idea.

"You know, she really likes the fried chicken from Jewel," he said.

So we began dipping into petty cash whenever Molly had a doctor's appointment. Shannon would roll up on her with some hot fried chicken sitting on the passenger seat.

Once I had to catch Molly. She agreed to take her meds and let me test her blood sugar while we sat on the hood of my car, but when her patience ran thin, she began screaming for the police. When that drew no attention, she began screaming rape.

The only one of our team who she fully trusted was Shannon, the man who showed up every day. Once, when he was on vacation, Molly showed up at the office and stuck her head into a team meeting.

"Do you know where he is?"

"He's on vacation," I said.

"I miss him."

"Molly, that's sweet."

"I have feelings, too, you know. Do you have a dollar?"

We had never heard her make any statement of emotional expression unless it was about her "boyfriend"—and panhandling partner—whom she wanted to marry. Molly said they had been together for twenty years, had a couple of kids, and used to go on vacations together. She didn't know his last name or where he lived. I wasn't sure he lived anywhere.

30

The police found Roger in the park, sleeping in a tent, filthy and covered in maggots. We picked him up from the hospital, moved him into a hotel, and threw out his clothes. He told me he wanted the bones in his arms replaced—the ones he had were faulty. The best we could do was a fresh set of clothes from our secondhand closet. He still wanted a tent in case he had to leave the hotel. Winter was coming and we suggested he stay indoors and that we'd get him more clothes.

Mariella took his case. When she went to his hotel, he would answer his door in sagging white underwear, a butter knife in his hand. Their exchange would go something like this:

"Why you answering the door with a knife?"

"I don't know. I forgot it was there."

"Put that down and we'll do this. You gotta take your meds."

"Well, come in then."

"No, you put your knife down and we'll do this right here."

They would stand for a moment at a stalemate in the doorway. Then Roger would put the knife down and Mariella would lay out the protocol for receiving visitors.

"Ask 'Who is it?' then put on pants, then open the door, and be polite."

If Roger didn't want to talk, he would pull out a transistor radio and flick the AM/FM switch like he was sending Morse Code. "You getting that?" he would ask Mariella. "Know what I mean?"

The hotel manager asked me to speak with Roger after the maid complained that Roger had defecated on the chair in his room. I went to the hotel and asked Roger if there was any particular reason for this.

"I was living outside for so long, I got used to going where I wanted to," he said.

"The bathroom is right here. That chair is farther away from your bed than the bathroom."

"But I was closer to the chair then."

"Some days we all have to work a little extra."

"Hey, can you get me a portable toilet? I could just take that around with me."

"No, you gotta get used to the nonportable ones."

Roger pouted. "Well, if you say so."

One day at the office, Mariella and I had to hospitalize Roger when he exploded during a psychiatric appointment. He ran out of the building, and we followed at a distance, calling 911 repeatedly to harass the operator because the police had failed to arrive while we had him safely at our building.

Down the street, Roger cursed out pedestrians and screamed at their little dogs as he made his way down Broadway. We kept following for several blocks until Roger flagged down a squad car because he wanted us arrested for chasing him. The cop cleverly offered Roger protection from us and told him to climb into the backseat. He politely got inside and agreed to go to the hospital.

This always made us look a little silly, calling for police assistance, especially when the person presenting the threat would calm down at the sight of a uniform, badge, belt, and gun.

After that hospital visit, Roger began taking his meds regularly. We also learned he was Molly's mystery boyfriend, the fellow she had been talking about. Roger confirmed their relationship had lasted more than twenty years and weathered homelessness, hospitalizations, and psychosis on the part of both parties. The state had taken their children but neither of them could remember how long ago.

We had all seen Molly with Roger in the past, but we couldn't be sure her stories about a boyfriend and babies were not delusional. They would sometimes meet in our waiting room and wait for each other to get their Haldol injections. The idea of a union between them just hadn't occurred to us.

Once the relationship was verified as clinical data, case managers would visit Roger in the morning and find Molly in his bed while he toasted stacks of frozen waffles.

One day, Molly asked Shannon: "Will you ask Roger to marry me?"

"We'll see about that," he said. If the relationship got that far, we agreed to have the wedding party in our office.

31

Shannon brought Lonnie to my office and demanded, "He needs ACT."

Lonnie had been sleeping in an alley after bolting from a nursing home a couple of months earlier. He had no money, no meds, and an old arson conviction from trying to warm himself in an abandoned building.

His chin displayed a thick scar that crawled up to the corner of his mouth and looked as if it had never received medical attention. A star pattern of fresh cuts marked where someone had broken a bottle on his face.

His brain had been hammered by psychosis, street drugs, and years of antipsychotic medications through most of his adult life. His physical reactions and verbal responses were terribly slowed. I had the feeling if I threw my car keys at his face, he wouldn't even begin to duck.

He described psychotic symptoms as physical pains or vague illnesses with no sense that they might be related to his paranoid ideas about people reading his mind. He said he suffered "anxiety about things." His case manager rolled her eyes and sighed whenever his answers were concrete or ambivalent.

"If you're homeless," I asked, "Where do you go to clean up?"

"Huh?"

Cleaning up hadn't been a priority. His fingernails were ringed black, and his clothes were filthy. I skipped ahead to his conviction record. I always prefaced this part of the intake with an explanation that I wasn't police or probation and was not concerned with the number of criminal charges a person had caught. I just needed to know the history so I could help.

"If we have to find housing," I told him, "I don't want to waste your money applying for places where they're going to say no. Some landlords want totally clean records, some don't care about murder, but they will refuse someone with an arson conviction. They're landlords—they want to protect their property, right? So, when's the last time you were arrested?"

"Maybe a couple months ago. When the police searched me, they found some crack rocks in my shoe," he said.

"Okay," I said, noncommittal.

"I didn't know they was there," he protested.

"All right."

"Really, I didn't know."

"I believe you."

"Why?"

"If you knew they were there, you would have smoked them, right?"

"Yeah!"

At least we could agree on that. But then he went ahead and told a grotesque falsehood—that he had been completely cured of his crack use. This garnered another eye-roll from the case manager.

"Then crack shouldn't be a problem anymore," I said. Even though I didn't believe him, there was no reason to argue.

"Nope."

I took Lonnie to Social Security to switch his payeeship to our agency. Shannon began scheduling all other services immediately—the psychiatrist, nurse, daily check-ins, and group counseling, but we had to have a way to find him every day. Since he slept in the alley behind a convenience store on Sheridan, we knew where we might catch him, but there was no guarantee the alley wouldn't be commandeered by others or ruined as a shelter due to the rain. We checked the alley each day. If we missed him early in the morning, one of the team would slip a note detailing his next appointment into a Ziploc bag and tape it to one of the dumpsters he slept between. To protect client confidentiality, we only used his first initial. We were shocked this worked. Lonnie started showing up to appointments and group sessions. Shannon got him into a room at the Men's Club. Lonnie couldn't afford anything better because his check had been reduced due to previous overpayments, but he wasn't sleeping outside.

Lonnie's talent for persuading others to extend credit to him presented a continual threat. He would gladly make all sorts of promises—well-meaning as they might be—in exchange for immediate gratification. He was constantly in debt for beer or crack purchased on credit. He knew everybody in the neighborhood and was half as slick as he thought he was. It seemed as if he owed money to someone on every corner. If he happened to be drunk when they demanded repayment, he cursed them out and got thoroughly stomped. His reflexes were lousy. He would take a shot to the face and hit the ground before he could get his hands out to break his fall.

Over two years, he settled into a schedule. He attended Health and Wellness and our substance abuse group and even did some spot work passing out flyers for restaurants. He moved up from the chicken-wire sleeping rooms to a hotel with a shared bathroom and then to a subsidized apartment, complete with a lease, guaranteeing him some security.

With a couple of brief stints of sobriety in the bank, Lonnie reunited with an ex-wife. She offered to act as his payee and to help him find a psychiatrist, but she would not let him sleep in her apartment. That was one bridge he had burned. She only allowed him to visit during the day or for dinner.

Before Christmas, Lonnie came to my office with Shannon.

"I've had enough," he said. "This is too much for me. I'm done," he said. "I've had it with exercise and the doctors and groups."

Shannon and I argued with him as gently as possible, prompting him to describe his plans for the immediate future. He wouldn't budge and wouldn't disclose any plans. His ex was going to take care of things, he promised. We didn't believe his ex was taking him back, but it was a respectable cover story for quitting the program. Christmas was coming and he wanted a holiday without any therapists or groups or doctors. This was a fine and admirable goal. All of our clients should have been working toward building a life where they would not need our entire team's support on a daily basis. But Lonnie didn't even want to plan. He wanted it done and believed that, magically, if he wanted it then he could wish it true.

Determined, he walked out of my office, shaking our hands like he was off to Afghanistan.

The team discussed what to do. We couldn't close his case immediately and we didn't think his plans would end in success. Lonnie had tried reuniting with the ex several times over the years and he'd ended up homeless every time. His ability to take care of himself was minimal if it existed at all. He could barely read or write, and his financial planning abilities were limited to whatever cash was in his hand.

• • •

We moved Lonnie from the flophouse to a subsidized apartment at the same time that we moved several other clients into the same building. The team figured the clients would either become a support system for each other—which we hoped—or they would create a psychiatrically disordered frat house. This particular gang found ways to do both. They pooled their resources, traveling in a pack to the church spaghetti dinners and food pantries, but they also drank and smoked together and fought in the lobby of their building over who got to make the run to the crack dealer. Rather than arguing over who would be saddled with the risk of arrest that came with carrying a pocket of crackdown Argyle St., they punched each other out for the opportunity to save five bucks by making the run while the others waited safely inside.

A month after Lonnie left us, his stumbling partners told us, "He's not doing good. You gotta help him." While these clients were Lonnie's pals, they weren't going to take up a collection to help him through a bad patch. At least they didn't silently watch him starve to death. Apparently, Lonnie's ex-wife vowed she would do just that. He had blown Christmas by getting high and selling the gifts he bought her. He'd come over drunk and she'd called the police.

Lonnie was ashamed of his stumbling, and we knew that, to him, appearing capable was more important than actually being capable. Magical thinking—if I say something enough times, it will become true—was his first line of defense. His only backup was denial. He told himself his ex would let him move in by Valentine's Day.

The team agreed the best way to pull Lonnie back was to stop in and see him over the weekend. Not a work-related visit; just stopping by to wish him Happy New Year.

I got into his building and pounded on his door. He was sitting in the dark. The television didn't work, the lights were out, and the only food he had left were honey mustard packets from the convenience store. In one month, he had lost twenty pounds, sold his Link card for crack and beer, and been beaten up on the street again. "I messed up," was the first thing he said. "I need food."

I withheld any lectures and said we'd start working together again on Monday if that was okay with him.

"Um, can you pay my cable bill somehow?" he asked. He had been watching static for the past two weeks.

Lonnie returned to the ACT program for six months, stepping right into his previous routine and decided, again, that he'd had enough therapy and exercise. Without a plan, Lonnie announced he would take care of his own business, for real this time. It was summer, so he figured that would help him take care of business. He started by immediately getting drunk and visiting his ex-wife. This time he left before she called the police. He wasn't violent; he simply wasn't welcome.

Lonnie came back to the program again after two weeks. For all of his horrible choices, he was not a malicious person, but he was deeply ashamed of his mistakes.

Lonnie realized he was stuck with us. He could no longer retreat, so he began coming to my office with complaints about his therapist. I reverted to my standard response.

"We don't talk about someone if they're not in the room."

I'd learned this the hard way when I was new on the job, trying to fix problems when clients came to my office. The team I'd inherited was long gone by the time Lonnie was on the caseload, but volunteering to solve whatever walked into my office hadn't won me any points with the staff.

After my first year on the job, I learned to sit with the anxiety of not fixing everything immediately. I circumvented some of the staff splitting by hiring people who were willing to prove in and let me do the same. We built trust with each other and never forgot two lessons: don't talk about anyone who is not in the room, and don't let anyone split staff—always have proof. The rules applied to everyone—clients and staff alike.

About once a month, Lonnie came to me with complaints about Shannon and his plans to quit the program without any realistic idea how to keep himself afloat in the world. I would call a meeting with Shannon, where we had to handle Lonnie gently, coaxing him to explain why he wanted to leave. We tried to reframe the discussion—nothing was so awful that he should avoid us. We had seen him in and out of jail, psychiatric units, and detox. We had seen him blind drunk, fighting with his pals, and wetting his pants in our waiting room.

"You're a man," Shannon said. "You have that right to go do all of this on your own. But for every right you have, you have a responsibility. If you have a complaint, if there's something you need, you have to say so. If you don't like groups, say so. That's your responsibility as a man to be direct and talk to us face-to-face. There are no rights without responsibilities."

"I'll do it," Lonnie promised after a moment of silence. "I'll stick around, and I'll be a man about it."

A day later I saw Lonnie on my block, walking past the coffee shop. I could see the familiar white-on-red cursive beer logo through the plastic bag hanging from his hand. Twenty-four hours earlier, Lonnie had added to our "rights and responsibilities" discussion a vow that he would also stop drinking again.

I saw him first and yelled a casual greeting. Lonnie recognized me and began to discreetly slide his grocery bag to the side, turning his body to block my view. He acknowledged my greeting and got around the corner as soon as possible.

Lonnie called that afternoon.

"Uh, I want to apologize," he said. "That was rude of me. I should have stopped and said hello when I saw you."

"No problem, Lonnie."

He paused and added, "Uh, Zak. That beer wasn't mine. I was running an errand for this little old lady."

"What beer, Lonnie?"

"Uh, never mind."

He hung up.

At least he didn't deny he was carrying beer. He and his drinking partners chronically told us stories about the "little old lady" for whom they ran errands. None remembered her name or room number. Whoever she was, she drank as much as four men combined.

In the substance abuse group, our therapists confronted the clients about their limited motivation for changing their lives. Sometimes the therapists would have to shove recent history right into the clients' faces.

"You all have been homeless; you think it can't happen again?" Shannon asked once. "How many of you have had to eat out of the garbage?"

This sounds like a cruel question, but our clients had grown used to living at the very bottom of the socioeconomic scale. They understood the unpleasant truth that some people are forced to eat from the garbage, trade sex for food, and break into abandoned buildings to stay warm.

Lonnie, without the requisite guile to protect himself from embarrassment, answered the question honestly, "Well, there was a chicken sandwich that was sitting on top of the fire hydrant once."

A couple of weeks later Lonnie left his wallet, keys, and cell phone at a crack dealer's apartment and came home to find himself locked out of his building. After spending the night in a doorway on the street, he confronted Shannon and referred to our "rights and responsibilities" talk: "I'm telling you what happened. Like you said, 'like a man.' Do you have spare keys to my room?"

He could have told us before he spent the night in the rain, but then he wasn't ready to admit he'd been at the crack dealer's place. That wasn't the image he wanted to present.

Once, as I walked through our waiting room with Yvonne, we overheard Lonnie talking with another client.

"You know, I'm not crazy," he said. "I just faked it for the disability check."

Yvonne, the stern queen bee who could scold and comfort a client at the same time, muttered under her breath to me: "Yeah, right. You wish."

32

Lucius came to us from the state hospital after he had already been discharged and set up at the Aragon Arms Hotel by another program. At twenty-two, he had only worked two jobs since high school—installing carpets and apprenticing in HVAC repair for a total of six months—but he was proud of both. He dismissed the idea of working retail because standing behind a cash register was not masculine. He wanted to be a mechanic but had never driven a car or looked at an engine. As a matter of routine, Lucius refused to answer any direct questions—they were intrusions from which he had to defend himself. I learned from hospital reports that he had attempted to assault his grandparents with a knife and the family had an order of protection against him. He denied this but said there had been spirits in the house, billowing out of his grandparents' bodies and permeating the walls and the furniture. He believed his grandparents were purposely releasing the spirits to haunt Lucius.

Lucius refused to allow any communication between our team and his family.

"I'm a man," he said. "You have a question, you ask me."

I learned later he had lied to his family about which community mental health program he was in. When his mother called the other mental health provider, that agency would, honestly, deny any knowledge of her son, which was what Lucius had told her they would do. During the initial interview, I spent an hour convincing him to sign the treatment agreement forms. He wouldn't sign unless I provided a time-limited period of treatment. In aggravation, I suggested we look at one year and revisit the timeline down the road. I would later regret this. Over that year, he kept the team at a distance, coming to psychiatric appointments but denying there was any reason to take medication. Nothing was wrong. His only complaints were he didn't have a job or a girlfriend. He refused to take meds in front of staff and had no interest in group or individual counseling. He was able to handle his money and made sure his rent was paid every month. He didn't drink, didn't do drugs, and struggled to present a controlled, confident image of himself. When he felt the anxiety and confusion building, he kept his answers to yes or no or refused to speak at all to hide his internal chaos from others.

His walk revealed a delusional self-image. He moved like a three-hundred-pound muscle-bound monster—shoulders back, chest puffed out—that would kill any man who looked at him wrong and could prompt near-orgasmic responses from women who dared to make eye contact. To anyone watching him, he merely looked awkward. His eyes flashed between panic and barely restrained rage, then back again before he would try to force a confident smile. The kid was untethered and struggled to keep anyone from suspecting this.

For weeks at a time, he wouldn't allow anyone in his hotel room, but he would step into the hall to meet us. After a couple of months, he tried to invite Holly inside for a visit with clear sexual undertones. Rebuffed, he became frustrated and asked her directly if he could kiss her. She reported back to the team, and we agreed that, from then on, no one would visit him alone. We kept trying to work with Lucius, but any interaction with him began to present risks for clinicians. He saw every man as a potential physical threat or conquest and every woman as a potential sexual threat or conquest. His paranoia and rage floated toward the surface more frequently and he wasn't doing a good job of masking it.

In the beginning his room had been OCD-level orderly but had grown cluttered. Forks and spoons were lined up on his dresser along with jelly jars and three brands of deodorant. Shoes were kept in a straight row across the middle of the room. His wallet and keys were laid out in some semblance of a geometric pattern, each object separate from the neighboring objects by an equidistant space. A variety of knives were laid out on washcloths, reminding me of surgical instruments, prepped and ready.

Lucius would dump out a glass of water if it had been poured incorrectly. If he saw the imprint of numbers on the side of a Depakote pill, he would throw the pill out. Trying to organize the pills in his med box only confounded him, and to such a degree that all of his Abilify would be in the Monday and Tuesday slots, and all the Depakote would be in the morning slots for the rest of the week. He had been organizing his meds by the color of the pills, which somehow correlated to numbers he had assigned to the days of the week. When we asked him about this, he said he didn't need his meds anyway because they would not address the real problem.

This cyst on his back, Lucius explained, trying to talk some sense into me, was a port where people could plug him in so he could get out of this world. He knew this for sure because he had seen the same thing happen in *The Matrix*.

The Matrix is to the person with paranoid delusions what *Catcher in the Rye* is to the celebrity assassin. The working mythology of the *Matrix* movies provided a justification for the protagonist's drab life: what he sees every day is not reality but only a scrim covering the real world. In the real world, he has special powers, not a psychiatric disorder. The paranoid person identifying with the movie sees that there may be a chance he doesn't actually live in an SRO room on Wilson Avenue, trying to survive off $674 a month.

The voices he hears and the ideas that pop into his head are transmissions from the real world where he is a person of value—where he and his girlfriend both are supermodel martial arts experts chosen to protect the rest of humanity from evil oppression. Of course, the rest of humanity doesn't know this and won't because society has been lulled to sleep with mundane distractions like rent, work, taxes, the internet, and social media. But in the real world, he is the next savior.

By the time I took over Lucius's case from the rest of the team, the paranoid delusions were taking up more of his waking hours and influencing his behavior in more obvious ways. Having been steered away from female staff, he became directly hostile with the guys. Every interaction was about power. He couldn't figure out what our team wanted from him. If anyone was going to be coming to his hotel room every day, it ought to be a woman, not some guy. That, in itself, was suspicious to Luscious.

His delusions broke the flow of reality, and to cover the discrepancy, he would offer up pieces of a narrative describing his unseen powers and who he really was.

"I can't explain," he told me.

"Why can't you explain?"

"I'm not allowed to disclose that."

"Is it complicated?"

"It would be for you."

The USB port on his back needed to be repaired, he said. And once that was fixed, he would be fine.

I was eventually contacted by Lucius's auntie—she'd found my business card in his wallet while he visited her one Sunday. I had to explain why I could not confirm nor deny whether any particular person was working with our program. HIPAA laws prohibited me from discussing clients without their written permission, I told her, but I could talk with people who merely wanted hypothetical advice.

The aunt told me about Lucius, whom she raised as well as she could despite interruptions by DCFS workers and his parents, who had prioritized their crack habits and abused the kid in their spare time. They'd forced him to kneel on dry rice in the corner of the kitchen to atone for the venial sin of spilling milk at the table. When he was still a minor, Child Protective Services had ordered Lucius to live with his auntie until his parents became fit to care for him. They didn't, and he stayed with his auntie until he was an adult, visiting her on weekends even after he moved out. Auntie told me that when Lucius came by the house people got scared because he kept demanding information regarding his parents, who were long gone. I gave her some basic tips on calling the police and asking for a Crisis Intervention Team if needed.

I could never get enough information from Lucius to verify any past abuse, but his hypermasculine demeanor gave me the sense he'd been dealt some, most likely by a man. He perceived any question of his alpha status as a potential sexual assault to defend against. He would rather stab someone than be seen as homosexual. He wasn't going to be a punk for anyone.

After months of knocking on his door every day, of attempting and failing to get him to discuss anything, he declared our time was up. He was done with the ACT program.

"That was our contract," he said. "Goodbye, good luck."

When I came around the next day, he barked at me through the locked door.

"I don't know you, sir! Consider this a request to quit harassing me! Any further attempts to do so will be responded to accordingly, sir!"

The following day he began yelling before I even knocked.

I knew he checked the peephole. His windows faced the afternoon sun, and I could see the shadow blocking the inverted fisheye lens. I heard him walk to the door and walk back. Whenever I was stuck having a conversation through a closed door with an angry, psychotic person, I thought of the gun that person might have on the other side.

On a Monday, the building manager told me Lucius hadn't come back over the weekend. I checked the Cook County Jail's inmate search. He'd been locked up for auto theft, which was not what I had expected.

I went to court the next week and met his auntie. She and the public defender explained that Lucius had walked up to an idling SUV in front of a fast food restaurant on Friday night, slid inside and driven off. He later explained he thought the truck was filled with explosives belonging to Al Qaeda. He said he was going to take the truck over to his auntie's place, but he couldn't explain why.

Lucius was not an ideal defendant. During the arraignment he repeatedly interrupted the judge with one question.

"So, can I have the truck back?"

A man a couple rows back hollered, "That's my truck!"

"You leave your truck running, you are giving up the truck," Lucius yelled to the judge. "That's the law."

"That's my truck!"

"I don't know him, your honor," Lucius said.

Then he pointed me out to the judge.

"I don't know him, either."

Lucius remained in Cook County Jail, extremely psychotic and refusing to take his meds, same as at home. His behavior became so disruptive—demanding an orderliness and privacy that didn't exist in jail—that they sent him to the state hospital, where the environmental stressors—threats of physical and sexual violence—were not so severe. This made sense considering Lucius's raging paranoia. Also, a hospital staff could invest more time in medication management than the jail staff ever could. When his psychotic symptoms decreased, he was sent back to jail where he would refuse his meds again, which eventually sent him back to the hospital. Back and forth he went for nine months, like a ping-pong ball, until a judge accepted time served and ordered probation.

Once Lucius was out, his auntie let him move into the basement apartment of her three-flat on the condition he take his meds every day—nonnegotiable. If he missed one day, he was on the street.

We didn't expect positive results from this arrangement, and we never saw Lucius again.

• • •

Meds suck. Or at least everything that goes with convincing psychotic clients in a broken mental health system to take their meds sucks. It sucks for the staff, and it sucks for the clients. Some clients take their meds with no hassles, either because they understand the negative impact of not taking them or because they have been worn down over the years by clinicians demanding compliance. Others maintain their critical thinking and have no reason to trust case managers they barely know, and they have every reason to distrust the medications they are instructed to swallow. The list of common side effects alone—impotence, high blood pressure, diabetes, high cholesterol, constipation, tremors, dry mouth, dizziness, insomnia, hypersomnia—can make street drugs look like nutrition supplements. The staff, meanwhile, works against heavily fortified barriers in the form of legitimate protests, delusion-fueled rage, and sophisticated or convoluted lies. We try to chip away at those barriers with justifications for coercing our clients to adhere to med regimens that have been forced on them and their whole disenfranchised client population for decades, with, at best, mixed results.

Some clients don't have the capacity to argue with psychiatrists about what medications they should take. Instead they simply decide that all medications are bad. It's when a client settles on that point of view that we start to see the classic nursing home coercion approach to med administration: if you take the meds, you can leave sooner. This prompts the resentful patient to adopt a new treatment goal: I'll do whatever I have to do to get out of here. The problem is that once that client gets out, they follow the obvious logic: I only have to take pills when I'm being held against my will. Now I'm out, I don't have to.

When some clients abruptly refuse all meds—effectively cleaning their system of a heavy regimen of antidepressants and antipsychotics—all of the previously blocked receptors open up and a honeymoon period can follow. Endorphins rampage gleefully through the brain and nervous system like a pack of pit bull puppies off the leash. Being off antipsychotic medications can feel good for a brief while, supporting the person's working thesis: I never needed the stuff in the first place.

In the staff-client battle over medication, almost nothing is trickier than managing a medication regimen when a person is off their meds and the symptoms have taken over. Delusions are convincing and they shift to deflect any argument and absorb any justification as to why one should not take meds. Arguing logic against delusions, logic always loses.

And mania can feel good: heightened creativity, euphoric bursts of energy, and seemingly more efficient thought processes. But mania can also escalate to grandiose, and even destructive, levels, resulting in aggressive behaviors that threaten the client and those around him, sometimes physically. At that point, intervention is difficult at best. In some cases the person comes to believe the pleasurable aspects of their manic episodes are the new norm and may feel no need for any medications until they hit a depressive downswing. There are no hard rules to any of this—the opposite experience can also occur, where the threat of mania is terrifying precisely because that's when bad things happen.

Ultimately, the med game is rigged because the basic human response to the positive effects of any prescribed medications—whether antibiotics or mood stabilizers—is to declare: "I feel better. I don't need this stuff anymore." For many people, that sentiment is confirmed once they stop taking medications because the side effects go away, and that feels pretty good, too. For some, the return of their psychosis, while still a terror, is comforting in its familiarity. When a person believes their psychotic symptoms are special powers or communications directly from God, the medications only get in the way.

33

Turner was drifting away from the ACT program when I took over. I saw him twice during my first few weeks while I was getting oriented, and the team decided to let him go. He didn't want any services from us. He refused his medications and adamantly, but politely, told his case manager from the original ACT crew that he did not want any help with housing. The case manager told him if he didn't take his meds, the team couldn't help him with housing. At the time I thought this was a bit harsh and kind of backward. If we kept him housed, it seemed, we would have more opportunities to keep him on his meds. The ultimatum gave Turner one last chance, and he turned it down. I saw him a few weeks later standing under an El stop to get out of the snow.

"I'm just watching people," he said.

He told me he would rather be homeless than take his meds. I didn't know the details of his case, so I kept my new-guy mouth shut.

Three years later I got a call from one of the state hospitals asking if I remembered Turner. I did. In the hospital he had been a "difficult" patient and had to be court-ordered to adhere to his medication regimen twice in the past year. The state was getting ready to discharge him and they wanted us to take him back.

During the intake interview he wanted to stay in bed, naked under the sheets. I told him I would wait until he was dressed, and we could talk about his discharge.

While I was waiting, a nurse told me, "He's like that all the time. He likes to try to walk around here naked."

Turner denied having any problems other than police harassment and deflected questions about what he had been doing over the last three years. Out of frustration, he signed all the appropriate papers to work with us and suggested I talk to his mother. He remained silent, with a Mona Lisa half smile, through the rest of the interview.

"What's funny?" I asked.

"Nothing."

"Looks like you're smiling."

"Nope. Not me."

I picked him up on discharge day and drove him into the city. We set him up in a hotel where the team had a good relationship with the desk clerks. They could at least monitor Turner's guests and let us know of any problems.

Some of the hotel managers were helpful like this, realizing that every time we showed up to intervene they would be expected to allow some slack for a client's disruptive behavior and, in return, keep collecting their rent money. It was a pretty solid arrangement. When things did go off the rails, we did the heavy lifting. Say we got a call from a hotel—your guy in 312 just shoved all the furniture into the hallway and is swinging a lamp at us, for example—we would come and hospitalize the person and, if necessary, call the police. Meanwhile, the hotel staff was able to keep track of our clients' comings and goings because all tenants had to turn in their keys at the front desk when they left for the day. In that way, the front desk clerks were providing auxiliary monitoring services for us and our clients.

Turner was aware of people watching him and he didn't want to look like a client. Before the audience of the hotel desk clerks, he tried to hold Mariella's hand and walk her up to his hotel room as if they were on a date.

"No, you don't," she said, telling him to go up the stairs first.

At his room, she stood in the doorway, mindful of safety, keeping the door open with her foot.

"I don't want people knowing my business," he said, trying to convince her to come inside.

Mariella noted that Turner had been more and more concerned with the government, the police, and people in general knowing his business. He said he knew things that went back to Biblical instruction, which he would have to enact personally in order to save the world.

Mariella began doing mouth checks to be sure, to some degree, that Turner was actually swallowing his meds. Turner began voluntarily opening his mouth after swallowing his pills rather than hiding them under his tongue or along his gums.

"You don't have to check me," he said. "But I'll let you."

One day Turner used a transparent cup rather than his usual opaque one. When he was done swallowing, Mariella noticed the pills stuck to the inside of the cup. He had been spitting them back into the water as he drank.

When we began having trouble finding Turner, the hotel staff told us he often left at night and wouldn't return until late in the morning, right after Mariella came looking for him. When questioned about this, Turner said he would wander the neighborhood, find a spot, and watch people.

"I'm not bothering anybody am I?" he said.

It was starting to bother us. He also began openly hanging around the parking lot at our office, asking team members which cars they drove and where they lived. His nonverbal responses and distant smile didn't comfort anyone. As Turner's delusions and sexualized behavior became more and more obvious, Mariella suggested he begin seeing me for therapy.

"I think you need to start talking to him," she said. "He's starting to scare me."

Mariella and I began interviewing his immediate family. His mother wouldn't speak to us, but we found a play cousin who had lived with the family. She told us there had been no father in the home per se, only various sperm donors who had stayed for a short time after Turner and each of his siblings were born, before disappearing.

The kids learned their mother's bedroom was open to all. They lived in a basement apartment with a drop ceiling. Turner and one of his sisters made a game of watching mom's bedroom at night, crawling along the solid half of the ceiling, with two-by-four supports, and peeking through the cracks to see who was in there and what they were doing.

The apartment had a revolving-door policy for mom's boyfriends and the "aunts" she brought home. The kids saw sex and violence between sex partners. They coerced the children into performing sex acts. Turner, we heard from one of his play cousins, had been sexually abused by several adults and was beaten by the main boyfriend when he wouldn't comply. The children—Turner and his cousin and her siblings—all replicated the behavior at school and at home. The play cousin described how she remembered Turner as an adolescent sneaking into his mother's bed during the night and staying through the morning. I began meeting Turner for individual therapy sessions while we were still culling the family history. When Mariella convinced Turner to start sessions with me she didn't call it therapy. Instead she danced around the subject of why we were meeting. Turner didn't want to do it. He saw nothing wrong. I would learn later that he believed it was the world that was skewed, not him. I was just trying to assess how dangerous he might be. Like Turner, I didn't think this was therapy, either. He wanted to talk, not to establish any kind of therapeutic relationship, but to see how close he could get to telling his truth without getting in trouble. We had two sessions in my office. After that, he refused to come, and I began visiting him in his hotel room. Despite his reluctance—I suspected he knew he should not be discussing anything real with me—he spoke as if he had to let some of the pressure loose. Turner knew how the world worked, he told me. The problem was other people kept trying to impose their rules on him. The rules other people followed were nonsense—just polite things people said to each other because they were scared of "sex stuff." "The sex stuff isn't like it looks," Turner said. "People are all different."

People were divided into all sorts of categories, he explained, not just male and female. Those categories were just man-made creations, like costumes made of skin that people had to wear. They had little to do with who and what people actually were. All people had currents flowing through them, electrical currents, but solid, a little thicker than water. The currents weren't warm or cool. They were either boiling hot or ice cold, but you couldn't feel them like you could the weather or water from a tap. He could tell whether a person was hot or cold even though there were no physical signs or behavioral cues. These currents were important because "things happened" when specific combinations of sexual currents came together. Turner was reluctant to say what things, but he squirmed in his chair and tried to change the subject. He later explained there were not two genders but six gradations of male and female. Two genders didn't really have sexual intercourse of any kind. If they did, nothing happened. For other genders, when coupled in the right combinations, their genitalia withered away and fell off. If not, then the genitalia were bitten off by the sex partner. But this only happened when specific combinations met, and sometimes required a threesome. He told me an old man he met on the street told him these secrets. He didn't create the rules and he wasn't responsible. He couldn't help himself if he followed these rules. He didn't invent the currents or the genders, but he knew they were true because he could feel their pull. Whenever he shifted from educating me to describing his own actions, a lapse in memory would blur out the details and he would give me a half smile and a shrug.

I warned myself not to get angry and tried to remember the rules of interviewing: be quiet and keep the person talking and be so nonjudgmental that the subject feels you are on his side. The lack of medications in his system may have had something to do with his inability to self-censor. He talked but I could feel how much he didn't want to. He denied any psychotic symptoms, but the delusions were obvious. His construction of gender and sexual roles was clearly psychotic but also appeared to be based on his experience.

"Are there other people who know this stuff?" I asked.

"Maybe. I think so."

"How would you know?"

"I don't know. I'm looking for them."

When he shut down completely, we would stop for the day and pick up again later.

"People don't want to hear this stuff," he said. "It scares them, but it's true."

Although Turner was our client, and we would, ideally, be on the same side, he was frightening. I made a note to myself: the team needed to know if we had to protect others, and ourselves, from Turner.

• • •

Turner said he didn't mind if people didn't believe him. He wanted to be left alone to follow what he knew to be true.

He stopped coming to the office entirely. I would find him in his hotel room early in the morning after he came home from his nightly walks.

"So, where do you go at night?" I asked once.

"I stay in my room."

"No, you don't. The night clerk says you go out and stay out. We've seen you coming back in the morning."

"I get out, get around."

The vaguer his answers became, the more patient I had to be in order to gather some information. "What neighborhood do you go to?"

"I stay around the hotel. There's people out at night."

"People you know?"

"Sometimes."

"What do you do when it's people you don't know?"

"I watch. I stay at the edge of the crowd. I watch over them."

"For what?"

"To make sure nothing happens to anyone."

"What might happen?"

"I don't know. I can't say." He would shrug and smile as if it were all too complicated to explain. I wanted to gather as much information as I could, so I would jump subjects to leave the line of conversation open for later. I met Turner every day in his hotel room, bringing his meds and fishing for information. He emptied his room of all furniture, telling the hotel manager to take it back. He had a television and an electric skillet on the floor. The bed, dresser, and chair were all removed because he wanted to be closer to the ground and away from any loose currents. "You're looking to put me in the hospital," he said, then proudly announced that he had thrown his meds in the toilet. The meds made him unable to feel the currents in people, he said, so that he couldn't read them.

"You want me to walk around like everybody else," he said. "That's not acceptable."

I left. We were done for the day. Turner was not going to say anything more. The next morning, Turner told me he was waiting for the right combination of gender, currents, and sexual partners. He needed two partners, and when he found the right ones his powers would increase, but only after they all had sex. The male partner's penis would shrivel up as he orally castrated Turner. Then the female partner would take on the sexual strength of both men. In exchange, Turner would get the female's power to see more clearly currents and secret genders. "This is theory," he said. "It won't happen."

I was listening closely. But Turner had been hospitalized so many times that he knew when to stop.

"I'm okay," he said. "I have food, shelter, and clothes. I don't want to kill myself."

That weekend the police picked him up for exposing himself in public.

Turner denied it. "I was just scratching myself," he said.

He turned his wrist to show me a set of thinly lined branding marks on his forearm. Three Xs and one diamond all in a row.

"This, I made over the weekend," he said. "With a paperclip and a lighter and cleaned it with iodine. I'm not even gonna explain it to you. The people who need to know what it is, will."

I felt like he was showing me just enough to make me worry, and pulling back so I had no justification to hospitalize him. Turner began riding CTA buses at night. The team suspected he was looking for a target and volunteered to watch him, setting up shifts to track him on foot and by car. I was proud of the dedication and tempted by the idea but ultimately, it would have been a waste of time. We had fifty-nine other clients to see during the day and we couldn't spare any of us to exhaustion from a mental health stakeout. He lived at night and was used to the patterns and rhythms of those hours before the sun comes up. And even if we had any skills to monitor him, we could never guarantee we would be on him every second. I spoke to the State's Attorney's office about Turner's case. We were worried he was building toward committing some physical or sexual violence. In fact we worried he might have already committed some ugly act and we just couldn't find it. Turner had a conviction record for assaulting officers and aggravated battery but no sex offenses. The ASA said his office couldn't step in unless Turner was arrested. Turner began loitering in front of his hotel wearing a string-strap tank top and tight satin shorts, making his sexual arousal obvious to any pedestrians. When I asked him about this he said people were lying about him.

I dropped the subject and drifted to other topics while he stirred a can of chili into his electric skillet.

The antipsychotic medications, he said, took away his powers and he needed them. He said he had to start looking.

"For what?"

"Now I have to find the right people."

"The right people for what?"

"For what I said before. I'll be with them and then I'll be castrated."

There was no breath behind his words. He looked down at his hands, looked away, and checked the corners of the room. Finally he brought his attention back to me, as if he had decided something.

"How do you know someone will castrate you?" I asked.

"I should be able to tell."

"What if they don't do it? Then what?"

"Someone has to. I'll make them, I guess."

"Again," I asked. "Why do you have to do this?"

"It says in the Bible that this is what has to happen. No escaping it. We're gonna die when we do it, I know."

"If you're taking the meds, do you still have to do it?"

"I'm not taking the meds. I don't want to argue it."

"You know I can't let you do this, right?"

"I don't know that. I'm done talking now. If you can't do nothing else for me than the meds, I don't want anything."

"Okay."

I got up and left his room. He went back to the skillet on the floor. Heading down the stairs, I called 911 to ask for assistance with an involuntary hospitalization. He had said the magic words—people were going to die. He knew enough not to directly announce that he would kill himself, or someone else. But given the context of the discussion, I had a valid argument for psychiatric hospitalization. Before the police arrived, Turner came downstairs with a bowl of chili. He looked at me without saying a word. Two squad cars rolled up and he shook his head.

"I knew you were going to do that," he said calmly, like some people just couldn't be helped. The police took him to the closest hospital, one where I had worked closely with the staff. I explained to them that Turner was a priority case that the State's Attorney's Office already knew about and that we were looking for a civil commitment. Our team had built a reputation for taking tough cases, so I hoped if we said we could no longer provide services, the psychiatric unit staff wouldn't argue. I told the attending psychiatrist we would not be taking Turner's case back. No matter how well I documented that Turner was delusional and potentially dangerous, the hospital would not hold him for long. To keep Turner for any real length of time, a psychiatrist would have to be willing to testify that he consistently presented a measurable threat to himself or others. The doctors would have felt more justified in doing this if Turner had been starving himself or stealing cars to run down pedestrians, but on the hospital unit, Turner knew how to behave. He took his meds. He went to groups. He was polite. He kept his delusions to himself. All of this proved to our team that Turner was dangerous because he was able to assess the consequences of his behavior and identify who had the leverage to stop him or punish him for it. I had informed the hospital that we would not take Turner upon discharge. We rarely did this, and I explained thoroughly why we were digging our heels in on this case. So, after two weeks on the unit, Turner was sent to a psychiatric nursing home, one of the few locked facilities in the city. He knew that to get out of there, all he had to do was threaten the staff, which he did. They sent him back to the hospital, which sent him to another nursing home, where he was allowed passes to leave during the day. The mental health system had few, if any, provisions or places for clients like Turner, not until after they committed a crime. We closed his case. I told myself there was little more we could do for him. The team was split. While all were glad to see him go, some believed maybe we could still help him. Ultimately, we were not structured to provide the help he needed without putting ourselves and our program at risk. Maybe we were wrong, and Turner was totally harmless. Maybe I had assessed a false positive, seeing risk where little existed. But the cost of losing that bet would have been too high.

From our assessment, Turner was building toward committing some sort of sexual violence and had begun testing boundaries. He knew they changed depending on his situation or environment—whether in the hospital, team office, nursing home, or his hotel. That his delusions were fixed and pointed toward his goal of increased psychic powers through the sexual mutilation of himself or another person didn't mean he could not control his behavior. He didn't want to get caught and was able to adjust his behavior to survive from one environment to the next.

Without any medications, Turner's delusions would continue to increase in severity until he could not safely assess his odds. Then he would get caught, but by then, he might also hurt somebody badly.

Closing the case, I felt helpless. We couldn't protect Turner from himself, and we couldn't protect others from him. For all of our efforts and worry, we couldn't find a solution.

After a couple of months Turner slipped out of the nursing home and chose to remain homeless. Sporadically, we would see him around the neighborhood, watching people.

34

The simplest definition of a sociopath is a person without empathy. They see the rest of us as objects to be manipulated that can either impede or assist them. Many sociopaths can mimic empathy in order to get by, but that's really just an exercise in cause and effect, a means of manipulating other people for personal gain. They possess the skills to live their lives and achieve their goals despite their lack of empathy.

A sociopath with those skills wouldn't come to the attention of the ACT team because he would be able to get what he wanted from others without getting arrested or hospitalized. A lack of those skills often results in behavior that creates a sort of chronic head-butting contest with society: incarceration, unemployment, substance abuse, and a volatile, or isolated, personal life. "It's the world, not me," the person might say, perceiving himself as perpetually victimized. This combination can lead to depressive symptoms, but those symptoms become secondary—born out of the problems and failures caused by the sociopathic behavior.

No one comes in for therapy saying, "I need help; I don't have any empathy." The sociopath doesn't see the need for treatment unless their complaint is that the world is not responding to them as they wish. This is a common aspect of any person's complaints, but the sociopath perceives the responsibility to be on others to act in a way that does not cause them distress. Without empathy, the understanding of one's own responsibility in the world is terribly skewed. Empathy connects us to each other and prompts us to act in ways that are not logical in a cold cost-benefit analysis.

The person without empathy does not have to be criminal or dangerous, though some clearly can be. But there are plenty of cowardly sociopaths who are very conservative in the cost-benefit analyses and afraid to take the serious risks associated with predatory behavior.

I'm sure there are psychoanalysts and therapists who can show that, given enough time and dedicated work with a person, empathy can be tapped and nurtured as long as it's already in there somewhere. I don't disagree with that, but if there is no empathy to work with, the best we can hope for is that a person leans toward imitating empathetic behavior. Either way, we were a triage unit working with a very different population than those individuals who had the resources to participate in insight-based therapy four times a week.

A person presenting with sociopathic behavior can meet the criteria for a diagnosis of antisocial personality disorder but does not qualify for disability benefits as recognized by the Social Security Administration. Sociopathy is not a mental illness like schizophrenia or PTSD. It's a choice of behavior, one made with an understanding of the difference between "right" and "wrong." The understanding exists, but the person places no value in it.

Our team caught a lot of referrals for clients who fit this diagnosis, but the diagnosis alone would not qualify anyone for ACT. Often the sociopathic behavior at this end of the socioeconomic spectrum is much less effective than at the other end, where the CEOs and politicians reside. For a sociopath, the one consistent criterion for measuring the success or failure of their behavior is always whether or not they got caught.

35

The ability to fake psychotic symptoms for personal gain is a skill that can, and should, be measured during intake assessments. I was getting a lot of practice at this. When the team was running smoothly, I didn't have to jump in on any crisis cases and had more time to hang out on the psychiatric units and interview potential clients.

One young man with a face tattoo that spelled out *Thug* under his right eye had an extensive history of ER visits. He described frequent suicidal ideation but had yet to make an attempt. During the intake interview, Thug said he brought himself to the hospital because he wanted to overdose on his pain meds and needed someone to stop him. He made certain to tell me he really needed his pain meds because he had been in a car accident and suffered chronic, debilitating back pain.

"I gotta apply for Social Security," he said. "I came here because I didn't have any meds."

"Then what were you going to overdose on?"

"I had other pills. I threw them out so I didn't overdose."

I explained the parameters of the ACT program. We would be seeing him every day for a couple reasons: to help him keep to his medication regimen, but especially to reduce any opportunity to overdose.

"We'll make sure you have your meds every day," I promised.

"What if the person with my meds calls in sick?"

"That's why there's twelve of us on the team. We don't miss."

Throughout the interview Thug carried himself with a sense of purpose, straight-backed, with full eye contact. No distractions, internal or external, pulled him from the conversation. He was measuring me up, so I made his options a little clearer.

"If you're working with us and you have a history of trying to overdose, we will hold your meds. We'll make sure you get meds every day, but you won't have enough to kill yourself."

"You gotta give me some of my meds when I get out of here," he said, specifically pointing out the trazodone, phenobarbital, and tramadol the attending psychiatrist had prescribed. "I have bad back pains. I gotta have the benzos, too."

"We'll see you every day and get you your meds."

I wanted to mention that I could see right through his story, but there would be little gain in that. He didn't fit the ACT program and I doubted he would accept my assessment.

I continued comforting him because I believed his story that he wanted to overdose on his psych meds. A couple of years earlier I would have taken his case and given him a chance with us, telling myself to go against my initial assessment because he might be telling the truth, even though I saw no acute symptoms.

"Listen," he said. "I'll be real. Just give me those bottles. I got to make a living. I don't take this shit, but I need to eat."

I explained that I couldn't hand over his meds if he was suicidal, as he claimed, or was going to sell them on the street, as he had just revealed. "You're bogus," he said. "This is weak shit. I don't want you all visiting me. I'll do this shit myself when I get out."

Only after getting burned too many times was I able to eliminate malingerers. Since ACT was seen—informally I believe—by the rest of the community mental health system as the container for all difficult cases, the referrals we received were often poorly thought out and terribly inappropriate.

• • •

Another potential intake was a man who had apparently attempted suicide by jumping out of a third floor window, fracturing his ankle. He was homeless, and informed the ER workers that voices were telling him to kill himself. I met him on another psych unit. Coming down the hall, I didn't notice the man, standing against the wall and tucked between two disheveled patients who were falling out of their hospital gowns. I should have noticed him, wearing a newsboy cap and standing at full attention. He stepped forward and introduced himself.

"Are you Zak? I'm Spencer."

He shook my hand hard and held eye contact, not trying for intimidating, but open to whatever I had to offer. Even with the air cast on his foot, he strutted, adding one hop every few steps to keep stride with me.

"I fractured my ankle like two weeks ago," he said as we looked for an empty office. Once we found an available room, Spencer took off his hat and folded his hands over his stomach. He looked like a working man who had accumulated a beer belly while the rest of his body had managed to work off the calories. His forearms were cabled with muscle and tagged with homemade tattoos. I went into the ACT spiel, describing what we do and why we do it, then asked Spencer what he thought he needed. He explained that he was born and raised in Chicago and had been homeless ever since he came back up from Kentucky in the spring. He was quick to show me his Social Security statements and had all of his paperwork organized into a file folder rolled up under his shirt. While he told me about the depression that crushed him every so often, I waited for a chance to discuss his criminal record. He needed an apartment, he said, and the hospital worker had told him I would be able to help. The hospital workers often told their patients we had apartments all rent-free and ready to go, a lie that was either a mistake or meant to motivate the patient to work with us when they left the hospital.

"We do help people find apartments," I said, "but I don't want to be wasting your time and money. These landlords want money to do background checks and there's no refunds. So, if they look you up in the system, what are they going to find?"

"Just some old stuff."

"Sure, but it depends on what it is. Some of these places don't mind a murder conviction, but anything that looks like arson or prostitution, they say no."

He was offended that I'd picked two potential freak convictions.

"No, no. Nah, nothing like that. I got an old home invasion that I did fifteen years for."

I played dumb. He expected me to stop questioning him once he named the charge and conviction.

"Burglary?" I asked.

"No, home invasion. There's a big difference."

"What's the difference?"

"Home invasion is when the people are in the house. Burglary is when nobody's home."

Spencer gave details about the job, told me the house had been right at the edge of Uptown, along Marine Drive.

"You just picked a house at random?"

"No. I had a guy who used to be in the business, and he knew who the people were and what they had in the house. He's not in the business anymore. He's down South, retired."

"How did you get caught? He turn you in?"

He looked a little shocked and then laughed it off. "No, he would never. I was so high I must've let the neighbors know. The police were waiting for me when I walked out the front door. But the family never woke up."

"How did you break your ankle?"

"This time?"

"Yeah."

He smiled, proud. "Ah, I got a lady who lets me stay with her. Her boyfriend came home when he wasn't supposed to the other week. I had to go out the window. She'll take me back. He's a long-distance trucker, gone most of the month."

"Good. Because I got to tell you, you don't qualify for ACT."

"Why not?"

"Listen, the people I work with are more like everyone else on this unit, right? You think you fit in here?"

"Well, there's one girl I can talk to."

"Yeah, one. But everyone we work with is functioning at a much lower level than you. Look, you're able to perform pretty organized crimes and know when to get out of a dangerous situation, right? I hate to tell you, but you're too much on the ball to work with us. And you've been able to do this without taking any psych meds at all, right?"

"I took them in prison."

"What did they do for you?"

"I felt a little calmer."

"Sure, and you know they do that just to keep things quiet. Lot of people sell the pills in there, yeah?"

"I did when I wanted to. But outside, I never took any."

I wanted to disengage gently, greasing the rails for my exit. We talked a little more and I found out he had another woman in the neighborhood he could stay with. We assessed that he couldn't have it too bad if he had a couple women willing to put him up.

"I couldn't find that second broad the night I came here," he said.

I gave him my card. "If things get bad for you again, give me a call and I can hook you up with another program at the agency."

As we were walking out the door, he made one more feeble attempt to bond, patting me on the back, "Well, you seem to be doing a good job. At least you've got a job. A lot of us don't, bro."

I was proud to tell the hospital staff and the attending psychiatrist I wasn't going to take Spencer's case. Jumping out the window can sound insane, but it was a decision that measured a possible suicide against a probable homicide when the husband came home.

• • •

A new staff member and I interviewed the wife of a potential client being referred to our program by a therapist within our agency. The client, they said, was going to be closed because no one could work with him. I agreed to give this guy another chance because I had been getting some complaints from other supervisors for refusing several referrals that were not appropriate for us.

The husband was in the hospital because he'd recently had what the wife called "an episode" and threatened her with a baseball bat. So we went to the apartment to talk to the wife first.

The wife said she hardly left the apartment due to anxiety and chronic back and leg pain. She took care of their rabbits, seven in all, whose cages took up most of the kitchen.

"We love our rabbits," she said. "Eric has threatened me, but never the rabbits."

Eric was in the hospital at least once a month. He would ask to be hospitalized whenever he blew his temper.

"He's done the same thing to his mother," Eric's wife said. "Said he'd set fire to her while she was asleep some night. He never did. From all the times here, the police know him well. He calms down as soon as they show up."

Eric's mother stayed in the back room of the house, past all the rabbits. She wouldn't speak to us and didn't want us coming back there. I had fleeting thoughts of Eric in the back room, doing his Anthony Perkins *Psycho* impersonation, as if this was a trick he liked to play on case managers.

The wife interspersed her complaints about her husband with proclamations of their love for each other and their shared faith in the Unification Church.

"He's a good man," she said. "We've been together for so long, I don't want to leave. My family cut me off anyway because of him. They said if I stayed with him they wanted nothing to do with me. He's had a million case managers. Whatever you do, don't send a woman case manager here alone, especially if I'm not here. He's inappropriate."

Eventually, Eric's mother came out and inspected us before climbing back over the rabbit cages and into her room. Eric's wife whispered that her mother-in-law was a bitch. She said Eric never really hit his mother; he only had temper tantrums.

We visited Eric in the hospital the following day.

"He's doing much better this time," one of the staff told us. Eric strutted down the hall toward us with another nurse in tow, like the psychiatric unit was his corporate office and the nurse was his personal assistant. He looked like a former bodybuilder who didn't make the height requirement for competition. We sat down in the baby-blue Isolation Room, pulling chairs around the rubber-mattressed bed frame bolted down in the center of the floor. A one-way mirror allowed a sightline into the quiet room from the nurses' station.

"What brought you to the hospital?" I asked Eric.

"I get symptomatic and start yelling," he said. "I'm bipolar."

"Who do you yell at?"

"My wife, mostly. See, I'm Mexican and I was spoiled by my mom. She spoiled me. I got used to getting what I want, so when I don't, I yell and scream."

He delivered this admission through a huge smile.

"I yell at my wife. I threaten her a lot."

"Did you want to come to the hospital?"

"Nooo."

"How did you get here?"

"She called the police after she locked me out. The police been taking me to the hospital most times."

"Did you yell at the police?"

"I can't help myself with my wife. She gets me so mad."

They had been arguing about dinner: who was going to make it and who was going to buy it. They were both living off disability.

"I want to get my way," he said, still smiling. "Sometimes I'm like a little boy."

"So did you yell and scream at the cops?"

"No."

"Did you threaten them?"

"No."

"But you didn't want to come to the hospital? Why didn't you yell at them?"

"It wouldn't have worked."

"Okay. So, you only yell at people when you think it will work?"

"Yeah."

"You didn't yell at the police because you didn't think it would work?"

He agreed again, impatient now.

"Then that's not mental illness," I said. "That's not your symptoms. That's you being a bully. I'm going to tell you about our rules. None of that is allowed. If you're going to work with our team, as soon as you yell at anyone, as soon as you make threats, we will kick you out. I don't care if we're in the car going down Lake Shore Drive. I will kick you out right there. I'm letting you know now that screaming and threatening don't work with us. Understand?"

"Yeah."

We shook hands, agreeing we had a deal. I suspected he would test it. We kept talking, covering sections of the intake interview as a friendly discussion rather than an interrogation. I found him repellent, felt the urge to back away during the interview, and hoped he would refuse to work with us.

On my way out, the hospital staff expressed their relief that we would be working with him. For all of his repeat visits to the psych unit, all the threats against himself and others, the staff had to really squint to see any progress: "He only had to go on restriction once for exposing himself to a nurse."

Tasha, the new team member accompanying me, had just joined ACT and was still learning how we operated. I told her I didn't think Eric would last long with us. The rules I gave him were the rules for any client, but I only spelled them out to suspected malingerers who blamed their violence on psychotic symptoms. I didn't think the guy was mentally healthy, but I didn't see any psychosis, either. I probably should have refused the case, but I had refused a string of recent cases from other agency programs—programs I resented for giving us such lousy referrals—so I figured I'd give Eric a shot. It was also a way to check myself since there was always the chance that my own feelings were getting in the way of assessments. But part of my brain knew I was setting myself up for the bureaucratic aggravation of justifying myself if I had to close the case. Eric's wife called me that night, asking if I could get her some benzodiazepines. She didn't like her psychiatrist and Eric had stolen her meds before he went into the hospital. She wanted either Xanax or Valium; she wasn't particular. Later in the week, Eric was discharged from the hospital, and I visited him at home. He opened the door wearing a karate gi tied with a white belt. Instead of a greeting, he made an announcement.

"I have good news. I have a lot of respect for you."

I suspected he believed I would challenge him on his behavior, so he was going to cycle through the typical sociopath approaches to relationships: intimidation or ingratiation. If he couldn't scare me, he would make like we were pals. This was a sadism of bureaucracy on a personal level—people were either stronger or weaker, dangerous or helpless. He was trying to size me up.

"What style do you study?" I asked, gesturing to the sleeve of his gi.

"Oh, general."

I tried to sound neutral. "You have a GED in martial arts?"

I saw a cloud pass his face. That was not the response he expected. I was screwing up, letting my hostility show. He hadn't caught it yet, but I didn't want him to see that he could provoke a reaction out of me.

He recovered and shifted positions, drifting into a litany of complaints as to how unfairly the world treated him. His father was never good to him; his brothers all have good jobs; he has to support his mother; his wife picks on him; people in the neighborhood pick on him, too. On top of all that, he said, he had been accused of rape by some girl who worked at the video store and her boyfriend was coming around making threats.

"But they had no DNA!" he yelled. "They can't prove anything happened and the police don't believe the girl anyway because we had consensual sex."

The wife giggled as Eric's rant grew more animated. I asked why she was laughing.

"Oh, he gets like this."

"I never do any sex stuff," he said. "I don't do anything; people just pick on me. These Latin Kings beat me up 'cause someone said I exposed myself to their mother. I never did it, but they beat me up anyway. In the hospital I did show it to one of the therapists, though."

Eric kept listing—and denying—accusations against him. I could feel my face getting warm. I focused on one of the rabbit cages behind his shoulder just to distract myself.

"I don't believe anything you say," I told him when he stopped for a breath. "You said you never exposed yourself, but then you said you did in the hospital."

"That wasn't my fault. She was wearing tight pants. You could ask the cops who pick me up all the time; they know me."

Maybe the cops who responded to his calls found it easier to transport him to the hospital than to write up reports. Some cops believe that anyone who appears to have a mental illness is ineligible for criminal prosecution.

"I don't got no record!" Eric bellowed. "You go look."

I did want to check his criminal record and said I would. His wife laughed hysterically at this. Maybe this was how they entertained themselves, screwing around with social workers. I felt my perspective shift as if I were rising out of my own head a little bit. My body became light, my face warm. This was not a good sign. I hadn't prepared myself to be mindful of my own anger before heading over to Eric's house. I'd been running from one thing to the next all day, an invincible to-do list swirling in my head. I was low on patience and in no mood to be manipulated by the most annoying couple on my caseload. Then Eric said one of the most infuriating things any client ever said to me: "I'm sensitive, like a little kid," he said. "My feelings get hurt easy, then I want to hurt someone else's feelings."

I let him keep talking but missed a bit of the conversation because a flood of pure adrenaline was drowning my senses. I took some deep, quiet breaths and countered every bogus claim he made, pointing out each juncture where one of his decisions collided with the fact of personal responsibility that he was so desperate to avoid. I told him we would keep talking on Monday and he was going to have to change some things.

When I was done, I let myself out. I didn't want to take his case. I should have turned him down the day I met him. Heading to the car, I could feel my hands shaking. My legs were weightless, from hips to ankles. Talking with Eric had set off all sorts of alarms, and my body wanted to do something to alleviate the adrenaline flood. There was nothing to do but start back to the office, where I would begin looking into his criminal record. I suspected he wouldn't be on parole, probation, or any sex offender registry. Clinically, I couldn't close his case yet. Driving back, I figured I'd blown it. I had recently talked to one of the case managers about checking his temper, how to visualize all the hot blood that went right to the surface of his skin and then draw it back down to the cool center with each deep breath. In two short meetings, Eric had tried to befriend me, impress me, intimidate me, and go for the pity play. There's no hard rule that a person has to go through the manipulation cycle in any particular order. If there is a rule, it's that the person will do whatever works most often for him.

I read Eric's old intake. He knew what to say to be accepted into a mental health program. He said he wanted a new psychiatrist, a therapist, and maybe neurological testing due to an alleged head injury. He also wanted group counseling and vocational training. The priority, he said, was to stop going to the hospital, but I suspected that his hospital trips would, in his mind, contribute to a not-guilty-by-reason-of-insanity defense if he was ever charged with anything serious.

I reviewed the referral paperwork again to see if I could console myself. Maybe he wasn't dangerous, and I was overreacting. I found, again, that Eric's goal for therapy was to discuss his "weird sexual stuff." That would be fine if his fantasies were not about hurting people, but from what I had already seen, he just wanted a noncritical audience to share his sadistic fantasies with. From the session notes, it appeared his therapist wasn't fond of challenging his clients. I figured I could keep Eric on our caseload for a few months, long enough to actually get a diagnosis. Or maybe before that he would decide that the ACT was cramping his lifestyle and bail out. I was certain that he'd noticed my slip in composure. I would have to start drawing boundaries again for him on Monday. At the office, I gave the team an update and said no one would deal with Eric but me. No one argued to take the case. Friday afternoons were quiet; everyone was tired and finishing paperwork. Clinicians turned off news radio and blasted their iPods while typing out their service notes.

Closing up for the day, Stella came into my office.

"He's here."

"Who?"

"The guy."

Eric now wore a down jacket over his gi. "I'm having a crisis," he said. "My wife is going nuts."

"I just saw you an hour ago. What happened?"

"Well, she doesn't have her meds."

"At your house, she told me she did."

"Well, basically, she's taking mine."

"So, what's her crisis, then?"

After a long pause, he said, "I got another card up my sleeve."

I tried to look as bored as possible. "What?"

"I don't want to work with the ACT. I want to keep my own doctor. You're fired. I want my paperwork back."

"Okay."

I had a folder with his Social Security statements and hospital discharges. I slid the folder over to him. He waited for an argument from me. I waved him to the door.

"You can go, then."

He did, smiling. He had gotten what he wanted, but I think he had expected me to fight more diligently to keep his case.

After he left, I checked his record—he wasn't on parole or probation or any sex offender registry. I later found out he had no criminal record at all. That didn't necessarily mean he was a harmless person. Maybe he just hadn't been caught yet.

36

I knew Cory by sight only, a wiry little man with an Abe Lincoln beard who performed his Madonna impressions in the dayroom. Agency staff viewed Cory as a harmless kook. He wasn't in our program, but a therapist in the agency referred Cory to ACT, so I sat down with him for an hour.

Worried by the recent media attention on sex offenders in nursing homes, Cory claimed the police would knock on his door at any minute.

"I went to prison one time," he said with the urgency of the wrongly condemned.

I knew enough to not ask, "What did you do?" because the only response would be, "Nothing." So I asked, "What did the cops accuse you of?"

Twenty-five years earlier Cory had been convicted of raping a seventy-year-old bedridden woman while he was visiting his mother in a nursing home. I asked Cory for specifics: Who called the police? What did the woman say? How did you know her? Were you even in the room? He didn't flatly deny the rape but equivocated away any pertinent details. He said he didn't really remember what had happened when he was in the woman's room. He did three years in Dixon Correctional Center "because of what people said happened." He had been treated like some criminal thug.

"You're not on the sex offender registry," I said. "What are you worried about?"

"That they're going to blame me for something else."

"Have you done anything else?"

Cory explained that he had been arrested twice for exposing himself to children.

"But the judge said it was a misdemeanor one time and the other time the girl scared me, he said. "She came right in the bathroom! I was scared!"

He gave me a tentative what-can-you-do grin, trying for haplessness and outrage simultaneously. Cory assured me he had done nothing improper since the last time he was arrested, and even then, he hadn't done anything because the kid had barged right into the restaurant's bathroom.

"So, when were you wrongly accused?"

"All of them."

"The old woman in the nursing home?"

"I don't want to talk about that."

If he didn't want to talk about it, he'd say he couldn't remember. Cory turned to faux-bashful mush when asked about the acts that led to the convictions.

"I told you just about all of them."

There was a difference between "just about all" and "all."

"So what about the kids?" I asked.

"The one surprised me. She walked right in while I was getting changed."

I let that slide and waited a couple of moments.

"So if you want therapy," I asked, "what are the goals? What do you want to accomplish? Are you worried about children walking by you?"

"No. I want to not worry about the police."

I asked Cory to describe his worry a little more concisely. He met no other ACT criteria for housing: psychosis or alcohol or drug use. From his own account, the worry was not keeping him from managing any of his responsibilities. No symptoms of depression or anxiety impeded his life.

"I don't want to be arrested," he said.

"Who does?" I said. "Did you do anything you could be arrested for?"

"No. But I didn't before, either, and they arrested me anyway. Those kids lied about me."

"Are there chances some kid is going to lie again?"

"I stay away from them all."

I didn't like the answer, but I kept prodding: What did he do during the days? Who did he socialize with? I justified the scrutiny of Cory by saying I didn't know anything about him and might be able to help if I knew his daily routine. I returned again to a timeline of arrests, probation, and probation violations, asking for insubstantial details as well as what he thought could have possibly happened. I may have sounded overly confused, but I eventually led Cory back to his offenses.

Again and again he omitted his own actions and replaced them with his version of his victim's intentions. He said people lied about him because they didn't like him or because they misunderstood what he did.

"What did they misunderstand?"

"Nothing!"

According to his own self-report, Cory had no urges or fantasies regarding children. He had been framed and saw no reason to change his behavior. His distress was not that he had these urges or might harm a child, but that he would get arrested again and he wanted someone to soothe this anxiety. I declined his case.

• • •

I went to a hospital in Evanston to assess a former client of the agency named Tom. I had never met him, but his records noted he had been "difficult," threatening staff and other clients in art therapy classes. There was no mention of violence, only threats.

Tom spoke eloquently and easily about his abusive childhood. He listed his past psychiatric diagnoses as schizoaffective disorder, antisocial personality disorder, and intermittent explosive disorder. Of the first diagnosis, he said, "I just act weird sometimes," but the examples he provided were affectations and not symptoms: "I would go to work in a smoking jacket sometimes or I would carry my cat around in a baby sling like I was nursing."

Of the antisocial personality disorder, Tom said, "I just don't care about other people."

Intermittent explosive disorder is, according to the *Diagnostic and Statistical Manual of Mental Disorders*, "characterized by discrete episodes of failure to resist aggressive impulses resulting in serious assaults or destructions of property."

Tom said this happened quite a bit.

"So, with the intermittent explosive disorder," I asked. "What happens when you get symptomatic?"

"I go off and want to kill someone for the slightest thing."

"Have you gotten violent with people?"

"It has happened where I've wanted to."

"What's the situation? What's going on when this happens?"

"When someone gets pushy."

"What do you consider 'pushy?'"

"You know, when someone pushes me."

"Like what?"

"Just when someone pushes me. You know."

"I don't know. What does it take to push you?"

"I get aggravated."

"What aggravates you?"

I kept pushing, but he didn't get symptomatic with me.

Tom had spent the last few months moving from one homeless shelter to another, appearing for intake interviews at community mental health programs and emergency rooms and claiming he was suicidal. At his most recent ER intake, he'd said he "wanted to walk into the lake and drown myself like Sylvia Plath." Literary misattribution aside, he knew his survival depended on staying out of the shelters. His physical appearance—scrawny and White—made him a target in the church basements where thirty men slept together on foam mats.

He had done prison time but said, "I'm not comfortable telling you what for. I don't trust you yet."

I informed Tom that I could not make a decision about helping him find housing unless I knew why he had been convicted.

"I'll tell you if you shut the door," he said. He didn't want people in the hospital to know his business and I suspect he wanted to see if I was willing to shut myself in a room with him. I closed the door.

"I was on an adult chat room—as far as I know," he said. "I didn't do anything wrong. The cops took me down outside this restaurant. I guess they figured that was a safe place to do it. They didn't want me to fight them. I pleaded guilty just to get it over with."

The more he talked, the more his story shifted and contradicted itself. He claimed his criminal conviction had absolutely nothing to do with what actually happened. He was just clicking around on an adult porn site and something strange happened with his computer. When I pushed for clarification, he said, "I don't know. I can't remember." All he knew was that he was smoking a joint in the park and plainclothes cops swarmed him. He alleged that this was a sting operation of some sort. The cops accused him of setting up a meeting with some girl. He claimed they raided his apartment and took his computers. The stories didn't match up and, in the gaps between, his memory simply failed him.

If I were to believe Tom's story, he did three years in prison for innocently signing into a chat room. When I got back to the office, I checked his previous intakes. Tom had told one clinician he was injured while serving in the first Gulf War. He told me he had two master's degrees, in biology and chemistry. No matter how I looked at the conflicting histories, the timelines didn't work. He might have done both of these things, but I doubted he did either.

I documented the interview, checked his criminal record—he did have a conviction for a sex crime against a child, but not for the internet stuff he had told me about—and opened and closed the case. I cited his sex offender status and lack of psychotic symptoms as the basis for the decision and made sure all of this was in the agency records now. I wasn't going to help him build an insanity defense if he ever got arrested again.

• • •

Not all sociopaths, or persons with antisocial personality disorders, are dangerous. Some easily measure the cost and benefit of being a responsible citizen, spouse, parent, or employee and are able to adjust their behavior to meet societal norms. Those who do not, end up causing a disproportionate amount of pain to those around them. They do this because, without empathy to impede them, they approach everyone in their orbit with the same question: how far can I push this other person to my benefit? For most people the equations determining interpersonal boundaries are a matrix of social mores, self-perceptions, emotions, and ideals we each learn throughout our lives. Among those factors is our own empathy—the ability to understand and feel another's pain. For a person without any empathy, the variables in the equation are minimal: can they get what they want at an acceptable cost?

We're socialized to think the best of others and, by extension, ourselves. By attributing our own empathy to a person who doesn't have any, we fail to see the volitional monster in front of us. It doesn't work to superimpose our values, desires, and motivations onto those of a sociopath because his are far less nuanced. And that distortion is amplified by our natural tendency to believe we can fix such people. We might want to believe a rapist is sick. How could a rational person do such a thing? Part of our work demanded that we differentiate between sick and evil.

• • •

Compared to other programs, ACT might have caught referrals for a disproportionate number of sociopaths. Some were severely psychotic, others were not. When the psychosis was severe enough to impair most factors of a client's life, we could not diagnose the antisocial behavior until the psychotic symptoms decreased.

We had one little man who claimed to have been a reverend

in the past. While his old storefront church was long gone, he still ranted religious ideations in a melodic baritone. He didn't want any interventions like medications or psychiatrists. If God thought he had a problem, God would fix it.

The reverend would steal to eat, which sounded reasonable to us. Theft was a necessity at the very bottom of the socioeconomic ladder, not a personality disorder. Still, we advised against it.

Several weeks of minor thefts and foul hygiene passed before he accepted the idea that God might be telling him something was wrong. Otherwise, he thought, he would have an apartment, a stocked refrigerator, and all the fine clothes he wanted. Maybe God sent the ACT team as a means for him to get what he wanted out of the world, we told him. Maybe God sent us to that hospital for a reason. He agreed and allowed us to find him a hotel room.

He was actually a charming and entertaining person, sweeping through the office with a cape and a fedora, a swirl of scarves and padded headphones over his ears.

"They're to hear the music my mama played me when I was in the womb," he said. "I've been an avatar of music since I was a baby."

The reverend never stopped talking. His tangential thoughts and loose associations could tire out any clinician, but as his medications took effect, he became an example of how psychosis and sociopathy are not mutually exclusive. As his symptoms subsided, more threatening behaviors came to the surface. We began collecting complaints from his landlord. He was bothering women in the building, knocking on doors, slipping notes into mailboxes. We had a talk and he agreed to leave the women alone. Then notes started coming to the women in the office. Disorganized and scribbled across ripped magazine pages without any sense of organization or of the page's boundaries, the letters alternated proclamations of love and demands for attention. The demands quickly shifted to threats.

The reverend became a stalker. The letters became vicious threats, rubber-banded to horror novels he stole from the thrift store. The threats became verbal. He dropped off packages of stolen books and DVDs for the female staff, each one wrapped in psychotic-scribble notes.

I sat down with him to give a warning. Undeterred, he let me see who he was for the first time.

"They all bitches," he said. "They never say they want it. I make 'em take it whether they want it or not. I'm a man. I do what I want when I want. But I understand. You gotta play the game like you don't know this."

He agreed to knock it off but didn't, so we closed his case. He tried coming around a few more times and we warned him again: any further contact from him and we would call the police.

We started filing criminal complaints. When he slipped into the building, we would force him back out and call 911 while crowding him back toward the door. He wasn't going to fight, only scream to see if we would back up.

"You call the police on me, punk-ass bitch!" he yelled at a therapist. "I want them here! I ain't scared of no police. I'll fuck them up, too."

The reverend always ran away before the police showed up. He only recognized power. Control belonged to whoever could make other people change their behavior. When he was unchallenged, he believed he had power. Unchallenged, he did have power. We could change that dynamic by calling the police because he didn't want to get arrested, and that proved he wasn't crazy. Adjusting one's behavior to avoid arrest is a sane thing to do. The reverend wasn't able to make that decision without medication, and we hadn't been able to diagnose his aggressive behavior until the meds had kicked in. Once the psychosis was gone, we saw his true character.

Sometimes our team worked for months to help a client curb their acute psychotic symptoms only to learn that they were, beneath the psychosis, a legitimate threat to us. The reverend liked that power and we had to revert to triage rules to protect ourselves first. We could not provide therapeutic services to someone who enjoyed hurting others. We have no pills for that.

37

Some days I would shut my office door and have to lie on the floor. The muscles around the L4 and L5 vertebrae would slam themselves tight and my body would start curling up, taking my legs out from under me. I figured it was nothing more than old injuries that never quite healed.

As a guy who'd humped furniture for a living for several years, I'd had my back go out on the job more than once, dropping me to my knees in someone's driveway. When I was a kid, the old-timers in my family bragged about ignoring injuries. My grandfather had given me what he thought was great advice, based on personal experience. "You hurt yourself picking up something heavy, pick up something heavier right after that," he told me. As a kid, I never pieced that together with the fact that the man had to use a cane to walk around and couldn't climb up a flight of stairs.

As an adult, I did keep trying to lift more and more weight, especially now that I wasn't doing manual labor. My hours at work were getting longer, I was adding more staff and more clients, and we kept expanding ACT to offer new therapy and life skills programs, a food pantry, and an emergency clothing supply. Beyond that, I had started a private practice, seeing a few clients a week in a rented office in the bank building on Lawrence and Broadway.

I told myself I'd always had a bad back and that it was no big deal. I remember looking in the mirror and seeing my back making a little S-shaped jog to one side as if I had been yanked out of alignment. But that was when I was carrying furniture up and down back porch stairs six days a week. I wasn't lifting anything heavier than a coffee cup now.

During my last semester of social work school I'd had an epidural. I blamed the dog. I would take her running in the morning and slipped on the ice once. I told myself that I had just reactivated an old injury and forced myself to push on. Attendance requirements in school were strict and I was already on the border, so I dragged myself to class and laid on the floor.

One day, a young woman in class said, "You actually look green." I hadn't considered that I could turn green from pain. Once I could no longer physically sit in a chair, I accepted defeat and went to the doctor for some painkillers and the epidural, which set me straight again, until ACT.

Now my bad back terrified me. I caught myself asking the questions we ask when we're in chronic pain: When will this go away? What if it keeps getting worse? Anxiety pushed my answers to catastrophic places. If I can't work, I'll lose my job. I would have to go on disability. I would not be able to support myself. I would lose everything, which would cause my back to tighten up even more.

I realize now, as I write this, that I had other problems besides my back. I had acclimated myself to sleeping lightly so I wouldn't miss emergency calls in the night. Even with no emergency, most mornings I would spring out of bed in a hazy panic.

I remember one morning when I shot straight up out of sleep and blurted, "Jamil's gotta get his fingers cut off today!"

I thought this was normal. I told myself anyone who said I was working too hard was simply not working hard enough themselves. I just had to keep going forward and find a way to not collapse. That plan finally went to shit when a tiny woman named Erin approached me at a conference after I gave a presentation.

"You're in pain, aren't you?" she said.

"Sure." I tried to shrug off my alarm that she could see into me.

"I might be able to help," she said.

I was expecting to hear some sort of New Agey meditation or yoga-type pitch, but Erin described her work so plainly that she appeared not to be selling it, like she was holding something back. The Grinberg Method, she said, was a type of bodywork developed by some Israelis meant specifically to address trauma that gets stored in the body. The first session was free.

She asked me what I did to relax. I could only visualize a pack of cigarettes and a diet Mountain Dew. Those, I expected, didn't really count. But I had nothing else. My life was pretty austere, and I thought this Grinberg Method sounded luxurious—but not in a good way. Giving myself a break like that seemed like some decadent self-care measure.

My first session was in Erin's house, and I was suspicious. She had me strip and lie face down on a massage table in the otherwise empty back bedroom, which didn't really relax me. When she started working on my back, I was not terribly impressed. It felt at first like a regular massage. But then I seemed to slide down into a tunnel—a nice, dark, comforting place. I saw things in the dark. A sort of psychedelic zodiac pinwheel. A diorama stage set that had something to do with the old newspaper columnist Mike Royko. I saw myself sailing in the air along a cliff's edge. Vivid images I was certain I could grab with my hands.

By the end of the session I was unconscious. To this day I don't know whether I passed out or simply fell asleep. Erin threw a blanket over me, shut off the lights, and left me alone for a few minutes. When she came back, I heard the click of the doorknob turning and I launched myself off of the table, totally confused as to where I was and why some stranger was letting herself into my apartment. She was polite about this. I wondered if others responded to the experience the way I had, but she didn't say.

I came back the next week and we continued. Even after a year of sessions, I wasn't sure how I felt about the whole process. But something extreme was happening. My body was somehow realigning itself. The pain was gone, and I noticed my posture and gait had straightened out. Other aches and pains came and went. Over time I learned the pain in my body had been functioning as a kind of trauma-alert system, signaling some confrontation in front of me that I was dreading—firing a staff member, trying to find housing for a client by the end of the day, confronting a client's drug dealer waiting in the parking lot. I was proud of this discovery and started connecting dots. For example, when I suspected one of my staff was committing Medicaid fraud, my back hurt like I'd been stuck from behind with an icepick. But once I made the decision to investigate, the pain went away. This old injury might be useful, I thought, another assessment tool, this one for my own self.

I was learning how stress and trauma, when avoided or dissociated, morphed into physical pain signals. I just didn't think that, like every other human, I was susceptible to it. Soon after, I tried going to therapy, a little scared of what I might discover about myself. It wasn't exactly revelatory at first, mostly false starts. But I felt physically better and kept working at my usual pace.

38

SPRING 2009

We got the announcement that our housing subsidies would be cut off in thirty days. This was a problem. If I were doing an assessment while a client was in the hospital and facing homelessness upon discharge, the money for housing allowed me to have the client's rent ready by the discharge date.

If I had to interview people in the hospital and convince them to work with us, I needed to be able to offer a concrete solution to a basic problem right away. Telling a person, "We can help you, but you'll have to stay in a homeless shelter for a while," felt awful and wasn't the way we could prove in with any client. We had to demonstrate that we could help them, not just promise that we could.

We needed our own emergency housing—a couple of SRO rooms where we could move someone in whenever we wanted without being dependent upon state money. A client could stay in the emergency apartment while they were waiting for their next check or for their benefits to kick in.

I wrote up a proposal for the agency and received a clear "nope" in return. They said it was too expensive, but if I could find a way to fund the emergency apartments, they would approve adding them to our program.

Our caseload had doubled in size in three years. New clients and new staff were coming in and we had room to be creative. We had already added things to the program—the Health and Wellness Program, Big Shop, a cooking class, a food pantry, a clothing closet, and a microlending program—that accounted for the little bit of petty cash we had. If we wanted emergency housing we were going to have to find the money ourselves.

I pitched the idea to the team and, understandably, they were not thrilled about becoming fundraisers. We had enough to do just balancing the ongoing crisis of the team caseload and keeping up with the billing notes required by the agency and the state. But we agreed we would throw some parties to raise the money. Big assistance came from the drug reps who made regular visits to the team. Drug reps worked for pharmaceutical manufacturers and were typically friendly, attractive women whose job was to create relationships with psychiatrists and clinicians and push the medications they were selling. A couple of drug reps trying to sell us on new medications took over the party planning. They called in favors for items to raffle and donations for the housing program. Had the party planning been left up to me, we probably would have raised enough to buy lunch.

The drug reps found a classy bar that would donate space for a night, and they filled the place with their friends and clients. It wasn't a bar or a neighborhood where I would have found myself otherwise. The crowd was mostly nicely dressed, upper-middle-class White folks. I wore what I usually wore for work—jeans and a T-shirt—and felt a bit out of place as the host. Most of my team was more uncomfortable than me and cut out really early.

During the party, I bumped into Dr. Khan, who ran the Cook County Jail psych unit. I had not seen him, really, since I had started my internship there. We'd had one conversation after I had gotten into an argument with a corrections officer on my second day. The guard had given his opinion of my usefulness in front of thirty inmates I was talking to on the unit. I told him what I thought his opinion was worth. We got a little heated, and some of the inmates told my supervisor. She asked if I wanted to file a complaint. I didn't and figured it would be forgotten. But Dr. Khan came by the unit a few days later.

"A funny thing happened the other day," Dr. Khan said. "I was leaving, and a guard came up to me in the parking lot and said, 'I didn't do anything! Your intern started it. If he says I did something, he's lying.' Now, I actually am a psychologist. I know when someone denies an accusation that wasn't made, it usually means he's guilty. What happened?"

I told him, but I was proud I hadn't filed a complaint. I think the incident had won me some points with the guys locked up, and my then supervisor probably appreciated that I hadn't bothered her with the extra paperwork.

At the party, Dr. Khan and I talked about the Chicago Police mental health trainings for the department's new Crisis Intervention Teams. He was glad to hear I had experience with cops who were doing a decent job not provoking violence when responding to mental health crises.

An old pal of mine, Kurt, from the moving company, strolled over during the conversation. Kurt had been crashing on my couch for a while. My dog was getting used to my pal's night terrors and Kurt was getting used to being awoken by a pit-bull body slam. Kurt had plenty of experience with the police, having been—in one night—clubbed, maced, and tased when a bar fight had turned into a chemical-fueled brawl.

"Dude," he said, "I was screaming at them, 'Gimme more of that!' I couldn't feel anything. Until the taser. I was crying like a baby."

This was a few years before the party and Kurt still had some legal problems. He joined my conversation with Dr. Khan, just to screw with the man.

"I myself have noticed the police are much more professional than they used to be."

"So, you're in the mental health field, too?" Dr. Khan asked.

"No, no I'm not. Not at all."

Financially, the party was a smash. We made enough money to pay a year's rent for both emergency apartments. And we never switched our clients over to the drug reps' products. After that, most of them stopped coming around the office with muffins for the team.

• • •

The emergency apartments were not actually apartments but furnished rooms in an SRO hotel. As fast as we could stock them with towels, soaps, and toiletries, we had potential clients ready to move in. I learned, though, that the offer of a free apartment seemed suspicious to people who had not yet worked with our team. This made sense—we were strangers, not to be trusted.

Mona, when I got her out of the hospital, demanded I drop her off by the Baptist Church on Wilson so she could get her shopping cart. The police had dragged her into the psych unit but had let her stash her cart before hauling her away. She grilled me the whole car ride from the hospital to the church.

"You're gonna just give me an apartment, huh, Mr. Social Worker? You gonna shoot me up with drugs like they tried in the motherfucking hospital, huh? I'm not taking that shit. This isn't mental illness like all those motherfuckers said. This is spirits following me. Huh?"

I introduced Mona to the front desk clerk, a strange little woman who smoked Newports and drew her eyebrows onto her forehead way north of where nature intended them. Behind the clerk was a wall of old wooden mail slots and a tiny black-and-white television blaring *Judge Judy*. The rest of what used to be the lobby of the hotel had been converted into the desk clerk's apartment, sectioned off by an accordion gate. In another setting, her cluttered apartment would be a fascinating art installation of couches, Tupperware storage bins, more televisions, and a stationary bicycle acting as a clothing rack. It was like a life-size diorama, a living space on public display.

The emergency apartment was pristine in comparison. We had made the bed with new sheets and stocked the bathroom with the basic toiletries. The television was new and there was a set of dollar-store pots and pans in the cabinet above the stove.

"This is it?" Mona asked. She took three steps, measuring the room, from the fridge to the bed. "Is there motherfucking cable?"

"No cable. But it's better than outside."

"We'll see."

I next introduced Mona to her case manager, Jennifer, who would help her get her benefits, schedule medical appointments, and find more permanent housing. I handed Mona's case off once I was comfortable that she was no longer in crisis. My job was to bring new clients in and do the triage work when a client started falling apart.

Mona continued to have complaints. As she had promised, she refused medications. I would get calls from her.

"I don't need this little motherfucking White girl helping me!"—"This apartment has bugs!"—"This is a shithole!"—"This place you put me in is just like the others. The motherfucking geeks followed me here! I got motherfucking Oprah and Johnny Depp fighting in my room! You gonna do something about this?"

I forwarded the messages to Jennifer.

• • •

Every year, I had an excess of paid time off, which I would opt to sell back to the agency rather than take vacations. I had grown to believe that if I heaped enough responsibility on myself I could control the program. In doing so, I had constructed the job so if I left for more than a day the whole enterprise would crumble. At least that's how I felt. I paid little attention to my personal life and every so often had to extricate myself from a relationship I should not have jumped into in the first place.

One day, Jennifer came into my office for our supervision hour. She quickly started crying, overwhelmed by the stress and breadth of the job. And just as one client appeared to be getting healthier and more independent, two others would fall into crisis. It was never-ending, she said, and she didn't know how much longer she could do it.

Jennifer was an excellent clinician—dedicated to the work and empathetic to her clients—but was putting in too many hours. I had, more than once, chased her out of the office at the end of the day because she was staying late to type notes.

"The work is unending," I told her. "We are not going to cure schizophrenia and clients are going to keep coming. You have to pace yourself."

I saw she was working way too much—staying late typing up notes in the office, seeing clients on her way home from work, fretting that there was more to be done. She was doing a stellar job with clients but was terrified she was not doing enough.

"Even if you don't pace yourself, the best case scenario could be you put in twelve-hour days all week, catch every crisis that comes around, make sure nothing slips by you. All your energy goes into this job, and you end up paying no attention to your personal life until you end up in a relationship with a person who has no business being in the same room as you."

She stopped crying long enough to ask, "Is this hypothetical?"

"Sure."

I waited for her to stop laughing before I went on.

"We're never going to clear our caseloads. We're swimming to the horizon here." It took a few more years before I listened to my own advice.

• • •

When Mona got her SSDI checks, we moved her into another hotel, the Chateau. After a couple of days without meds and refusing services, she called me.

"I still got these motherfucking geeks in my apartment, coming up through the floor and fighting. I got these geeks. The place is haunted."

She was adamant that her perceptions were not psychotic symptoms but evidence of the paranormal. She cursed out her caseworkers and the doctor every time they mentioned medication. She wanted a seance or her hotel room cleansed by someone who "knows what they're motherfucking doing."

So I asked a friend who was a Wiccan if she would be willing to perform a ritual cleansing of Mona's room. I had been in dozens of crappy hotel rooms, but I was starting to feel like Mona's room might be haunted. Maybe because Mona was so fervent in her belief. She never turned on the lights, and more than once she scared the hell out of me by answering her door in a bathrobe, a towel wrapped around her head, and with her face covered in a gray death mask of mush she had made out of newspapers soaked in the bathroom sink.

My Wiccan friend came to the hotel with me. She was dressed in a flowing white suit and carrying a little wooden box. I introduced them and my friend asked me to step into the hallway during the cleansing.

When they let me back in, the room smelled of candles and sage. The space felt calmer. Mona said to the Wiccan, "Thank you, ma'am. It feels a little better in here."

Mona called me the next day.

"Well, Mr. Social Worker, Mr. Problem Solver, the motherfucking geeks are back. Motherfuckers screaming at me and fighting and coming from the TV and up from the motherfucking floor. So, what you gonna motherfucking do about it, huh? What am I supposed to motherfucking do?"

I wanted to say, "How about you try taking some motherfucking meds?"

But I had no answer for her and told her so. She cursed me out some more, but less intensely, like it was comforting to her that I had no solutions. Then she hung up.

• • •

Another call from Mona: "Okay, Mr. motherfucking social worker. This shithole apartment you put me in is such a shithole there's motherfucking dogs running around the motherfucking hallways. I got enough motherfucking bullshit to deal with and now I gotta worry about getting my ass bit by motherfucking dogs."

She went on until I said I would come by. I told the team, "I have to go hospitalize Mona. This time there's dogs after her in the Chateau."

No one was surprised or particularly upset. Mona was not the most pleasant person.

The desk clerk at the Chateau ignored me as he always did unless someone was behind on their rent, and I walked the stairs up to the fourth floor where Mona was staying. The Chateau was one of the places where the elevators were more dangerous than the stairs; you never knew who would be in there or if the thing would just break down.

I stepped onto the fourth floor and there they were, two German shepherds, just standing there in the hallway. The dogs ambled into an open doorway, and I went and told Mona I would complain to management.

"You know you have dogs up on the fourth floor," I told the desk clerk on my way out.

"They ain't supposed to have no dogs up there."

"They do."

"Okay. I'll look into it."

• • •

The other emergency apartment went to a client named Timothy, who had never been in the mental health system. He had made it to his midforties without any apparent mental health interventions at all, but when his family money ran out and he lost the three-flat his deceased parents had left him to foreclosure, his mental health took a dive. He descended into homelessness as his psychotic symptoms kicked up. He was so paranoid that it took me hours to get the most basic information out of him.

I got a call from a shelter on the west side of Chicago, a notoriously tough neighborhood that has done more than its share to give the city its reputation as the national leader in open-air gunfights. The shelter supervisor asked if I could come out and assess Timothy.

"He really needs some mental health treatment," the supervisor said. "He's scaring people here."

"What's he doing?"

I expected the worst.

"Nothing. He doesn't bother anyone. He just sits here and reads, but he's a little scary."

I took Jennifer with me. She was new and we had to fill her caseload. Part of my job was to train them on the basics, including how to start working with a new client.

The shelter was clean and open, full of light, and smelled like they had just served a decent lunch. Men either dressed for lives of homelessness or making raggedy attempts at looking like gangsters were still milling about the tables. In the middle of the crowd, with a table all to himself and plenty of space around him, was one lanky, blond-haired, blue-eyed White man wearing one of those Bill Cosby dad sweaters from the 1980s. Timothy. He was reading a book.

The supervisor explained that Timothy was about to hit his time limit at the shelter—and had done nothing to try to find housing or benefits or a job or anything—then walked us over to him. I began my usual sales pitch: what we did, what services we offered, and what we expected of people working with us. I never used the word "client" but made it sound like a partnership of sorts, which wasn't untrue.

Thus began a brutally slow two-hour conversation, during which Timothy stopped me to question just about every other word that came out of my mouth like he was a lawyer performing a cross-examination. Without any emotion in his voice, he wanted to make sure I knew what I was talking about. His paranoia was so prevalent that he was also seeking the meanings beneath anything I said. I would learn later he felt he had been cheated somehow out of a home, career, and any relationships. That paranoid conspiracy explained, in his mind, how he'd ended up in a shelter on the West Side. His fear of being cheated again made him hypervigilant in his dealings with me.

By the time Timothy agreed to work with us, Jennifer was falling asleep in her chair.

"I want to see the housing before I sign anything," Timothy said.

"Legally, I need you to sign this stuff first," I told him, "before I even let you in my car."

We went in circles. Then he had to think about it more, so we sat there quietly.

I gestured to the Bible he had closed.

"Are you religious?"

Timothy thought for a second. "I would probably interpret that question to mean you are not. You're probably a liberal atheist who thinks religion is for the weak, even though atheism is simply nihilism dressed as intellectualism. I could take it like that, and we could be real uncomfortable, but this is the only thing to read here. And I'm not comfortable telling you anything about myself. Whether I'm religious or not should have no bearing on whether you're going to do anything for me."

"Okay. You want to check out this apartment, see if it might be better than the shelter?"

"I guess."

I have no idea why changing the subject worked, but it did.

We walked out to my car, a 1995 Chevy Cavalier, which I had bought for a thousand dollars cash right before I took the job. It had taken a beating: the antenna was ripped off, one side mirror was taped together, and one smashed window had been replaced with a sheet of clear plastic for the time being. But it ran perfectly fine. I was hoping to hold onto the wreck long enough to celebrate an odometer reading of two hundred thousand miles.

Timothy looked at the car and said, "I see you're doing real well for yourself."

We moved him into the apartment, and he soon had the place rigged with questionably functional Rube Goldberg devices designed to alert him in case anyone snuck in while he was gone. He told us the desktop computer he had brought with him was wired to electrocute anyone who tried to turn it on.

Timothy was paranoid that we were breaking into the place while he was gone and, at one point, refused to let anyone in. I had to remind him we held the lease on the place and were paying the rent.

"We could let the courts decide," he said.

"We could," I agreed.

I was dreading this. We already had a guy threatening to become a squatter.

Timothy put that threat away and, soon after, demanded to work with a clinician other than Jennifer.

"I don't think she knows what she's doing," he said.

Jennifer was okay with that since he "creeped her out."

Timothy went back to refusing to allow case managers to visit him, ducking out when they were coming by or refusing to open the door. I had two male clinicians tag-teaming him to find the guy and provide some damn clinical services.

Timothy called me to complain, "Do you only hire knuckleheads?"

He wasn't enjoying this but was truly frustrated by our rules. He said he did not feel safe in the apartment and wanted to get his gun out of a storage locker. I told him guns were not allowed. This turned into a discussion of his perception of my dictatorial leanings, as there were no written rules regarding firearms. In fact, I was apparently making up rules as we went along. He wasn't incorrect about this.

As far as I knew, Timothy never went and got his gun, but our team knew he was refusing all services, refusing medications, and making vague claims of ownership of the apartment. Three months passed like this before he got his first disability check. He wanted to stay at the apartment and save up money by not paying rent to any landlord. It made sense to him. It was infuriating to us.

I had to write up a formal thirty-day eviction letter informing Timothy he would have to begin paying rent for the apartment since he was receiving a monthly check. Proud of myself that I had thought of this possibility, I was able to show Timothy the agreement he had signed where this was clearly spelled out.

"You know, you and these dumbbells are going to make me go live in a storage locker," he said.

I had to adjust my criteria for emergency apartment candidates.

39

Amos, a naturally intelligent kid and a degenerate crack user, had stolen from every family member who had ever offered to help him. Even without crack pumping through his brain, his thoughts tangled themselves like wire coat hangers. His mind was a mash-up of concepts and information: the Old Testament, video game design, psychoanalytic babble, and political theory. He expressed even his simplest thoughts in such personal, code-laden terms that a cryptologist would have thrown a fit trying to decipher them.

For example: "You're like those Greek restaurant owners; everything is a special, everything is in quotes, but all with that construction-cone orange sauce out of the can. Homemade, but mass marketed."

By that, he meant a person was insincere.

Sometimes the sound of the words held more weight for Amos than the meanings of the words. In speech, the alliteration and sibilants matched his moods, even when the words were out of context. Once, he told me, "Oh, the great Gogamog is going to projectively identify and make me the bad Grinch."

Amos said he felt verbal directives coming from electrical outlets, commanding him to scream out the window of his hotel or to line up his cigarette butts to match the pattern of his carpet.

He had navigated his way through nursing homes, group homes, Cook County Jail, various girlfriends, and his stepfather's garage, all while refusing his meds and smoking crack.

He held a fierce resentment against the point systems of the group homes that had housed him. Residents would get ten points for brushing their teeth, maybe five points for brushing their hair, five more for making their bed, and at the end of the week these points could be traded for candy and pop kept in a locked refrigerator. Now that Amos was on his own, he linked any suggestion of rules with the old, hated point system. To his mind, all rules were bad.

When the urge for drugs struck Amos, which it did every day, he would steal anything he could carry to pay for them. Living in a flophouse and shoplifting from convenience stores for crack money was not the life he wanted. But he flaunted his opposition to our advice, walking the neighborhood early in the morning, looking pensive and carrying a glass crack pipe like he was Sherlock Holmes. If there were a painless way to quit drugs, he might have tried, he said. But giving up the sixty seconds of godlike serenity that crack provided just to return to sober psychosis and poverty was not worth the effort.

"I'm not trying to be noncompliant or anything," Amos said, having learned the clinical lingo long ago, "but I personally disagree with this and I'm trying not to use my vocal cords in that certain way that freaks people out."

During every visit, the doctor pressured Amos to swallow at least one pill each day. Amos picked his nails during the lectures. Once, he interrupted to ask, "Do you think you could give me a pill to give me ADD so I don't have to listen to people talk so much?"

We were the last stop for the kid. Every other agency had tried to help him and passed him along. He was a smart kid, doing what he had to do to survive and feed his addiction. As frustrating as his behavior was, we had to console ourselves that the best we might ever be able to do would be to keep him from falling into the legal system. He appeared to be actively fighting against this goal by stealing stuff from Target and selling it on the next block, but that was the operative definition of addiction—the goals of the addiction trumped everything else.

We were all in a holding pattern, waiting for him to make the effort to either run from us or begin taking care of himself in some slight way. We couldn't expect our clients to recognize the efforts we made on their behalf. That was unrealistic. Our job was to provide motivation and safety for clients until they were able to internalize some basic goals of self-reliance.

"I shouldn't be working harder than the client" is a maxim for some clinicians. But it assumes—often incorrectly—that the client is able to work as hard as the clinician. It doesn't take into account the interference caused by psychosis, personality-disordered behaviors, and addiction. For our team, the maxim couldn't be applied across the board. When a client would clearly continue falling down without our intervention, then the clinician had to be the one to work harder. We did have to respond differently to a malingerer fighting for control of the clinical relationship than we would to a client who was testing boundaries with us, for example, by replicating the awful relationships that had marked their life.

Amos made it tough on everyone around him. In the moments when he could describe what he wanted from his life, he was no different from a lot of young men with a vague plan to design video games and get an IT job. But there were so many barriers surrounding him and keeping him from making any progress. Looking back, our frustration with him echoed his frustration with what the world had done to him. Such parallel processes played out often—what we experienced with a client told us something about how they experienced the world and what they demanded of it.

Establishing boundaries—as hard as it was when psychosis diffused the boundaries of a client's sense of self—was one way we had to create some sense of safety in the world.

· · ·

One young woman, Sharonda, made multiple suicide threat calls to our emergency line, repeatedly claiming she had slit her wrists, overdosed on painkillers, or had a gun to her head. Often they were hang-up calls, leaving no room for discussion, so we had to respond by calling police and EMTs to her place. She denied any suicidality and fought against hospitalization, even though she had been hospitalized so many times most emergency rooms knew her by sight—and ambulance crews knew to check her mouth for razors, as she would cut herself once she was safely in her hospital room. She had burned through several mental health programs, agencies, and residential facilities. Our agency's administration had sent her to ACT as a last-chance effort.

But Sharonda's threats and hospitalizations continued. The suicide calls would come in and we would find her watching TV with her cousin or passed out in the bathtub. Sometimes she would call and refuse to tell the team where she was. I would have to explain to clinicians that we could not do anything about this except acknowledge that she was putting us in a position to only feel helpless. Her suicide threats and self-harming behaviors were not "manipulative" or "bullshit," as some team members complained, they were her rageful and desperate attempts to get other people to care for her. She was simultaneously in charge and totally helpless—as we were in this situation. She was seeking the safety that she had been deprived of in childhood.

Still, I had to set a new boundary with Sharonda.

"The emergency line is no longer an option," I told her. "If you can call us, you can call 911, which is what you have to do from now on. Any calls you make to this number will not be answered."

After that, we had to reset the boundaries in all sorts of ways—meds, doctor's appointments, the number of clinicians she had access to—which meant I had to take over her case. I saw her four times a week for therapy as she continued to cut herself and overdose on pain medication.

When a psych unit tried to send her to a psychiatric nursing home, she walked right out, back to her SRO room. And she and I went back to our four-times-a-week routine. She was therapy-savvy, having worked with therapists since she was a little kid. She was the victim of multiple sexual predators in the family, and she was blamed for all of it by her mother and siblings. They told her she "broke up the family."

The only way I could determine whether we were making any progress with Sharonda was when the frequency of her hospitalizations decreased. What had once been a weekly trip to the ER for an assessment dwindled down to once a month. She was able to acknowledge that she didn't really want to die but wanted to bring her family back together.

All of her traumatized—and traumatizing—behavior was an effort to get her family to act like a family, as if she could make her pain obvious enough to them that they would take her back.

Over the years, Sharonda's family had offered the same response to her cries for help as some of our staff, accusing her of faking it and trying to get attention. At the kitchen table, her father once dared her to kill herself. I met with the parents once. Their assessment was that their daughter ought to "toughen up" since no one needed all this therapy, and the girl was just "playing a fool." Personally, I hoped Sharonda could get about a thousand miles away from her parents, but even if she did, they were deep in her head.

Sharonda and I were not following the ACT model for treatment. She didn't need multiple case managers visiting her and helping with basic life skills impeded by psychosis and drug abuse. But there was nowhere else for her in the system, so I went with the intensive-one-on-one-therapy plan. She was able to accept some new boundaries and we wanted to find a way to stick with her. We couldn't treat our clients as if they were automatons and we couldn't perform our job duties as if we were working on an assembly line. Our approach had to be malleable and individualized, not geared toward changing the behavior of clients to appease the clinicians. By definition, ACT clients were prone to rejecting clinical suggestions—such as taking meds—and could require months of work by our team to make any measurable progress at all. If that weren't the case, they wouldn't have been referred to us in the first place.

We had to hospitalize Sharonda less and less often, which I considered immense progress. But I started celebrating too early. During her next hospitalization, a charge nurse told me Sharonda had rescinded her release of information, meaning I did not have her permission to talk to her or the doctors or the staff. She also informed me that Sharonda would be going home to her family. It felt like a failure to me.

40

On my day off, I received a call from a client's mother who explained that she was driving her boy home from the grocery store when he "started talking crazy." Before I could ask for more details, she said she was pulling up to the office. The client, JJ, was nearly thirty years old and a former high school athlete, a community college walk-on football player who didn't survive summer tryouts. He had two children somewhere but lived with his mother until his violent behavior forced her to kick him out. Since his initial psychotic break he had been hospitalized multiple times and kept trying to talk his way back into his mom's place.

I had taken over his case since he began wrapping his primary clinician into his paranoid delusions, daring the case manager while pointing to the threshold of his apartment door, "Cross that line, I might think you're trying to get sexy with me. I didn't invite you in." While JJ's mom talked to me on the emergency line, I called Stella on another phone and asked her to have the team stick around. I was heading over to help assess the kid.

JJ and his mother were already in the waiting room when I showed up. One of the clinicians, Bethanne, had heard the announcement and slipped out the back door after telling Stella she had something else to do. Bethanne saw her time on the team as a begrudging requirement to getting her supervision hours before going into private practice. One of the criteria for a person to be accepted into the ACT program was frequent hospitalizations. Every team member comes aboard with this expectation spelled out during the initial interview—hospitalizing clients was not an optional duty.

Still furious at Bethanne's sense of entitlement, I sat down with JJ in a treatment room while Mariella and Stella took JJ's mom into the team office. I had Shannon watching the treatment room, ready to call 911. JJ kept swearing he did not understand why his mother had brought him to the office—she was acting crazy, not him. He wanted to go home and if anyone got in the way, he said, he would kill them.

"I'll go to prison before I go to another hospital," he promised. "Look at these sad eyes. You know who I am? I'm Jesus. Don't I look like him? What I need you to get me is a chrome .45 so I can start blowing the domes off some motherfucking sinners." I gave Shannon the signal to call the cops and stayed with JJ, listening to his plans to rid the world of evil.

It felt like it took forever for the first two cops to show up, but when they did, they approached us gently, doing a fine job of saying all the right things to keep a person calm. JJ had already made his decision, though. He started rolling his wrists to avoid being grabbed, warning the police, "Whoever touches me is going to get hurt."

Three more cops showed up and the treatment room—meant for two people to have quiet conversations—was filled to capacity. Shannon pulled me out by the sleeve as the police crowded JJ and blocked the door. The young man kept his word. As soon as one cop grabbed for his wrist, JJ flew forward, trying to get an arm around the cop's neck. Three cops grabbed JJ after he hip-checked the first two in different directions, putting one through the drywall. The third officer tackled him, and they went over the office desk. The fourth cop stepped back and yelled, "Taser! Taser! Taser!" Only one needle stuck JJ and he kept throwing punches as the other needle flopped around at the end of its spiral cord. The cops piled on and brought him to the ground. Yanked back up to a standing position with cuffs on his wrists, JJ looked around and whooped, "Damn, that bitch was angry!"

A couple of days later, I visited him in the hospital. He was much calmer with a couple Haldol and Thorazine injections coursing through his bloodstream. "You remember Wednesday?" I asked.

"Yeah."

"What do you think?"

"I was saying some stupid shit."

"You remember what happened, right?"

"Yeah."

"You know why you should take your meds now?"

"I will," he promised mechanically.

"Here's why. You weren't really in control of yourself, right?"

"I don't know."

"You had five cops in our office. They were pretty pissed. Some of them got hurt. They're going to remember this. If they have to take you to the hospital again, what do you think they're gonna do?"

"I don't know. Fuck me up?"

"If they fuck you up, they're going to do it when they have you alone. Not in our offices, not in the hospital. That's why you have to take your meds. They're gonna hurt you bad next time." He did start taking his meds for a while, but I attribute that to the work of Shannon and Jennifer, who followed up after JJ was discharged. His aversion to medications, and any clinical assistance, continued to keep him away from our offices. He would avoid our phone calls or slip out the window when we came to his front door. Last we heard, he had grabbed some money from his mother and left the state.

• • •

Hospitalizing JJ, violent though he was, was not as upsetting to me as Bethanne choosing to leave the office rather than assist in a potentially dangerous situation. During job interviews I told every potential ACT candidate that one of their most important responsibilities would be to support teammates—whether in a crisis or in everyday duties. The support has to be quantitative, not just in spirit. To run away from a potential hospitalization increases the risk for the clinician who stays and places the client in crisis at greater risk, too.

I wanted to fire Bethanne on the spot. I called her into my office and as I asked questions, she gave me a series of shifting rationales: "I didn't think I needed to be there."—"Last time his mother thought he had to go to the hospital, he didn't have to."—"I didn't hear the instructions."—"The instructions weren't clear."—"I didn't know what to do, so I left."

Each excuse contradicted another and, ultimately, put the blame on someone else. The commonality was: I don't want to get in trouble now. I will give you multiple answers—pick one.

Rather than call Bethanne a liar, I asked her to pick an excuse. Based on that excuse, we made a plan for any future incidents where she might be confused. She began looking around for another job and left soon after.

• • •

Burnout often stemmed from a clinician's unrealistic expectations of their clients or of the job itself. Focusing on daily tasks without looking at the big picture can help the day go by more quickly, but it may not help the clients with anything. Trying to impose one's will—My job is to get you to take your meds—without considering why the client is fighting it leads to nothing but frustration.

Fighting for that kind of control, the clinician has to work extremely hard while the client merely has to say no. The fight becomes an expense of energy, which drains the clinician long before the client gets tired. The clinician who goes all in with Do it! No! Do it! No! runs out of tricks very quickly.

On bad days, the same dynamic existed between me and the clinicians. Initially, I internalized any team member's shortcomings as a sign of my own deficiencies as a supervisor. If I couldn't fix the problem, then I was doubly a failure. I had to learn to back off and contain my urge to have a hand in everything. I would be annoyed if I wasn't updated on some client issue, but I would be equally annoyed if I was updated on every little thing. On those days I become the boss who couldn't be satisfied. This was lousy for the rest of the team. I had to follow the same advice I had once given a frustrated clinician about his overblown need for control: grab what you can control and let go of what you cannot.

As tempting as it was to say to the team, "Do your job!" I found it ineffective. Making that demand doesn't even feel good except in the fleeting moment it takes to say the words. More importantly, it didn't work.

I always had to gauge whether I was being too hard on the team or whether I was being played by clinicians who had decided that their best bet was to get over by doing the minimal amount of work required for the job. By assessing myself, I could better assess what was going on around me. To check myself I would measure a clinician's workload against those on the team in whom I had complete trust. Usually I found that my suspicions were born out of my own exhaustion, that I had been working too hard for too many days and, in response, was begrudging others for not matching my stress levels over their own job duties.

But sometimes the problem wasn't me. Sometimes I could feel a drop in a clinician's motivation, a growing sense of entitlement, where the clinician's needs came before the client's. For example, some clinicians resented unscheduled contact with their clients, as if the clients were supposed to bend to the clinician's schedule. This wasn't that kind of work. But when it went that way, the triage model became inverted and the reluctant clinician prioritized paperwork and phone calls before client outreaches. Sometimes the clinician began subtly shifting their share of the caseload onto others, using excuses like, "I'm doing notes; I can't see him."

It was infuriating.

41

Charles had been with the ACT team longer than me. As staff came and went over the years, Charles remained a constant source of dread to anyone who worked with him. He could be charming and entertaining but his dedication to his crack addiction was so pervasive that every clinician questioned whether we should close his case for our own sanity.

Nothing mattered to Charles except picking up his allocated budget so he could buy crack. If he didn't have any money, he panhandled for crack, in sideways rainstorms if he had to, his clothes whipping against his ninety-nine-pound frame as traffic blew past on Broadway. If panhandling was too slow, he would shoplift. When he couldn't shoplift successfully, he would find someone to sell him crack on credit.

Thirty years earlier, Charles had been a crossdressing regular in the drag bars of Chicago and LA. His career was interrupted when he committed a burglary that turned into a hostage situation with one little old lady hanging in the balance. He was found not guilty by reason of insanity and spent years in the state hospital. He denied remembering anything other than being locked up in a hospital.

Charles was always fastidious about his appearance. During the summer, he would find linen pants or short-shorts to go with mesh T-shirts. If he were feeling celebratory, he'd cover himself in glitter. In the winter he would come to the office wearing an ankle-length white leather duster and sunglasses that covered half his face. He would not waste money on laundry. When his clothes were too filthy, he would go steal more.

Charles's voice was an effeminate whisper until the pressure of no money and no crack got to him. Then he would fire off a barrage of curses in a Fred Flintstone baritone at whoever he believed was between him and his money: "This is bullshit! Get me my money now! Where's my motherfucking money? I want to be my own payee! I want my money! That's my motherfucking money!"

He would panhandle on the corner in front of our office, determined and oblivious, approaching our cars as we came and went. Only after rattling his 7-11 cup in the window would Charles recognize me and then feign nonchalance at our chance meeting.

"Oh, hi. How're you? You look nice today."

Then he would move on to the next car in line.

Once, I was sitting in a Starbucks—with a client who hated the agency building so much that we had therapy sessions in the neighborhood—when I saw Charles out of the corner of my eye, sauntering up to the register. He nodded and smiled at the baristas, intertwined his fingers under his chin while he perused the menu, then grabbed a handful of CDs from the display rack and ran out the door.

At the grocery store, he ordered food from the hot deli and tried to wolf it down before he got to the register. He would smile—toothless—while stuffing hot potato skins into his mouth.

He was picked up for shoplifting so frequently the local cops knew him by name: "Aw, you again, Charlie?"

He used his apartment as storage space for stolen items he could not have carried on his own. On some days he would have four televisions in one corner and three sofas stacked on end. Piles of dirty clothes consistently blocked the doorway and Charles had to slip in and out sideways. Not even a walking path existed in his room. He had to climb an obstacle course every morning. He balanced his microwave and crockpot on the back of the sofa where he slept. We tried to clean the room with him, but he had fits if anything was going to be discarded. This was not hoarder's distress. Charles simply hoped everything had some resale value.

When the dealers in his hotel realized they would never be repaid for the crack they sold him on credit, they sprayed his room with lighter fluid and set it on fire. Charles was out for the day, but he had left his door open because he kept losing his keys and refused to pay the hotel for any more replacements.

The only power Charles could exercise was his refusal to cooperate with the world. He fought to defend his right to smoke crack, which he wanted formally allocated into his budget. And he reserved the right to say no to everything.

One morning, he passed out in our lobby, empty crack baggies falling from his pockets as he hit the floor. When he woke up, he denied using any drugs that morning, even when confronted with the thumb-size Ziploc baggies scattered around him.

"What are these for then?" I asked. "Tiny sandwiches?"

"I don't know what those are."

I pulled copper scouring pads out of his pockets, and he denied knowing any drug paraphernalia was in his pants.

"Someone else put that there! These are borrowed pants!"

Once, he jumped out of Phillip's car when he felt he was being lectured. They had just left the HIV clinic downtown and Phillip called me, wanting to know if he should chase Charles.

I had to say, "Leave him alone; he'll find his way home."

If Charles felt he was being treated poorly, he would stay away from the office for a day or a week but would always return, unable to find anyone else who would manage his money or his housing. He quit our program repeatedly but came back each time within the week.

When he came to the office, it was to demand money. He was scheduled to get paid twice a week, but he wanted money every day. Clinicians would take the opportunity to give Charles his meds, which he took sporadically. Along with a heavy regimen of antipsychotic meds, he also had an HIV medication regimen.

Charles became an unfortunate—but important—learning opportunity for new staff. When Phillip first started, he tried to tell Charles, "You have to take your meds before you get your money."

Charles had learned to flip the script long before Phillip came around.

"Give me my money first."

"You have to take your HIV meds."

"Give me my money first."

"Your meds are more important."

"No, they're not. Gimme my money. I want my money."

"You have to take your meds."

"I want my money. I want my money."

This would become a chant.

Charles would spin clinicians around, claiming, "I'm not going to take my meds unless you give me my money. If you don't give me my money, you're making my HIV worse. You're gonna kill me because you won't give me my damn money!"

Charles would quickly escalate to screaming, threatening to sue, and pounding on my office door, demanding a new case manager. Other clinicians would have to intervene to try to talk him down from his temper tantrum. Charles illustrated why we could not link the idea of meds and money as a cause-and-effect equation—if it supposedly worked in one direction, it should work in the other. And Charles was all about the money.

Because of his history of psychiatric hospitalizations, incarcerations, and homelessness, the state determined that Charles would always need a payee. That didn't stop him from trying to circumvent the requirement. Once, he announced he had found a mystery uncle who would be his new payee.

"Who's your uncle?" I asked.

"Uncle . . . Charlie."

Whenever staff members were in my office at the end of their Charles rope—and this happened frequently—I would ask them a question.

"Do you think you have more patience than him?"

They would get slightly offended, but the answer was always the same.

"Yeah!"

"Then that's what we have to have," I'd say. "Forget today; try him again tomorrow."

• • •

When staff would pick Charles up for his appointments with the HIV doctor, he regularly answered the door in a housedress, still needing time to get ready. To exercise one little bit of control, he would take his time answering the door, as if he were crossing a great dining hall rather than a ten-by-twelve-foot flophouse room.

One impatient case manager didn't get the joke. She yelled through his locked door, "Charles, I'm in a hurry."

" . . . Just a min-ute."

"Let's go, Charles!"

" . . . I'm com-ing . . ."

"Charles, I'm double-parked!"

" . . . That's stu-pid."

It was not his problem that his case manager was parked illegally.

We had to work with him on a rotation simply because he burned through case managers the same way he burned through car-antennae crack pipes. He was exhausting. Shannon summarized him once. "Crazy don't get tired, Zak."

Sometime after we had grown accustomed to Charles's daily outbursts and chronic panhandling, and his outrageous conduct in the office no longer cranked the staff's anxiety and adrenaline, his body began to betray him. His kinetic energy seemed to have drained from his whippet-thin body and the team was alarmed to see him one morning with his face and stomach swollen almost past recognition. His strut gone, he walked carefully. Charles denied anything was wrong. He wanted his money.

When he had difficulty walking out of the office, we called an ambulance. Mariella, who was especially pit bullish when it came to clients' medical issues, took over.

We learned that Charles's kidneys were failing. A strict diet and medical regimen might help him, but Charles would only go to the hospital when the pain kept him from making his crack rounds.

He tried to run when we had to hospitalize him. Only his physical deterioration allowed us to catch him halfway down the block, leaning against a newly planted tree.

"I'm not sick," he said. "Just tired. This damn coat is too heavy."

"Charles, if you're too tired to run from us, it's time to see a doctor," I told him.

When he didn't appear at the office for his money one day, we went to check on him. He agreed to let us call an ambulance when he didn't have the strength to climb past the stolen goods and dirty laundry piled inside the apartment.

He referred to his therapist, Jennifer, as "the girl" since she was the newest staff member. She did a fine job convincing him to keep an overnight bag ready for the increasingly frequent hospital trips. Charles was starting to understand he couldn't avoid the hospital.

"Have the girl carry my bag," he ordered while the EMTs carried him out of his room.

His overnight bag held a sub sandwich, a battery-operated toy dog, and a child's microscope. Charles was hoping to sell the latter two items while in the hospital, not wanting to waste an opportunity to pry money away from people.

ER visits would, more often than not, end in a walking chase through the hospital as Charles grew frantic. "Fuck this, I'm leaving!" he would say and stomp off in his hospital gown.

Psychiatric units do not have bedside phones, but medical units do. When admitted to a medical unit, Charles abused the phone, calling our office constantly throughout the day. In the office, we would watch the phones take turns lighting up as Charles tried every line we had.

Like an invisible bird flitting about, Charles left a whispery message at each desk one day, talking to the voicemail as if it needed time to respond: "This is Charles . . . Hi. Hello. How are you . . .? Send someone to Illinois Masonic with a beef sandwich, fries, and a orange pop. No, pizza . . . No. A combo sandwich. With cheese and onion rings. And a Snickers . . . No, Twix. And hurry. And don't send that Mariella. She never did nothing for nobody!"

He was feeling better.

When we would visit Charles in the hospital, the staff would complain that he was sneaking cigarettes behind other patients' oxygen tanks or setting himself a table in front of the nurses' station because he didn't want to eat in his room.

One doctor gave us his baffled excuse for a diagnosis: "I don't know how he's alive."

Over the summer, Charles was in the hospital more than he was out. When he was out, he kept moving in his usual circles through the neighborhood, looking to score crack and panhandling for change at the intersection in front of our office. We tried to coax him onto dialysis, but he couldn't sit still and pulled the IV out of the collarbone port and walked out of the first session.

Then he disappeared. He wasn't at his apartment, and he wasn't coming to the office. Mariella called all the hospitals, and I called the morgue. Someone finally checked the Cook County Inmate rolls and there he was, in Cook County Jail.

The only concepts of time Charles could adhere to were now and never. His wants obliterated everything in between. Until this point, he had been able to chase down what he wanted, oblivious to any consequences. When he needed grooming supplies, he would shoplift. He was not going to show the gray roots in his hair, no matter what. This last arrest was for stealing hair dye from a drugstore. We missed the court date. Jennifer was set to attend, but another client went into a crisis, and I made the decision she should handle that first. Charles had been in court so many times for so many misdemeanor theft and trespassing charges, I figured they would let him go with just time served or a fine he would never pay, like all of his other arrests.

Tired of seeing Charles month after month, the Cook County judge that day decided Charles was a chronic case and sentenced him to a year in prison.

After Charles went to Statesville Prison we didn't see him again. Mariella put in calls to the prison superintendent and staff social workers, asking for an exemption due to Charles's health. He was too sick to stay in general population. Even the prison saw he was dying and had already moved him to the prison hospital right from intake.

Charles never called us. He passed away at the end of October. A hospital worker at the prison called Mariella. At first the team stayed quiet, uncertain what to say. A couple of days went by before Mariella, Yvonne, Holly, and Jennifer were in my office, fighting back tears and stoically comforting each other. They began listing all of the opportunities we had missed to keep him out of prison.

We could have gone to court.

We could have visited him in jail.

Maybe we could have forced him into inpatient drug treatment.

I had to counter their doubts. For years, we had gone above and beyond for Charles. He was one of the people who we weren't going to be able to save. We weren't able to help him build many skills or gain any insight into his behaviors or motivations. He fought us on every point. The best we could do, maybe, was keep him safe on some days. He fought like a wolverine against the idea of recovery. He wanted crack and anything else was secondary or nonexistent. We actually ended up admiring his tenacity. He would not quit.

Charles had a begrudging respect for people who set limits. He would never acknowledge this, but he steamrolled anyone who didn't stand up to him. I listed every clinician who had asked to never work with him again, including most of the women in the room.

Charles had, in one moment of insight, confided in Mariella that he knew he was dying. In the end, he knew there wasn't anything else to do. Without us, he wouldn't have lived this long. He never said this, but we each knew it was true.

As infuriating as he was, we protected him the best we could. Our greatest fear was always that he would die on the street, drop dead in traffic or alone in his lousy room. Throughout the past year we talked about impending death whenever Charles's name came up, trying to prepare ourselves for the day we would find him lifeless in his room. We had kept trying to throw him in the hospital, hoping that when the moment came, he would be in a bed, not in the rain. He had no family, no friends—only crack acquaintances who had set his room on fire.

"The only way Charles would stay in the hospital," I said, "was if it were a prison hospital."

"They did say they had to ankle cuff him to the bed," Mariella said, proud of his truculence.

No private hospital could hold Charles. Of course, he wasn't going to stay in any bed.

The cloud in my office lifted a bit as we acknowledged Charles's willfulness. Physically healthy, he would have tunneled out of Statesville with a spoon. He would have harassed the guards with an array of temper tantrums until they killed him or helped him escape. It helped the grieving to fantasize a bit about Charles's potential indestructibility. If he had passed away in the neighborhood, he would have risen from the dead to get the last of his Social Security checks and to ask for a loan against next month's.

In Statesville, he hadn't had the resources to score any drugs and he no longer had the energy to fight. We told ourselves things we couldn't confirm. We hoped he had stopped fighting everyone for at least a few days. We hoped he had passed with enough medication to obliterate the pain. We hoped, despite his surroundings, that his last moments were peaceful.

While he was in prison, and even after his death, when we would be at various hospitals with other clients, the staff would ask us about Charles, saying, "We haven't seen him in a while . . ."

We would share the news, and inpatient workers would share stories. Everybody had one about Charles. "This one time he rolled up someone's art project and smoked it," a hospital nurse told us. "The smoke alarm's going off and he's hiding in the bathroom with a construction paper cigar! Ooh, he made me so mad!"

We all told Charles stories. Once when I had to hospitalize him as his body started breaking down, he slipped out of the ER. I ran a full circuit around the outside of the hospital, looking for a man sporting an orange afro and hospital gown. I eventually found him in the hospital cafeteria. He had panhandled his way through the hallways until he had enough for a full lunch. When I caught up to him, he was wistfully looking at his Polish sausage sandwich, too sick to eat it. We took it back to the ER.

Mariella, Yvonne, and Holly traded Charles stories and quotes in my office: "He accidentally flashed the whole lobby because we took his belt and shoelaces. He was holding up his pants and they dropped when he grabbed for the free coffee."

"Remember when he had all the nice clothes, the dry cleaning he stole?"

"The glitter in his hair and the kimono."

"He told me, 'I don't wanna work with no smelly girls!'"

"He stole other patients' clothes and would walk around like he was doing a fashion show on the unit!"

"He stole his roommate's clothes and tried to put them on under his own!"

Almost every story ended with the admission, "I'll sorta miss him."

We were trying to process the loss. We wanted to believe we had done everything we could for him, but Charles was with us for years and had still died in prison, so it was hard to believe we had done enough. As brutally unfair as the man's life was, though, as awful as he could be to other people, and as despairing as his situation often seemed, I think we were able to give him a little bit of hope while he was around—some sense, each day, that he was not alone. The evidence of this? He never quit. And we took pride in never quitting on him. With some clients, it was stunning to see how much they could suffer and not lose hope for a better life, whether we agreed with what that might look like or not.

We never abandoned Charles. That was maybe the most important thing we could promise anyone.

42

SUMMER 2018

I ran the ACT team for seven years and my resignation was an anticlimactic nonevent with one month's notice. Most of the clinicians I was close with had left already and we were breaking in a new crew. I wasn't very excited about teaching rookies anymore. I was tired and busy building a private practice at night.

My private practice was still in the neighborhood, but it took months to get used to the solitude and the lack of crises and familiar faces. My life felt very quiet.

Walking from my office to get coffee, I would see ACT clients on Broadway, strolling or loitering, panhandling or cadging cigarettes. But less and less over the years. I don't know where most of these folks are. Where I had once been intimately involved in almost every aspect of their lives, our conversations were now cursory, mostly regarding recent housing issues in the area. The SROs and flophouses were being renovated into luxury microsuites and people on fixed incomes were being shoved out of the neighborhood.

Gentrification was in full swing. The shelters were being closed—or at least threatened with closure—and the homeless camps under the viaducts were being cleared away by city ordinance. The homeless problem has not been solved, but the homeless are being shuffled elsewhere by the sheer pressure of real estate money that does not tolerate threats to property values. The Wilson Men's Club closed, the Salvation Army shut down and the neighborhood's first Target went up. Slow-pour coffee shops, vegan delis, and sushi joints replaced some of the old standard grease pits where fried chicken and egg rolls were the staples of the menu. The neighborhood was becoming quiet and clean, a slow shift I only seemed to notice once I began to see fewer and fewer of the homeless people and loiterers I used to work with every day.

I missed that part of the job—being known on the corners, in the shelters, and on the hospital units—as much as I missed the daily opportunities to be an effective person. I even missed the crises and jumping into unpredictable, sometimes awful, situations. But during my last year with ACT, I had burned out—doing too much and not enjoying any of it.

On my last day on the job, I had to walk a fairly new client, Reginald, down from an El platform after he called me in a panic saying he couldn't get down to the street.

"I'm not going to make it to my doctor's appointment," he said. "I'm on the Bryn Mawr platform and all these people want to push me in front of the next train."

When I got up to the station, Reginald was by himself at the narrow end of the platform where the north and south lines come together. He was spinning himself in circles, swinging his briefcase with his outstretched arm.

While I was hospitalizing him, he cited a litany of evidence that, to his mind, proved his IQ was much higher than mine. I really wanted to argue. The calm and malleability I needed to keep the situation from escalating was in short supply, threatening not just the moment but the core philosophy of the job. It was a good time to go.

• • •

I originally told myself I took the job because no one else wanted it, but the deeper truth was I wanted to prove myself by doing the toughest job I could get better than anyone thought it could be done. At the time, I had been drifting and didn't realize the job was a connection to the world—and a role in it—that I needed. In an agency of several hundred employees, almost no one wanted to deal with ACT clients. But over the years I was able to hire some people who were truly dedicated to what we were doing and for similarly personal reasons.

The core team and I used a lot of gallows humor to bolster morale and get through our days, but sometimes we needed to remind ourselves that we had developed some serious skills and had accomplished a lot with our clients. For a couple of years, I organized the ACT Annual Awards Dinner to acknowledge each clinician's success in facing the seemingly impossible jobs we had. One year, I presented diplomas awarding each clinician a paramilitary ranking. Shannon became the ACT field marshal. Our nurse, Yvonne, was righteously acknowledged as the deputy chief queen bee. Mariella became Lieutenant Uhura—Dean's favorite character from *Star Trek*. I designated Stella the ACT subcomandante. I was proud when she hung her diploma at the front desk where visitors could view her credentials. At the bottom of each ACT diploma was the phrase *Illegitimi Non Carborundum*, which creatively translated from Latin means "Don't let the bastards get you down."

Another year, the team earned boxer's robes with their names and fight monikers embossed across the back:

"The Lion of Zion."

"Ice Pick."

"No Justice, No Peace."

Of course trinkets and annual awards didn't keep our people from leaving their high-stress, low-pay, thanks-for-nothing positions. But those who stayed with the team took pride in working with the population we served.

Outsiders to ACT often thought we were nuts for doing the work we did. They tried sometimes to praise us for our efforts, but they weren't very good at it. When other clinicians would say they would never do that work, what they really meant was that they couldn't do it. I would remind the team of this. Like judging a high-diving contest, degree of difficulty counts for a lot. Our credentials were determined by our accomplishments, not by the degrees or licenses we held.

It worked the other way, too. When people would say they couldn't do that work, they actually meant they wouldn't do that in a million years.

I think many people in the mental health field work under the bogus assumption that a correlation exists between the level at which a client functions and the skills of the clinician. I was taught when I started that the better clinicians work with clients who come in and sit down for polite fifty-minute sessions. But that type of thinking is anathema to a team—like ACT—that works with clients who might demonstrate extraordinary progress simply by managing to shop for their own groceries or refrain from smoking crack for thirty-six hours. The implication that clinicians who serve higher-functioning clients must be higher-functioning clinicians is snobbery.

Now that I spend my days sitting still, providing the kind of therapeutic services I used to dismiss, I see how much I had to relearn. During the ACT years, I felt I had to have all of the answers, a move to make in every situation. But the control I had insisted upon to keep my ACT clients safe is a detriment here, useless in this setting. In order to keep learning, I had to accept how much I still didn't know or understand about my work and myself. Doing that led me to my own analysis three times a week and studying to be a psychoanalyst.

Here's something I've learned: the chaos of running the ACT team—which was very real—was also really in my head. It was then and it is now. I dealt with it back then by finding a job chaotic enough to camouflage or displace the chaos I was carrying around inside. It was a complicated way to learn that fixing external problems doesn't necessarily fix the internal ones.

These days, I sit with patients in my office, just like my analyst sits with me while I lay on the couch. Everyone is sitting still yet all of our chaos is still there. I'm just starting to see how much I don't know and how much is left for me to take apart and put back together again. Some moments still feel like my first day on the job.

Sometimes I have this heavy little stone of joyfulness in my chest—it feels like a sob combined with a burst of laughter. It tells me it's okay that I don't have an answer for everything and that I'll be learning this stuff for the rest of my life.

When the stone is there, I feel like I'm a million miles beyond anywhere I had expected to be in my life.

ACT was a great place for me to start, though. We didn't have much of a psychoanalytic vocabulary, but I see now that the actions of the team mostly did the job that needed to be done. Shannon, Mariella, and others were consistent, supportive forces in the lives of their clients. With that, they created a connection to the world, and that connection fostered hope for a better life. Humans are social, emotional creatures, and we need all of that stuff, even if some of us can only measure progress toward it in millimeters.

• • •

Our clients did not come to us because we were their first choice for therapeutic care. We were their last option once all other options had failed. Precisely because of this, we refused to put them on some bottom rung, as though only personal resources equaled worthiness for treatment. Just because they faced more barriers than most people to the standard therapeutic goals of insight and self-actualization did not mean they were less deserving of dedicated clinical care. Had we thought that way, we would have been supporting the social and cultural ideals that had forced our clients to the bottom in the first place.

To see the ACT population as less deserving of the best care reflects the puritanical idea that wealth and health are concrete signs of God's favor. Just as each of us fits somewhere along a socioeconomic continuum—from most to least—we can also exist along a psychiatric continuum that measures our overall mental health. For some, their place on it—their diagnosis—is not determined by valid clinical assessment but rather by the value of their resources or perception of their public personas.

Celebrities, for example, occupy a world where they get to define mental health. What their publicists describe as exhaustion, I suspect, would be referred to as detox for the rest of us. Whoever has the ability to create definitions has the power.

A privileged few get to make their own diagnoses, but the majority of us are stuck in a health care system that has stigmatized mental illness to the point that people are afraid to ask for help. The impact of any illness or crisis ripples deeper through a person's life when available resources cannot absorb the shock, so the poor tend to suffer the most. ACT clients only came to us once they had become a problem that could no longer be ignored by police, hospitals, and landlords. Before that, they often suffered in isolation while most of the community tried to pretend they didn't exist.

That the mental health system even needs an ACT team suggests strong evidence that the standard of care provided in most programs fails often. ACT has only survived because intensive programs save the government a lot of money. At the least, ACT minimizes the time that some of the community's most disruptive and desperate people have to spend in jails, nursing homes, and hospitals, all on the taxpayers' dime.

Meanwhile prosperity and good health remain barometers of moral standing in our culture. We adopt all sorts of mantras to explain tragedies and illnesses in order to alleviate our own pain and anxiety. If bad things happen to bad people we can console ourselves with the belief that if we are good we are somehow safe from the chaos of the world. But life is unfair. Our clients learned that a long time ago, and it's particularly true in their world. If fairness reigned, we would run out of ACT clients before we ever had the chance to retire.

But there are always more clients. I used to tell the team that we were swimming to the horizon, and eventually we would all quit or drown. But that's not as grim as it sounds. Those of us who saw the work as more than a job were also able to create some of what we needed to see in the world—hope, compassion, some justice maybe.

There was an implied promise within ACT that I'm sure wasn't spoken out loud enough. It was that no one in these complex relationships is alone in the world. No one gets abandoned in this connection.

• • •

On a recent coffee run I ran into an old client, Little Stewart. He looked like he had been homeless for a while, wearing several layers of sweatsuits and picking cigarette butts from the ground. We were never able to get him stabilized in an apartment. Our program was always too restrictive for him, and he only had a couple of short stints with us before his obsequiousness became a rage fit that landed him in the hospital and a nursing home.

The last I had seen him we were in the ACT office. He'd thrown an unbelievably weak karate kick at me. It was no physical feat to catch his ankle and hold our pose while explaining why he was going to the hospital.

But now, standing on the corner of Broadway and Bryn Mawr, we chatted like old neighbors bumping into each other. He couldn't remember my name but was trying to be polite.

"Oh, hey buddy," he said. "Wow. I forgot all about you people. You still working over there?"

"No, I haven't been there in years."

"Oh, no," he said. "I'm so sorry to hear that. Don't worry, buddy. Things are gonna turn around for you. Things'll be looking up soon enough. But I'm getting out of here. I've had enough of the city. A friend of mine is gonna wire me a bus ticket to Arizona and I'm gonna stay with him. It's lousy here. I'm sick of Chicago."

Stewart always had vague plans to get out of town and there was usually an improbable payday or life-changing score right around the corner. Maybe it was true this time. How would I know? Things happen.

I wished him luck, he wished me the same, and we each went back to work.

www.ingramcontent.com/pod-product-compliance
Lightning Source LLC
LaVergne TN
LVHW091714070526
838199LV00050B/2394